Empathy
A Social Psychological Approach

Mark H. Davis

Eckerd College

WestviewPress

A Division of HarperCollinsPublishers

Social Psychology Series
John Harvey, Series Editor

Empathy: A Social Psychological Approach, Mark H. Davis

Violence Within the Family: Social Psychological Perspectives,
Sharon D. Herzberger

Social Dilemmas, Samuel S. Komorita and Craig D. Parks

*Self-Presentation: Impression Management
and Interpersonal Behavior*, Mark R. Leary

*Experimental and Nonexperimental Designs in Social
Psychology*, Abraham S. Ross and Malcolm Grant

Intergroup Relations, Walter G. Stephan and Cookie White Stephan

Copyright © 1994, 1996 by Westview Press, Inc., A Division of HarperCollins
Publishers, Inc.

Published in 1996 in the United States of America by Westview Press, Inc., 5500
Central Avenue, Boulder, Colorado 80301-2877, and in the United Kingdom by
Westview Press, 12 Hid's Copse Road, Cumnor Hill, Oxford OX2 9JJ

Davis, Mark H.
    Empathy : a social psychological approach / by Mark H. Davis.
        p. cm.
    Madison, Wis. : Brown & Benchmark Publishers, c1994.
    Includes bibliographical references and index.
    ISBN 0-8133-3001-7 (pbk.)
    1. Empathy. 2. Sympathy. 3. Altruism. 4. Helping behavior—Social aspects.
I. Title.
BF575.E55D37   1996
152.4'1—dc20   96-422
                                                                  CIP

The paper used in this publication meets the requirements of the American
National Standard for Permanence of Paper for Printed Library Materials Z39.48-
1984.

10   9   8   7   6   5   4   3   2

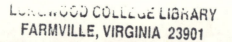

For Linda

CONTENTS

PREFACE

I have a confession to make. After studying empathy in one form or another for over 15 years, I am *finally* beginning to feel as though I have some understanding of the topic. Part of the reason it has taken so long, I fear, is dispositional as there are, no doubt, many others who are quicker studies than I. But some of the reason also lies in the nature of the topic itself; empathy is a multifaceted phenomenon of interest to psychologists of many different stripes (i.e., clinical, developmental, sociobiological, personality, social) as well as to a variety of non-psychologists including anthropologists, philosophers, and theologians. In my defense, therefore, I would suggest that one reason it is difficult to get a good handle on empathy is that it *has so many handles*.

One of the best ways to learn about a subject, of course, is to teach it, and that has certainly been my experience while writing this book. Organizing the multitude of investigations relevant to this topic, explaining them to an unseen audience, and placing the findings within a coherent organizational framework have been enormously educational. It is my hope that this book will provide readers with much of the understanding of empathy that I have gained while sparing them the considerable inconvenience of writing a book on the topic!

Although empathy has relevance to many different disciplines, my approach to the topic has unabashedly been that of a social/personality psychologist. What that means, at the most general level, is that my training in this tradition has inevitably influenced the course of this project: not only the selection and interpretation of the material included here, but also the kind of organization imposed on that material. What it means, more specifically, is that some topics not central to a social/personality approach—most notably empathy's role in the clinical setting—are not included at all. While such matters are important, they are somewhat peripheral to a mainstream social psychological approach; more importantly, perhaps, there are already books on those topics. Thus, the clear focus in this endeavor has been on doing something new: examining empathy from the standpoint of contemporary social/personality psychology—emphasizing these disciplines' traditional subject matter (e.g., emotion, cognition, helping, aggression) and its research techniques (survey research, laboratory experiments).

As I wrote this book, the primary readers that I had in mind were advanced undergraduate and graduate students. Thus, my goal was to provide a thorough, readable, even-handed summary of contemporary empathy research, more advanced than that in a basic textbook, but not as technical as one intended solely for a professional audience. Even so, my hope is that non-student, professional readers will also find something of value in this work. If nothing else, it may suggest some ways in which empathy, broadly defined, can be relevant to their more traditional research interests.

Finally, I would like to offer thanks to several parties who were especially helpful to me as I worked on this project: to Eckerd College for the sabbatical leave during which I wrote most of this book; to my psychology colleagues at Eckerd, Sal Capobianco, Jeff Howard, and Jim MacDougall, who were helpful in numerous ways both large and small; to Cathy McCoy of the Eckerd College library for her unflagging willingness to locate yet another reference; and to Nancy Eisenberg, Arizona State University; Bob Hogan, University of Tulsa; Paul Miller, Arizona State University West, and Linda Kraus, University of Tampa, who read some or all of this book at various points and who provided me with a host of very useful comments. To all of you, my deepest thanks.

Mark H. Davis

History and Definitions

The fact that human beings are capable of enormously selfish behavior can hardly be disputed. One need only peruse the daily newspaper for evidence. In fact, in today's morning paper there were stories about a 14 year old girl stabbed to death by her ex-boyfriend, two teenagers who bludgeoned to death an acquaintance, prison guards who beat up a prisoner in restraints, a young man who stabbed and killed a 62 year old woman, threats of renewed violence in South Africa, an impending Ku Klux Klan rally in Florida, and a man whose home was virtually cleaned out by two house-sitters, people he considered ''among my best friends.'' Admittedly, newspapers publish ''news''—that is, what is considered unusual. Even so, the widespread evidence of our capacity to act in ways that serve our own interests at the expense of others seems undeniable.

Moreover, we are fundamentally not very surprised to read such stories. The fact that we are capable of ignoring the unpleasant consequences our actions have on others seems sadly self-evident. A robust hedonism, a willingness to maximize our own outcomes no matter the cost to others, unfortunately seems to have a considerable survival value. It's hard for most of us to imagine a successful species whose members did not display this kind of powerful self-interest. In fact, if anything needs explaining, it's why we don't act in completely egocentric ways all of the time.

This question has been around for quite a while, of course, and one early answer to it can be found in Thomas Hobbes' *Leviathan* (1651). Hobbes argued that the nature of humans is such that the inevitable outcome of social living is a state of virtual warfare, with each against all. Because there are no internal reasons to willingly curb our desires, everyone strives to maximize personal gain at the expense of others, producing a human existence which is, in Hobbes' famous phrase, "solitary, poor, nasty, brutish, and short." In fact, the only forces said to impel people toward peaceful existence at all are a fear of death and a desire for creature comforts. In practical terms, this means that peace and social order only result when all individuals in a society are willing to surrender individual rights and freedoms to the state, which then exerts the kind of control over individual egoistic actions that the individuals themselves will not.

A less pessimistic possibility also exists. Writing a century after Hobbes, Adam Smith (1759/1976) offered a different vision in which the regulation of egoistic behavior comes not from an external source like the state, but springs instead from limits that individuals place on themselves. What makes us place these limits on ourselves? The answer, for Smith, is what he calls **sympathy,** and what is often today termed **empathy.** What Smith means by sympathy is the shared feeling that results when we observe other people in emotional states, the compassion we feel for their sorrow, the resentment when they are slighted, the joy when they triumph. This affective bond between individuals changes the whole equation that Hobbes was trying to solve. If the feeling states of separate individuals are linked, then the Hobbesian view of humans as fundamentally isolated and selfish does not hold, and the existence of some external agent enforcing a grudging cooperation is no longer necessary. Instead, pro-social actions can be internally generated rather than externally coerced, allowing us to act in a seemingly selfless fashion.

Although Smith (along with Hume, 1739/1968) was among the first to write explicitly about this phenomenon, many others have done so since. The remainder of this chapter will review some of the major definitions of empathy which have been advanced over the years, focusing on those which continue to influence contemporary thinking. Following this, I will attempt to organize the various definitions of empathy into a tidier taxonomy within a conceptual framework which treats empathy as a multidimensional phenomenon. First, however, it's necessary to start at the beginning.

Historical Views of Sympathy and Empathy

Sympathy

Although sympathy and empathy are deeply intertwined today, the two concepts initially grew out of separate traditions (Wispé, 1986). One of the first, and best, accounts of sympathy came from the economist and moral philosopher Adam Smith (1759/1976). Smith felt that we are imbued by nature with an ability, in fact a near irresistible tendency, to experience a "fellow-feeling" when we observe someone experiencing a powerful emotional state. This fellow-feeling can take many forms: pity for the sorrowful, anguish for the miserable, joy for the successful, and so on. Thus, we might experience an affective state which more or less matches the state we observe, such as sharing fear with a frightened person, or we might experience an emotion such as pity for a beggar, which seems broadly compatible but is not precisely the same. Both kinds of reactions are placed by Smith, however, under the general heading of **sympathy.**

What is the source of these fellow-feelings? Smith argues that it is solely through the power of imagination that sympathy is possible, because our senses alone can never fully inform us of the physical and affective experiences of another. Specifically, Smith argues that through imagination we "place ourselves in his situation . . . enter as it were into his body, and become in some measure the same person with him." By means of imagination we come to experience sensations which are generally similar to, although typically weaker than, those of the other person.

Another influential view of sympathy came over a century later, in Herbert Spencer's (1870) *Principles of Psychology.* Spencer started with the idea of an underlying sociality said to exist in many species, including humans. In such species, Spencer argued, a tendency to affiliate with species-mates served an adaptive function, particularly in the area of self-defense, because of the safety provided by numbers. It followed, he believed, that over time there developed in these species a feeling of pleasure in affiliation and a commensurate displeasure when deprived of such social interaction. The net result of these feelings is a high level of social contact among these species. Given this high level of social contact, sympathy develops as a result of repeated association.

Consider, for example, the case of sympathetic fear. Spencer argues that the stimulus which creates fear in one member of a species (the sound of an approaching predator) also produces in that creature a "fear reaction" (alarm cries, escape). Other members of the species present at the time not only experience fear in response to the predator, but also experience simultaneous associations between the predator's sounds, their own fear, and the fear reactions of others. Over time, the fear reactions of others come to elicit fear in the individual even in the absence of frightening stimuli. One implication of Spencer's ideas is that sympathy is largely a means of communication, with the reactions of others coming to signify important information regarding environmental conditions. This phenomenon, which prompts all members of a group to quickly experience the same affective state, helps make it possible to coordinate the behavior of many individuals.

McDougall's (1908) *Introduction to Social Psychology* provided another influential treatment of sympathy which focused on the mechanism by which target and observer actually come to share emotional reactions. In McDougall's instinct theory, there are two ways to induce an emotion. The first is through the "biologically adequate" cause, such as a loud noise or frightening animal. The second way is through the perception of that emotion in action in another person, what he termed *primitive passive sympathy*. Observing emotion in others tends to produce the same emotion in an observer, McDougall argued, because for each of the primary emotions there exists a specific perceptual mechanism, called a "perceptual inlet," which is designed to receive particular affective cues of others and to translate those cues into a shared emotional response. For McDougall sympathetic reactions were not the result of "imagining ourselves into" the experiences of another (Smith), or of learning based on repeated prior experiences (Spencer), but were the automatic result of built-in, "hard-wired" perceptual mechanisms. Despite these differences regarding mechanisms, however, all three approaches focused primarily on the same basic phenomenon—the sharing of affect between two individuals—and all three used the term "sympathy" to describe it. During that time, however, a different way of conceptualizing self-other connections was emerging.

Empathy

Sympathy, as we have seen, had its earliest roots (Hume; Smith) in 18th century moral philosophy. Empathy, in contrast, came from the term *Einfühlung,* initially used in German aesthetics. In its original usage it referred to the tendency of observers to project themselves "into" that which they observe, typically some physical object of beauty. Lipps (1903, 1905) appropriated the term for use in more psychological contexts, first applying it to the study of optical illusions and later to the process by which we come to know other people. The English word *empathy* was actually invented by Titchener (1909) as a "translation" of Lipps' *einfühlung.*

Both Lipps and Titchener believed that the mechanism through which empathy occurred was an inner imitation, or *inner Nachahmung,* of the observed person or object, a process referred to today as motor mimicry. Lipps (1926) argued that witnessing another's emotional state prompts the observer to covertly, internally, imitate the other's emotional cues (for example, tensing our muscles when witnessing someone under stress). The result of this process is the production of similar, though weaker, reactions in the observer. This sharing of emotions between target and observer was said to foster a better understanding of the actor as well.

There is an important yet subtle difference between the older concept of sympathy and the newer concept of *einfühlung*/empathy. Sympathy as conceptualized by Smith, Spencer, and McDougall had a largely, though not entirely, passive flavor to it. The emphasis was on ways in which an observer came to feel what another felt, or was moved by another's experience. In contrast, empathy suggested a more *active* attempt by one individual to get "inside" the other, to reach out in some fashion through a deliberate intellectual effort. This distinction is not perfect, of course; Smith's explanation for sympathy did hinge on an imaginative process of placing ourselves in others' situations, a process which seems active rather than passive, and thus closer to the essence of the newer term. Overall, however, the new concept of empathy put a different, more active spin on the question of emotional sharing.

One result of conceptualizing empathy in this more active fashion was that it placed a greater emphasis on deliberate cognitive processes. While shared affect had previously been seen as resulting from largely passive associative learning (Spencer) or biological mechanisms (McDougall), empathy as conceived by Lipps and Titchener identified the observer as a willful agent deliberately making an effort to step outside the self and "into" the experiences of others. Within such a theoretical stance the active process of empathizing is highlighted, and a series of theorists began to focus on this process in their work.

One of the first to argue in this more cognitive vein was Kohler (1929). Rather than continuing to focus on "feeling into" the experiences of another, Kohler held that empathy was more the understanding of others' feelings than a sharing of them. One implication of this view is that the mechanisms by which the affective sharing was said to occur, such as motor mimicry and "perceptual inlets," were to some degree beside the point. Understanding other people, as opposed to feeling what they felt, could be accomplished merely by viewing and interpreting the actor's actions, movements, and physical cues. Processes leading to affective sharing were no longer essential.

At that time two highly influential theorists separately addressed, in their own ways, the question of empathy, and both offered views which emphasized the cognitive over the emotional. George Herbert Mead's (1934) work placed a huge emphasis on the individual's capacity to take on the role of other persons as a means of understanding how they view the world. The ability to do this was seen as an extremely important component in the developmental process of learning to live effectively in a highly social world. In fact, meaningful social organization would be largely impossible without the ability to anticipate the reactions that one's behavior will evoke in others, and to use those anticipated reactions in tailoring one's behavior to fit a variety of different social circumstances.

At roughly the same time Jean Piaget (1932) was advancing his theories of child development, with a similar emphasis on a crucial cognitive skill—the ability to decenter. In Piaget's view, the child begins as a creature incapable of differentiating between the experiences of self and those of others. Only as children progress through the stages of cognitive development do they become capable of making this distinction. The ability to decenter, or to abandon the child's original and literally "self"-ish perspective, is thus an integral part of social development.

The similarity between the constructs of role taking and decentering is clear. Both emphasize a primarily cognitive process in which the individual suppresses his or her usual egocentric outlook and imagines how the world appears to others. In both cases this process is said to underlie later cognitive development, and in both cases it is thought to make possible more effective, less contentious social interactions. The essentially simultaneous appearance of these two complementary, fundamentally cognitive, views signalled an important shift in the direction taken by subsequent empathy research.

One evidence of this shift is the emphasis by later developmental psychologists on the study of children's role taking. Treatments of this topic have typically distinguished between *perceptual* role-taking, or the ability to imagine the literal visual perspective of another, *cognitive* role taking, the ability to imagine others' thoughts and motives, and *affective* role taking, the ability to infer another's emotional states (Eisenberg, 1986) with the latter two receiving the most empirical attention. It should be noted that affective role-taking in this context refers only to an awareness of others' emotional states and does not necessarily include any affective reaction in the observer. Eventually an impressive series of techniques were developed to assess individuals' levels of role-taking capacity in both the cognitive (e.g., Chandler, 1973; Flavell, Botkin, Fry, Wright, & Jarvis, 1968) and affective (e.g., Chandler & Greenspan, 1972; Feshbach & Roe, 1968; Rothenberg, 1970) realms. As predicted by both Mead and Piaget, the evidence suggests that role-taking skill generally increases with age throughout childhood (Eisenberg & Mussen, 1989).

A second evidence of the cognitive shift was the strong emphasis, especially during the 1940's and 1950's, on empathy's role in enhancing accuracy in person perception, what is sometimes termed *social acuity*. Much of the research during this period was predicated on the idea that empathy consists of an ability to accurately imagine others' viewpoints (e.g., Chapin, 1942; Kerr & Speroff, 1954). In fact, some of these approaches essentially equated empathy with the accurate perceptions of others (e.g. Dymond, 1948; 1949; 1950). As we shall see in later chapters, however, research on interpersonal accuracy came to a rather abrupt halt in the 1950's when the most popular technique for assessing accuracy was found to have some serious methodological problems. It was partially as a result of this, in fact, that more recent theorizing about empathy began to re-emphasize the emotional side of the empathy coin.

Contemporary Views of Empathy

Among contemporary empathy theorists, Ezra Stotland and colleagues (Stotland, 1969; Stotland, Sherman, & Shaver, 1971) were perhaps the first to again conceive of empathy in solely affective terms. Stotland (1969, p. 272) defined empathy as "an observer's reacting emotionally because he perceives that another is experiencing or is about to experience an emotion." Thus, Stotland specifically distinguished affective empathy from cognitive processes related to accuracy, although he also discussed ways in which the two separate constructs might be related. Stotland's view of empathy therefore bears a strong resemblance to the historical definitions of sympathy discussed earlier. As did they, this definition also focuses exclusively on the affective responses experienced by one person in reaction to the experiences of another. It should be noted, however, that while the earlier views explicitly or implicitly assumed that the nature of the observer's emotion would parallel that of the target, no such assumption is made in Stotland's definition. For example, an observer's gleeful reaction to the pain of another would still qualify as empathy. Stotland et al. (1971) refer to this as *contrast empathy*.

More recent contemporary theorists have also tended to define empathy solely in terms of affective responses, but unlike Stotland, they have also generally restricted the term empathy to emotional reactions which are at least broadly congruent with those of the target (Barnett, 1987; Eisenberg & Strayer, 1987; Hoffman, 1984; Gruen & Mendohlson, 1986). In fact, the influential contemporary approach of Dan Batson (Batson, 1991; Batson, Fultz, & Schoenrade, 1987), is even more limited. Empathy, for Batson, consists specifically of other-oriented feelings of concern and compassion which result from witnessing another person suffer. Thus, in Batson's view even an empathic match of emotions is not empathy; that term is reserved for compassionate feelings alone.

One exception to this recent consensus which defines empathy as a congruent affective reaction is the position of Lauren Wispé (1986, 1991). Emphasizing the two separate traditions from which sympathy and empathy developed, Wispé argues that sympathy is the "heightened awareness of the suffering of another person as something to be alleviated" (Wispé, 1986, p. 318). It thus seems very close to Batson's view of empathy as other-oriented sympathy, and reasonably close to the most common modern conception of empathy as an emotional response congruent with that of the target. In contrast, empathy for Wispé (1986, p. 318) is an "attempt by one self-aware self to comprehend unjudgmentally the positive and negative experiences of another self." It is a more active, effortful process in which the observer tries to understand the target by deliberately "reaching out" to the other. Thus, Wispé's definition of empathy stays close to empathy's original roots (e.g., Lipps, 1903, 1905; Titchener, 1909), and has a markedly more cognitive tone than most other contemporary views.

The most ambitious of the modern empathy theorists is probably Martin Hoffman (1984; 1987), whose ideas will be explored in more detail in the next chapter. At this point it will suffice to only briefly outline Hoffman's position. Hoffman defined empathy in a fashion similar to most other contemporary theorists as "an affective response more appropriate to someone else's situation than to one's own" (Hoffman, 1987). Within his larger theoretical framework, however, Hoffman also addresses a number of other important constructs related to empathy. In brief, children are said to move developmentally from a stage in which they have no sense of a self-other distinction, reacting to the distress of others with a personal distress of their own, to a more advanced state in which the growing cognitive sense of self allows the child to experience both a self-oriented distress and a more advanced distress experienced for other people. As role-taking skills develop, this other-oriented distress increasingly becomes a form of true compassion for others. Thus, Hoffman's theoretical framework encompasses cognitive role-taking, personal feelings of distress created by others' distress, and feelings of sympathy/concern for the other, all of which qualify as empathy in one or more theoretical schemes.

Problems with Contemporary Views

The nature of empathy has been and continues to be a matter of some disagreement among those who toil in this vineyard. In particular, there is one central, recurrent, and seemingly intractable problem: the term empathy is routinely used to refer to two distinctly separate phenomena, cognitive role taking and affective reactivity to others. Despite virtually universal recognition that these two constructs must be distinguished from one another, the label "empathy" continues to be applied to both constructs, a fact which contributes in no small way to the continuing semantic confusion in empathy research. The two related factors which seem to be most responsible for the persistence of this state of affairs are the semantic problem resulting from the fact that key terms have long carried extra meaning, and the fact that there has been a long-term confusion between empathy as process and empathy as outcome.

Consider the semantic problem first. The two key terms in this area are empathy and sympathy, and both have been weighed down with extra meaning from the very beginning of their use. Consider Smith's (1759/1976) discussion of the meaning of sympathy:

> "Pity and compassion are words appropriated to signify our
> fellow-feeling with the sorrow of others. Sympathy, though its
> meaning was, perhaps, originally the same, may now, however,
> without much impropriety, be made use of to denote our
> fellow-feeling with any passion whatever." (Smith, 1759/1976, p. 10)

In this passage Smith identifies a phenomenon in which observers experience fellow-feeling with a wide variety of observed emotions, but acknowledges using a term to describe this—sympathy—which more specifically refers to feelings of compassion for another's sorrow. Unfortunately, the choice of such a meaning-laden term set the stage for later confusion. Because the more specific meaning of sympathy as compassion is the more common, colloquial usage, recruiting the term to refer to the more general experience of fellow-feeling ran into some difficulty. In fact, as Wispé (1986) notes, the term sympathy (used in Smith's sense) essentially disappeared from social psychology by the 1950's. Without this generally recognized term to refer to the phenomenon of shared affective reactions, the newer term empathy was increasingly used for this purpose.

This process was made easier because the newer term was itself fraught with extra meaning. From the beginning, empathy was seen as a means of "knowing" another through a projection of the self "into" the other. This process is noticeably more active than the rather passive sympathy process described by Spencer and McDougall. At the same time, however, there was also an element of affective responsiveness inherent in the term; the process of projecting oneself into another was, after all, said to produce affective changes in the observer. Given the dual cognitive/affective nature of the term empathy, and the gradual loss of the term sympathy to denote affective sharing, it was perhaps inevitable that such sharing would increasingly be labelled "empathy." The end result is that today this term carries a surplus of meaning, being routinely used to characterize phenomena both cognitive and affective, both active and passive.

The other factor contributing to the current confusion has been the pervasive mingling of *process* and *outcome* in thinking about empathy. The distinction is an important one. Process, in the sense that I intend, refers to something that happens when one is exposed in some fashion to another (usually distressed) person. Attempting to entertain the cognitive or emotional perspective of the other, for example, is a process; unconsciously imitating the other's facial or postural movements is another. An outcome, in contrast, refers to something that results from these processes, for example, emotional responses in the observer or a more accurate cognitive understanding of the other. Definitions of empathy or sympathy which focus on affective responses are, therefore, outcome-oriented definitions. Approaches which define empathy as role taking, however, more typically focus on the process rather than the outcome. Viewed in this way, it can be seen that part of the definitional confusion regarding empathy results from the fact that theorists and researchers, while all studying "empathy," are in fact frequently addressing quite different parts of a larger phenomenon. Thus, failing to distinguish between process and outcome also contributes to the ongoing confusion regarding the "true" nature of empathy.

Like the blind men with the elephant, each of whom was convinced that the part of the creature he was holding defined its nature, empathy theorists and researchers have grappled with what is ostensibly the same subject yet reached sometimes dramatically different conclusions about what it really is. Is it the cognitive act of adopting another's perspective? A cognitively based understanding of others? An affective reaction to the emotions of another? If so, what kind of emotion? The same? Similar? Must it have a compassionate tone? The answer to all of these questions is "yes"—and that is the problem. Despite empathy's important role in a variety of contexts, many of which will be discussed in this book, the topic has generally suffered from the lack of a clear, compelling organizational framework. In large part this failure has been the result of the fragmented way in which the key constructs have been conceived and communicated.

The consequences of this state of affairs are easy to recognize. Separate research traditions have grown up around each of the major constructs, ostensibly investigating the same phenomenon but most often pursuing one "brand" of empathy with only a tangential recognition of the other. When other approaches have been recognized, it has frequently been in the context of explaining why they do not "truly" qualify as empathy. Only a few efforts (e.g., Hoffman, 1984, 1987) have been made to explicitly consider the ways in which the two phenomena, separated by a common label, might actually fit together. As a result, the study of empathy, as much as any topic in psychology, has been marked by a failure to agree on the nature of and relations among its core constructs.

Given this state of affairs, a highly useful tool would be an organizational model which makes clear the similarities and differences between the various constructs that fall within empathy's roughly defined domain. To that end, the next section lays out such a model of empathy-related constructs, with an indication of how historical and contemporary approaches fit into this system. Parts of this framework are borrowed from Hoffman (1984) and Staub (1987), with additional original elements freely added. This organizational scheme provides a conceptual framework within which the remainder of the book will be organized. Figure 1.1 contains the major elements of this model.

Empathy: An Organizational Model

One danger posed by the current multiplicity of empathy definitions is the possibility that when empathy is defined in a particular manner, any constructs excluded by the definition are in some sense seen as peripheral. Thus, if empathy is defined as an affective response, then cognitive role taking isn't empathy and becomes less important. If empathy is more specifically defined as experiencing similar affect, then dissimilar feelings fall outside the area of interest. The unintended result of such a series of exclusive definitions is to Balkanize the study of empathy. The spirit of this model is just the opposite; its goal is to emphasize the connectedness of these constructs.

To do so, the model is based on an inclusive definition of empathy. Empathy is broadly defined as a set of constructs having to do with the responses of one individual to the experiences of another. These constructs specifically include the *processes* taking place within the observer and the affective and non-affective *outcomes* which result from those processes. This definition therefore includes under the heading "empathy" a much wider range of phenomena than is typical. This is done deliberately in order to highlight the connections among constructs which are sometimes overlooked. Based on this definition, the organizational model conceives of the typical empathy "episode" as consisting of an observer being exposed in some way to a target, after which some response on the part of the observer, cognitive, affective, and/or behavioral, occurs. Four related constructs can be identified within this prototypical episode: **antecedents,** which refer to characteristics of the observer, target, or situation; **processes,** which refer to the particular mechanisms by which empathic outcomes are produced; **intrapersonal outcomes,** which refer to cognitive and affective responses produced in the observer which are not manifested in overt behavior toward the target; and **interpersonal outcomes,** which refer to behavioral responses directed toward the target.

The relations among these four constructs appear in Figure 1.1. As the figure illustrates, associations are hypothesized to exist between a construct (e.g., antecedents) and all those constructs appearing later in the model (e.g., processes, intrapersonal outcomes, and interpersonal outcomes). However, the logic of the model also

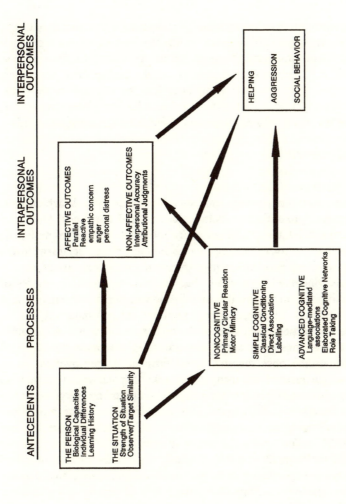

FIGURE 1.1
The organizational model

implies that stronger associations will typically be found between constructs which are adjacent in the model such as between antecedents and processes, between processes and intrapersonal outcomes, and between intrapersonal and interpersonal outcomes. Thus, the most powerful influences will be exerted by the most proximal constructs, with distal variables having a more modest effect. With this in mind, let us now consider each construct in turn.

Antecedents

The Person

All observers bring certain characteristics to an episode which have the potential to influence both processes and outcomes. One such characteristic is the simple *capacity* for empathy, for example, the intellectual ability to engage in role taking or the species-wide capacity to experience affect in response to witnessing affect in others. Also included here would be the previous *learning history* of the individual, including the socialization of empathy-related values and behaviors. Finally, a very important set of characteristics involves *individual differences* in the tendency to engage in empathy-related processes or to experience empathic outcomes. A variety of individual difference measures have been developed over the years for the purpose of assessing the stable dispositional tendency to engage in empathy-related processes such as perspective taking (e.g., Davis, 1980; Hogan, 1969) or to experience empathy-related affective responses (e.g., Davis, 1980; Mehrabian & Epstein, 1972). These measures fall under the heading of person variables because they represent stable characteristics of the individual which influence the likelihood of engaging in an empathy-related process or experiencing an empathy-related outcome during any particular empathy episode.

The Situation

All responses to another person, whether cognitive or affective, emerge from some specific situational context. Whether a face-to-face encounter with a family member, witnessing a handicapped child during a telethon, or reading about refugees in the newspaper, all reactions to others are rooted in specific situations which vary along certain dimensions. One such dimension is what we can call the *strength of the situation*. Especially with regard to affective reactions, situations vary tremendously in terms of their power to evoke a response from observers. Strong displays of negative emotion, especially by weak or helpless targets, are particularly able to engender powerful observer responses. In fact, faced with such extremely strong situations, other variables, both situational and dispositional, may recede in importance. In less powerful situations other factors, including characteristics of the observer, may play a larger role.

A second situational feature is the *degree of similarity* between the observer and target. (Similarity is actually a joint function of both the target and the observer, but for the sake of convenience we will consider it here.) Greater observer-target similarity is generally thought to increase the likelihood and/or intensity of the observer's empathic response, whether affective or non-affective. Research addressing this issue is reviewed in Chapters 5 and 6.

Processes

The second construct within the organizational model consists of the specific processes which generate empathic outcomes in the observer. Building on the work of Hoffman (1984), and Nancy Eisenberg (Eisenberg, Shea, Carlo, & Knight, 1991), I will argue that three broad classes of empathy-related processes can be identified, chiefly distinguished from one another by the degree of cognitive effort and sophistication required for their operation. These processes can be considered empathy-related because they frequently occur during episodes in which an observer is exposed to a target, and because they often result in some empathy-related outcome. However, it should be emphasized that these processes can occur in other contexts as well, and need not produce an empathy-related outcome when they do.

Noncognitive Processes

Some processes which lead to empathic outcomes seem to require very little cognitive activity. Newborn infants, for example, tend to cry in response to hearing other infants cry, a phenomenon that occurs so early in life that it seems unlikely to be the result of any learning. This apparently innate tendency, which Hoffman (1984) refers to as a *primary circular reaction,* can therefore be considered a non-cognitive process which produces an affective outcome in the infant "observer." McDougall's innate "perceptual inlets," which virtually automatically transform witnessed emotion into experienced emotion, also appear to qualify as a noncognitive mechanism.

Another noncognitive process is *motor mimicry,* the tendency for observers to automatically and largely unconsciously imitate the target. The hypothesized result of such mimicry is the production in the observer of an emotional state consistent with the target's. This process can be seen in the work of Lipps (1926) and Titchener (1909), who also argued that mimicry by observers has the effect of producing shared affect. Although these early conceptions of mimicry (or *inner Nachahmung*) viewed it as a somewhat deliberate strategy for "feeling into" the other, more recent approaches (e.g., Hoffman, 1984; Vaughan & Lanzetta, 1980) have treated it as a relatively automatic, largely non-cognitive process. It is therefore included under the non-cognitive category in the model.

Simple Cognitive Processes

In contrast to the noncognitive processes, other processes, such as *classical conditioning,* require at least a rudimentary cognitive ability on the part of the observer. For example, if an observer has previously perceived affective cues in others while experiencing that same affect (perhaps because both observer and target are simultaneously exposed to the same unpleasant stimulus), then the affective cues of targets may come to evoke that emotional state. This is precisely the process described by Spencer (1870), and it relies on the existence of quite elementary cognitive capacities—simply the ability to distinguish stimuli and be conditioned. A similar but more general version of this process, *direct association,* has also been proposed (Hoffman, 1984), and is more fully described in the next chapter. In addition, Eisenberg, Shea et al. (1991) identify a process of comparably modest sophistication, called *labelling,* in which the observer uses simple cues to infer something about the target's experience. For example, an observer may know that certain situations (like college graduations) usually produce happiness. Witnessing someone graduating may lead to the inference that the person is happy, regardless of other cues which may be present. This rather simple inference process therefore requires a fairly low level of cognitive sophistication.

Advanced Cognitive Processes

Finally, some processes require rather advanced kinds of cognitive activity. One example is what Hoffman refers to as *language-mediated association,* in which the observer's reaction to the target's plight is produced by activating language-based cognitive networks which trigger associations with the observer's own feelings or experiences. For example, a target who says "I've been laid off" may exhibit no obvious facial or vocal cues indicating distress, but an observer may respond empathically because personal relevant memories are activated by the target's words. Such a process requires a more advanced level of cognitive sophistication than the processes previously discussed. Eisenberg, Shea et al. (1991) have described a very similar process, the use of *elaborated cognitive networks,* in which observers also employ target cues in order to access existing knowledge stores, and use this information to form inferences about the target.

The most advanced process, however, is what has been termed *role taking* or *perspective taking*: the attempts by one individual to understand another by imagining the other's perspective. It is typically an effortful process, involving both the suppression of one's own egocentric perspective on events and the active entertaining of someone else's. Earlier theorists who have argued for such a process include Smith, Mead, and Piaget, all of whom emphasized the importance of imagining others' perspectives. Among more recent approaches, Wispé's definition of empathy also seems to fit here.

When considering the terminology frequently used in this field, it seems clear that attempts to entertain the perspective of others, what we have described as an advanced cognitive process, constitutes a substantial part of what has often been referred to as "cognitive empathy." It is not, however, the only thing which has been included under that heading. It is important to re-emphasize that in the organizational model the term role taking refers specifically to the *process* in which one individual attempts to imagine the world of another. The *outcomes* of perspective taking, both affective and cognitive, are excluded from this definition. With all of this taken into account, the contemporary definitions of empathy which most closely correspond to role taking in this model come from Wispé (described earlier) and Hogan (1969, p. 308), for whom empathy "refers only to the act of constructing for oneself another person's mental state; the versimilitude of the resulting construct is not a necessary part of the concept's meaning."

Intrapersonal Outcomes

The third major construct within the organizational model is **intrapersonal outcomes**—the affective and non-affective responses of the observer that result from exposure to the target. In particular, these outcomes are thought to result primarily from the various processes identified at the previous stage in the model.

Affective Outcomes
This category consists of the emotional reactions experienced by an observer in response to the observed experiences of the target.

Worded in such a broad way, this definition can therefore encompass even Stotland's (1969) approach, which allows any sort of emotional reaction (even an opposite one) to another person to qualify as an empathic response. However, because most contemporary approaches employ much narrower definitions, affective outcomes are further subdivided into two forms: *parallel* and *reactive* outcomes.

A *parallel outcome* may in a sense be considered the prototypical affective response—an actual reproduction in an observer of the target's feelings. This sort of emotional matching is clearly the focus of several historical approaches. For example, Spencer's and McDougall's treatments of sympathy both emphasize observers coming to experience the same affect as that of the target. Smith's treatment does not focus quite as tightly on an exact match of emotion, but the experience of parallel affect quite clearly would be included within his definition of sympathy.

An interesting problem is posed by the cluster of recent definitions (e.g., Barnett, 1987; Eisenberg & Strayer, 1987; Gruen & Mendolsohn, 1986; Hoffman, 1984) which generally define empathy as an affective reaction which is congruent with, but not necessarily the same as, that of the target. Obviously such definitions would apply to those occasions when an empathic match occurs; an exact match does, after all, seem congruent with the observed emotion. Thus, when the affect of observer and target are closely matched, at least at the broadest level, these definitions would seem to fall under the heading of parallel outcomes. At other times, when observers experience affective reactions, such as sympathy, which go beyond those of the target, another way to conceptualize these responses is necessary.

Such a conceptualization is provided by *reactive outcomes,* defined as affective reactions to the experiences of others which differ from the observed affect. They are so named because they are empathic reactions to another's state rather than a simple reproduction of that state in the observer. Responses clearly falling into this category are the feelings of compassion for others referred to variously as sympathy (Wispé, 1986), empathy (Batson, 1991), and empathic concern (Davis, 1983b), and the empathic anger that observers may experience when witnessing someone being maltreated. In each case the observer's affect differs from the target's but is a direct reaction to that target's experiences. One additional affective response which has received recent attention is personal distress, the tendency to feel discomfort and anxiety in response to needy targets. As we shall see, it is difficult to categorize this affective state as purely parallel or reactive in nature. However, for reasons described in Chapter 6, we shall place it in the reactive outcome category.

A reactive outcome in many cases will result from more sophisticated cognitive processes than a parallel outcome. For example, a parallel affective response may result from fairly primitive motor mimicry and/or conditioning history. However, to experience an emotion or reactive affect different from the target in all probability requires some higher order processing to recognize and interpret the target's cues. Parallel outcomes will also tend to be more *self*-centered reactions (distress, for example), while reactive outcomes will tend to be more *other*-oriented (e.g., sympathy for another, or anger on another's behalf).

Non-Affective Outcomes

Not all outcomes resulting from exposure to others are affective in nature; some are primarily cognitive. One such outcome is *interpersonal accuracy,* the successful estimation of other people's thoughts, feelings, and characteristics. In general, such interpersonal judgments have been viewed as resulting to a considerable degree from cognitive role-taking processes (Dymond, 1950; Kerr & Speroff, 1954), a view which is consistent with the theoretical work of Mead and Piaget. More recently, empathy-related processes have also been implicated in affecting the *attributional judgments* offered by observers for targets' behavior (e.g., Regan & Totten, 1975; Gould & Sigall, 1977). In keeping with the process-outcome distinction outlined earlier, attributions for target behaviors and accurate judgments of others are classified as *outcomes,* and are clearly separated in this model from the *process* of role taking.

Interpersonal Outcomes

The final construct in the model consists of **interpersonal outcomes,** defined as behaviors directed toward a target which result from prior exposure to that target. The outcome which has attracted the most attention from empathy theorists and researchers is *helping behavior.* Both cognitive and affective facets of empathy have long been thought to contribute to the likelihood of observers offering help to needy targets. *Aggressive behavior* has also been linked theoretically to empathy-related processes and dispositions, with the expectation that empathy will be negatively associated with aggressive actions. The effect of empathy on behaviors that occur within *social relationships,* a topic which has only recently begun to attract consistent research interest, also falls into this category. As Figure 1.1 illustrates, interpersonal outcomes are viewed by the organizational model as resulting most directly from cognitive and affective intrapersonal outcomes, and less directly by various empathy-related processes and antecedent conditions.

Advantages of the Organizational Model

Using the model as represented in Figure 1.1, it is possible to examine previous theoretical and empirical approaches to empathy in a slightly different light. For example, consider the early theorists who focused attention on "sympathy." Smith, Spencer, and McDougall were all interested in essentially the same intrapersonal endpoint—the experience of parallel affective outcomes. That is, all three defined sympathy in terms of the observer coming to share the affect of the target. Interestingly, however, each of them proposed a different process by which this outcome was reached. McDougall's innate, automatic "perceptual inlets" seem the epitome of a non-cognitive process; Spencer's emphasis was clearly on simple associative learning processes; and Smith's view that sympathy results from the power of imagination clearly implicates the most cognitively advanced mechanism.

Contemporary approaches also favor an affective definition of empathy, but a major concern of these approaches is drawing distinctions among the various affective reactions, especially regarding their implications for behaviors such as helping (e.g., Batson, 1991). The process most frequently considered in these approaches is cognitively advanced role taking, which is sometimes manipulated via instructional sets in an explicit effort to create specific affective reactions (e.g., Stotland, 1969; Toi & Batson, 1982). In this approach attention is also occasionally given to antecedent characteristics of the situation, for example, degree of similarity between target and observer, as influences on affective reactions (e.g., Krebs, 1975; Stotland, 1969). Non-affective outcomes are typically ignored by such approaches.

Theory and research taking a more cognitive view of empathy understandably focuses on different portions of the model: primarily the non-affective outcomes. The accuracy research of the 1940's and 1950's is one example of such a focus, although some of that research blurred the distinction between process and outcome. Another example is the spate of interest in the 1970's concerning the effects of role-taking manipulations on observers' attributions for a target's behavior and outcomes (e.g., Regan & Totten, 1975). For the most part, however, cognitive perspectives on empathy have paid little attention to either affective outcomes or to characteristics of the situation, tending instead to focus rather tightly on role-taking, non-affective outcomes, and the links between them.

The value of an approach such as Hoffman's (1984) is that it deals simultaneously with several elements of the model. For example, Hoffman argues that at very young ages there is a virtually automatic link between situational factors, such as strong distress cues in others, and the evocation of parallel distress responses, with few meaningful cognitive processes operating at all. With the development of role-taking capacity, however, more of the affective empathic experience is transformed into a reactive outcome such as empathic concern for the distressed other. Hoffman's approach therefore has a wider scope than most approaches, incorporating antecedent conditions, several different processes, and a variety of affective outcomes, and therefore attempts a more comprehensive explanation of the empathy domain.

A Multidimensional Approach to Empathy

The logic of the organizational model presented here, and the advantages afforded by models such as Hoffman's, point clearly toward one conclusion: the study of empathy is best served by adopting an explicitly multidimensional approach to the topic. As noted earlier, previous approaches have in general tended to identify a relatively small portion of the overall model, define that portion as the topic of interest, and then investigate it in a fairly focused way. With relatively few exceptions, then, this strategy has led to discrete, well-bounded bodies of information without much insight into the connections among empathy's various facets.

This has not gone completely unnoticed by those working in the field. For two decades the literature has seen periodic calls for more comprehensive approaches to empathy which would recognize its multifaceted nature (e.g., Davis, 1980, 1983b; Deutsch & Madle, 1975; Iannotti, 1975; Strayer, 1987). Some movement in this direction has in fact taken place. Hoffman's model is one example, and some of Eisenberg's (Eisenberg et al., 1991) work addresses this problem as well. At least one individual difference measure of empathy explicitly guided by such a view has also been developed and used (Davis, 1980; 1983b). Despite these examples, however, the dominant approach continues to be the separation of empathy into largely discrete areas of theoretical and research activity.

The approach taken in this book will be to examine the empirical work in a variety of empathy-related areas, clearly recognizing the theoretical context(s) in which it was conducted. In addition, however, an effort will be made to interpret this work in terms of the organizational model presented here, with the goal of fitting the various pieces of the puzzle into a larger and more coherent picture. The next three chapters will deal with what the organizational model refers to as antecedents, focusing on the question of empathic capabilities and tendencies in particular. Chapters 5 and 6 will address both affective and non-affective intrapersonal outcomes, and include a discussion of various empathy-related processes. Chapters 7, 8, and 9 will separately examine the interpersonal outcomes of helping, aggression, and behaviors occurring within social relationships. The final chapter will offer a broader perspective on empathy theorizing and research, will evaluate the utility of the organizational model, and will offer suggestions for future work. The first step in this journey, however, is the question of origins: where does empathy, in all of its different facets, come from?

2

Evolutionary Origins of Empathic Capacities

We have seen that the term empathy encompasses a variety of processes and outcomes, and that a comprehensive understanding of the topic will require a broad multidimensional approach. Addressing the question of empathy's origins, moreover, will require making further distinctions as well. In discussing where empathy in its various forms "comes from," it is important to distinguish between three different levels of analysis: empathy as an innate capacity, empathy as a stable dispositional characteristic, and empathy as it occurs in specific situations.

How one asks and answers the question of origins depends upon the particular level of analysis that is chosen. Explanations focusing on the inherent human capacity for empathic responding must address the functional nature of such capacities; in short, why would such capacities evolve in humans at all? What evolutionary advantages would they provide? Explanations focusing on dispositional tendencies to think or act in empathic ways must address the factors which contribute to individuals' stable likelihood of utilizing the capacities they possess. The two primary contributors would seem to be inherited propensities (genetic component) and socialization experiences present during childhood (environmental component). Finally, explanations focusing on empathy as it occurs within specific situations must examine features of both the particular setting and of the individuals involved. At each level of analysis, of course, it will be important to carefully distinguish among the various kinds of cognitive and affective processes and outcomes. This chapter will discuss the origins of empathy at the first level of analysis—empathy as an innate capacity. The other two levels are discussed in subsequent chapters.

Empathy as an Innate Human Capacity

The subject of this chapter can be summed up in two questions: 1) Why would the capacity to experience emotion in response to others' experiences ever come to exist?; and 2) What purpose would be served by the evolution of an ability to imaginatively adopt the visual, cognitive, or affective point of view of others? Any attempt to understand the origins of empathic capacities must grapple with both of these questions. As it turns out, efforts to do so have tended to fall into two traditions—one which focuses on the evolutionary question of how altruism might be selected for, and the other on the evolution of primate intelligence. Let us examine the altruism tradition first.

Empathy as a Mechanism for Altruism

The question of altruism has intrigued philosophers and theologians for centuries, and it is not difficult to see why. The issue of whether or not humans are capable of truly non-selfish actions, meaning whether or not we are fundamentally and irreversibly egoistic, cuts to the heart of human nature. One recurring issue in this debate has been how behavior which sacrifices self-interest in order to benefit others could be consistent with the logic of Darwin's (1859/1966) theory of natural selection. The two appear quite contradictory. Darwin's picture of existence as a life-long struggle for survival, with each individual organism competing against the rest, does not seem on the surface to be compatible with the existence of altruistic behavior, typically defined as acting "in such a way as to increase another entity's welfare at the expense of its own'' (Dawkins, 1976, p. 4). Surely organisms which practice self-sacrifice must become less likely to survive and reproduce, with the genes contributing to their behavior becoming less prevalent in the population. How, then, can the widespread incidence of seemingly altruistic behavior across a wide variety of species, from bees to elephants to humans, be explained in evolutionary terms?

The answer proposed by Hamilton (1964), and championed more recently by sociobiologists (e.g., Wilson, 1975), is that we must look beyond the survival or demise of the individual organism to fully understand how altruism might evolve. In particular, it is useful to think about evolution not from the standpoint of the individual at all but from the perspective of the gene. In a fascinating book, *The Selfish Gene,* Richard Dawkins (1976) argues that the proper level of analysis in most discussions of evolution is the genetic level; individual organisms—plant, fish, reptile, or mammal— are nothing more than ''survival machines'' created over eons of history to house and serve the genes. Thus, individual organisms, including you and me, are simply a means to the end of successful gene replication. It is also important to keep in mind that the genes we possess are not unique to us. That is, genes identical to ours exist in varying proportions in other people, with those most closely related to us (parents and siblings) sharing the greatest percentage of our genetic material.

From this vantage point, it can be seen that the ''true'' evolutionary battle for survival is taking place at the genetic level rather than at the level of individual organisms. In the struggle by genes to ensure their propagation, the survival of the individual organism is actually somewhat of a side issue. This analysis leads to the following conclusion: rather than considering simply the *individual fitness* of organisms, their ability to produce their own successful offspring, we must also consider their *inclusive fitness,* the production of successful offspring by these individuals and by their relatives. If the essence of natural selection is the survival of the gene rather than the individual, and if many of the same genes are shared by close relatives, then actions by individuals which benefit these relatives will generally increase the genes' chances of survival.

This logic has led to the concept of *kin selection,* one of the major sociobiological explanations for altruism (Hamilton, 1964). Because individuals and their close relatives possess a relatively high proportion of identical genes, altruistic behaviors which endanger the individuals but benefit their kin may be superior, in evolutionary terms, to behaviors which simply maximize the individuals' own chances for survival. For example, imagine a bird which attracts the attention of a predator and leads it away from the nest containing the bird's three offspring. Because each baby bird shares, on average, 50 percent of its genes with the parent, this altruistic behavior by the parent bird is advantageous. Although it risks 100 percent of its own genes by attracting the predator, it also saves the "150 percent" $(3 \times 50$ percent) of its genes represented by the three offspring. While the survival chances of the parent are reduced, survival of its genes, some of which presumably prompt this altruistic act, becomes more likely. Therefore, according to the logic of kin selection individuals who do the most to promote the survival of their genes, regardless of where these genes "reside," will be at an evolutionary advantage.

More recently, Rushton, Russell, and Wells (1984) have proposed an extension of the logic underlying kin selection in the *genetic similarity theory* (GST). In short, Rushton et al. argue that a gene "may ensure its own survival by acting so as to bring about the reproduction of *any* organism in which copies of itself are to be found" (p. 181). Thus, according to GST altruism towards *non*-kin may also be evolutionarily advantageous if the non-kin recipient of the altruism bears enough genetic similarity to the altruistic individual. GST is therefore a more general statement of the principle underlying kin selection and can be seen as subsuming it. One clear advantage of GST is that it can help account for the altruism often observed between non-related individuals. GST also prompts interesting questions concerning the ways in which an organism would recognize genetic similarity in others. Krebs (1983) has noted that most animals, humans included, do not possess an innate ability to recognize kin, much less the presence of genetic similarity in non-kin. As a result, they are probably forced to rely on visible cues which are associated with kinship such as physical similarity, geographical proximity, and in-group status. Because physically similar others, or in-group members, are relatively more likely to be genetically similar, helping them is advantageous. If this is true, then the long-term evolutionary advantages of relying on such cues would help explain the heightened level of empathic response to similar targets found in laboratory experiments (e.g., Krebs, 1975; Stotland, 1969).

In addition to GST, *reciprocal altruism* (Trivers, 1971) is another mechanism explaining non-kin altruism. According to this view, acting so as to benefit unrelated species-mates can be advantageous to the individual as long as such altruism is later reciprocated. Thus, rather than relying on hypothesized increases in inclusive fitness, reciprocal altruism continues to emphasize individual fitness.

An example frequently used is that of social grooming—a common behavior in many species in which one individual grooms the other's fur or feathers, removing burrs, insects, and the like. The behavior has some small but real cost to the groomer (time lost from eating, mating, etc.) and some advantage to the "groomee" (greater health as disease-carrying parasites are removed). An individual who grooms others but never receives reciprocal grooming is in fact operating at a survival "deficit," paying a cost but never receiving a benefit. Such a genetic tendency would not survive over time. In contrast, individuals who groom only those others who return the favor would have increased fitness; they would pay the cost but also reap the benefit, and the genes of the reciprocal altruist could increase in the population. Those who simply refuse to groom would eventually be shut out by the reciprocal groomers, and non-grooming genes would suffer an eventual decline.

Patient readers may be wondering where empathy fits into all of this. The answer is that empathy may be one key mechanism by which altruistic behaviors are directly produced. It is one thing to say that genes "for" altruism produce altruistic behavior, which in turn leads to greater survivability for those genes in the population. However, the altruistic behavior is still undertaken by the individual organism and not the gene. Some mechanism must exist within that individual, between the gene level and the behavioral act, to prompt the individual to act against its own short-term interest. In the case of simpler organisms it seems likely that innate fixed action patterns might serve this purpose; among humans, however, it seems unlikely that this is feasible. Empathy, it has been argued (Hoffman, 1978; Leak & Christopher, 1982), may be the proximate mechanism which generates altruistic behavior in humans. Specifically, if witnessing another organism in distress produces distress in the observer, then that distress may be most effectively alleviated by the observer offering help.

Hoffman's (1978) argument is that any mechanism responsible for producing altruism in humans must be reliable, but also flexible. That is, it should not be so automatic in operation (like a fixed action pattern) that behavior could not be modified as a result of environmental conditions. In particular, the mechanism should allow the behavior to be affected by judgments regarding costs to the individual and benefits to the recipient(s). Thus, Hoffman argues that what must have been selected during evolution was a biologically-based predisposition to act altruistically, but one which was still subject to control by cognitive processes. In his view, empathy, defined as a vicarious affective response to the experiences of others, meets these criteria.

In arguing the case for empathy as the altruism mechanism, Hoffman cites evidence consistent with the idea that humans possess an innate capacity to react affectively to others. For example, infants as young as one or two days old display a response which appears to be empathic in nature—the tendency to cry in response to another infant's cry (Sagi & Hoffman, 1976; Simner, 1971). Importantly, the infants do not react as strongly to equally loud but non-human noises, reinforcing the interpretation that this is a special sensitivity to human affect. Hoffman also notes that the tendency for humans to automatically imitate the posture, gestures, and expressions of others with slight movements of their own may be a species-wide response and thus consistent with the evolutionary argument. Because adopting facial expressions does tend to induce emotions consistent with the expressions (e.g., Laird, 1974; Vaughan & Lanzetta, 1981), this tendency toward motor mimicry provides a means by which emotions witnessed in targets come to be experienced in observers.

If affective empathy is indeed a long-standing evolutionary mechanism through which altruism is fostered, then the existence of a neural substrate for the process by which affect comes to be shared is strongly suggested. In fact, a recent review of the evidence by Brothers (1989) is consistent with this suggestion. This review focuses first on studies in which monkeys were exposed to a variety of stimuli while the activity of single neurons, primarily in the superior temporal sulcus of the temporal lobes and in the amygdala, were recorded. Results of these investigations indicate that some cells indeed seem to "specialize" in responding to faces, and respond more strongly to pictures of a whole face than to individual elements (e.g., eyes). There is also evidence that individual neurons react differentially to specific facial expressions and body postures as well (Baylis, Rolls, & Leonard, 1985; Perrett, Rolls, & Caan, 1982; Perrett, Smith, & Potter, 1985). Taken as a whole, these findings support the idea that a responsivity to others, and in particular to their affective states, is innate to each individual.

Moving beyond the results of single neuron studies, Brothers (1989) also suggests that the crucial brain structure, insofar as affective empathy is concerned, may be the amygdala. This highly interconnected cluster of neurons, part of the limbic system, receives most of its inputs from the high level sensory cortex, including the superior temporal sulcus. Importantly, major outputs of the amygdala go to brain stem centers which control heart and respiratory rates and to the hypothalamus, which is critical in regulating endocrine activity. As Brothers observes, the amygdala is therefore "strategically located for generating rapid and specific autonomic and endocrine patterns in response to complex social signals" (p. 16). In short, the amygdala may be the neurological link between observing affect in others and producing physio-affective reactions in oneself.

To recap, the argument advanced thus far is that the evolutionary fitness of an organism is advanced by altruism in two ways: 1) an individual's inclusive fitness is maximized by acting altruistically toward others with a high degree of genetic similarity (especially kin); and 2) individual fitness is maximized through reciprocal altruism. In either case, however, some proximate mechanism is necessary to actually prompt the organism to take the altruistic action. Empathy has been proposed as one candidate, and seems to possess the features one would expect in such a mechanism (Brothers, 1989; Hoffman, 1978). It is important to be specific, however, as to what constitutes empathy in this scenario. As implied by the discussion thus far, empathy in this context falls generally under the heading of parallel affective outcomes.

Parallel outcomes seem the most appropriate characterization because the emphasis in these analyses is clearly on the fact that distress in others produces distress in the self, and this self-distress prompts the altruistic act. In making his case for empathy as the mechanism producing altruism, Hoffman (1978) states this connection quite clearly: "Empathy is uniquely well suited for bridging the gap between egoism and altruism since it can transform another person's misfortune into one's own distress, which in turn can usually best be alleviated by helping that person" (p. 333). This analysis therefore suggests that the empathic response selected for by eons of evolutionary pressure is the sharing of negative affect. To understand the evolutionary basis for "cognitive empathy," the capacity for role taking, it is necessary to examine a separate tradition, one which essentially ignores the question of altruism and focuses instead on explanations for the development of human intelligence.

Empathy as a Variety of Social Intelligence

Just as the question of altruism has attracted the attention of evolutionary theorists, so too has the issue of human intelligence and especially the question of what evolutionary forces have led to its advanced development. While no universally accepted explanations currently exist, the fact that humans differ so dramatically from other primates in both intelligence and their sophistication of tool usage has led many scholars to argue that technology was the environmental factor promoting the development of intelligence (Wynn, 1988). That is, with the advent of human bipedalism and the consequent freeing of the hands, the ability to make and use sophisticated tools came to have significant fitness advantages. More intelligent humans came to flourish at the expense of the less intelligent because of their facility at tool production and innovation (Oakley, 1959; Washburn, 1960). More recent versions of this approach (e.g., Tobias, 1983) have tended to deemphasize tool use per se and focused on the importance of the tool-using "culture" as a whole in promoting the development of intelligence. In either case, however, the central point is that the fabrication and use of technology, along with the cultural changes it produces, are the most important selective environmental forces. According to this view human intelligence was largely shaped in an environment which put a premium on technological problem-solving abilities.

Another more recently formulated view is that the evolution of primate intelligence occurred, at least in part and perhaps primarily, because of the pressures inherent in living within complex social organizations. According to this view, heightened intelligence resulted not from evolutionary pressures to develop better and better tools, but because the environment systematically rewarded in tangible ways those individuals most capable of successfully maneuvering through complicated social situations. The ability to succeed in the social arena, to prosper at least in part because of one's ability to manipulate other social actors, is sometimes referred to as "Machiavellian intelligence" (Whiten & Byrne, 1988a). As we shall see, an important component of such intelligence must certainly be a capacity to understand the perspective of others. Before reaching that point, however, let us examine the claims of the social intelligence hypothesis.

Precisely what is it about primate social life that places such a premium on social competence, and what evolutionary advantage would be gained by those possessing it? In his seminal paper, Nicholas Humphrey (1976) argued that the problematic nature of social life for the higher primates stems from the fact that while individual members undoubtedly profit from the continued stable existence of the group, they also benefit from successful "exploitation" of other group members through social maneuvering. As a result of this inherent tension, they must become "calculating beings," able to anticipate the consequences of their behavior, especially the responses others will have to that behavior. The purpose of these calculations is to allow them to act in ways which will maximize their own status relative to others but, more importantly, in ways which will not prove so disruptive as to threaten the stability of the group. Furthermore, the fluid nature of social interaction ensures that the information on which calculations are based is constantly changing, necessitating a continuous calculation and recalculation of the odds, and, it would seem, a considerable level of intellect.

Importantly, Humphrey emphasizes the give and take nature of social interaction, in particular the game-like form that it often takes. Consider, for example, an individual attempting to affect the behavior of another person, one who is also intelligent and resistant to change. Success in such endeavors will largely depend on what Humphrey calls "forward planning," or the ability to anticipate the likely response of the other to a variety of one's possible actions. Such planning allows individuals to consider, discard, and then select behavioral strategies with the greatest possibility of success. The most successful forward planning will result if one is able to look two, three, or four moves ahead, just as good chess players do, and in fact Humphrey explicitly makes this comparison. For the purposes of our discussion, it is important to recognize the strong similarity between the "forward planning" that Humphrey describes and the cognitively advanced process of role taking. What Humphrey describes is exactly what empathy theorists have termed role taking: the ability to understand the psychological point of view of another being, including the other's likely reaction to one's own behavior.

What sort of evidence can be offered for the social intelligence view? The fact that humans possess considerable intelligence and simultaneously demonstrate substantial role-taking capacity is consistent with this formulation, of course, but cannot really be considered proof of it. More intriguing, though not without problems, is the rich body of anecdotal evidence indicating that non-human primates with complex social structures are capable of behavior strongly suggesting the kind of role taking described above. Our nearest genetic relatives, though much less developed in terms of overall intelligence (Passingham, 1982; Wynn, 1988), have shared many elements of our evolutionary heritage, including highly similar social organization. If they are found to possess cognitive role-taking abilities, it will strengthen the argument that the demands of social living select for a social intelligence that includes role taking.

Frans de Waal, in his 1982 book *Chimpanzee Politics,* gives a number of fascinating examples of such behavior. In one instance, the chimp Yeroen suffered a slight wound during a fight with a rival, Nikkie. For nearly a week thereafter Yeroen limped pitifully but only when within Nikkie's visual field! Outside of Nikkie's view Yeroen acted in a completely normal fashion. de Waal's interpretation is that Yeroen was playacting, deliberately attempting to make Nikkie believe that he had been hurt more seriously than he in fact had, probably because Yeroen had previously learned that he received better treatment from Nikkie when injured.

The supply of such examples is nearly endless (see also Whiten and Byrne, 1988b), and because they so tellingly illustrate the thesis, the temptation to report more of them is strong. I will content myself with one more, an example of the "furtive mating" which often takes place in chimpanzee society between a receptive female and a male ranking low in the group's status hierarchy. Higher-ranking males reserve mating rights to themselves, and typically do not tolerate such activity by low-status males. They enforce this prerogative by attacking the unlucky couple if they are discovered, a not uncommon occurrence since females sometimes emit a distinctive high scream at the point of climax. de Waal reports several cases in which one or the other of the "lovers" displayed behavioral changes strongly suggesting a deliberate intention to conceal evidence of the illicit liaison. The female chimp Oor, for instance, displayed a pattern of behavior in which she would scream loudly only during mating sessions with the dominant male; when mating with lower status males, with secrecy at a premium, she showed the same bared teeth and open mouth associated with screaming, but emitted a relatively noiseless expulsion of breath from the back of the throat. As in the case of Yeroen, what this seems to indicate is an understanding of how others will respond to one's behavior, and an alteration of the behavior as a result.

Before leaving this discussion of the evolution of social intelligence, mention should be made of another, independent approach which is generally consistent with the Machiavellian intelligence hypothesis. Robert Hogan (1983) has proposed a *socioanalytic theory of personality,* based in roughly equal parts on evolutionary theory, depth psychology, and Mead's (1934) views on the relationship between self and society. What is of most relevance to us is Hogan's emphasis on considering human personality in terms of our evolutionary heritage. In particular he focuses on the fact that humans have always lived in groups and that all groups are organized in terms of a status hierarchy. Following this logic, he argues that the most important and universal problems in life therefore revolve around the attainment of status (relative position within the group) and popularity (being liked by other group members), both of which have considerable survival value. Higher status, of course, produces increased access to resources, especially reproductive opportunities. Popularity offers survival advantages as well, and rather direct ones. Hogan (1983) cites the high homicide rates among hunter-gatherer societies as one clear indication that it is good to remain popular with one's peers!

Hogan believes that our present-day conceptions of personality are heavily influenced by our evolutionary heritage. In fact, the major trait dimensions recognized today (e.g., neuroticism, extraversion, agreeableness) represent a societal consensus regarding the most important social dimensions. More specifically, it follows from socioanalytic theory that characteristics which are instrumental in attaining status and/or popularity, such as role-taking capacity, will confer an evolutionary advantage. Consistent with the Machiavellian intelligence approach, socioanalytic theory also argues that evolutionary pressures probably encouraged the development of a role-taking ability useful in obtaining status and popularity. Thus, two different theories, one concerned with the development of intelligence and the other with personality theory more generally, both reach the same conclusion: evolutionary pressures in all likelihood selected for a cognitive capacity to imaginatively adopt the psychological point of view of others.

Evaluation of the Evolutionary Argument

Based on the preceding discussion, it seems possible to make a prima facie case for the two central propositions of this chapter: that evolutionary pressures have led to 1) the development of humans' capacity for affective sharing, and 2) the ability to adopt others' perspectives. Despite the plausibility of the evolutionary arguments, however, there are limits on the applicability of the sociobiological approach, especially to humans. In particular, there are two related problems which typically work against it: 1) the almost complete absence of direct evidence for its claims, and 2) the resulting overreliance on plausible but untested explanations of the way in which environmental forces produce specific behaviors (Gould, 1980).

The first problem, lack of evidence, stems from the extreme difficulty of directly studying the genetics of behavior in humans. For example, the most common form of evidence for genetic influences on human personality and behavior comes from twin studies, a topic addressed in more detail in Chapter 4. As we shall see, these studies indeed suggest that many characteristics, some of them empathy-related, are influenced by inherited predispositions. Unfortunately, however, such studies reveal nothing about the evolutionary forces which may or may not have shaped the development of those characteristics in the species. Thus, they do not address whether or not the particular forces described here, kin selection and inclusive fitness, are responsible.

This lack of direct evidence exacerbates the second problem of the sociobiological approach, which is the overreliance on plausible-sounding explanations. As Gould (1980) notes, sociobiological explanations frequently begin with the assumption that the existence of a behavior is de facto evidence that the behavior is adaptive (Why else would it exist?), and then proceed to spin a genuinely plausible explanation of the ways in which the behavior increases fitness. Because the ideas are so difficult to test empirically, frequently "virtuosity in invention replaces testability as the criterion for acceptance" (Gould, 1980; p. 258). The end result of this process is a kind of theoretical "storytelling" which produces plausible, often fascinating, but typically unsupported accounts of the development of many different capacities, traits, and behaviors.

Do these two problems invalidate the sociobiological accounts of empathy presented here? The question is impossible to answer with certainty, but I would tentatively suggest that they do not. One reason for this conclusion is the inappropriateness of other mechanisms frequently offered as substitutes for natural selection by critics of sociobiological explanations. One special problem regarding humans, for example, is that even clearly adaptive behaviors need not have a genetic basis. Such behaviors may in fact be discovered by trial and error at some early point in history and then passed on through cultural transmission (Caplan, 1980; Gould, 1980). Thus what may appear superficially to be a behavior selected for through evolution can turn out to be simply taught to succeeding generations.

To the degree that the behavior in question can be shown not to be learned, however, this argument loses force. Thus, the fact that affective responsivity to the distress of others appears in newborns (Sagi & Hoffman, 1976; Simner, 1971) suggests that this behavioral response is innate and not learned. The physiological evidence regarding primate sensitivity to emotional expressions in others (Brothers, 1989) further supports this conclusion, at least with regard to affective responsivity. Thus, while the limits of sociobiological accounts must be taken seriously, they appear to provide in this case a plausible, though not proven, explanation for the origin of empathic capacities.

There is another kind of critique, based on the particular view of human nature seemingly implied by these analyses, which may also be advanced against the evolutionary interpretations presented here. In a nutshell, the argument is that these explanations suggest that the sole or primary human motive is a selfish one which excludes the possibility of truly altruistic behavior. This view of humans can be seen, for example, in the argument that perspective taking evolved in order to allow a successful manipulation of one's peers. It is also inherent in the argument that the mechanism which evolved to permit altruism (parallel affect) operates in a largely egoistic manner by prompting prosocial behavior because it reduces one's own distress (Hoffman, 1978). Taken together, these explanations do not seem to allow for the possibility of more genuinely altruistic, cooperative human motives.

Although we will return to this issue in Chapter 7, it is appropriate at this point to examine exactly what sociobiologists and psychologists mean by the term altruism. The typical sociobiological definition which we have been using thus far is quite narrow, focusing only on the behavior and its consequences. A representative view is that of Dawkins (1976): an organism is said to be acting altruistically if it "behaves in such a way as to increase another such entity's welfare at the expense of its own" (p. 4). Contrast this with Batson's (1991) definition: "a motivational state with the ultimate goal of increasing another's welfare" (p. 6). The essence of Batson's definition is the motive for the helper's act; in order to qualify as altruistic the "ultimate" goal must be the other's welfare. Thus, the same physical behavior could be viewed as altruistic if the proper motive is present, or as egoistic if it is not. The sociobiologists' view of altruism deliberately excludes such questions. They are only concerned with the consequences of the behaviors, in particular the effect that altruism has on the survival chances of those involved.

Is this sociobiological definition of altruism appropriate? Given the wide scope of sociobiological theory, and in particular its need to explain species other than human, it is frankly hard to see how an explanation of altruism within this tradition could take as its definition anything other than a behavioral one. The key mechanism for the natural selection analysis is the survival of genetic material resulting from altruistic acts. From the theory's point of view the conscious or unconscious motives of the individual "survival machine" are quite beside the point. In fact, using a definition which included a consideration of the helper's motives would have been impossible in the case of non-humans—how could the motives of the bee, or whale, be assessed?

What then is the significance of the kind of genuinely selfless altruism described by Batson? As we shall see in Chapter 7, it is a difficult task even to demonstrate the existence of a truly non-egocentric form of helping. Assuming that such helping does in fact exist, however, it does not seem to be necessary in order to explain the evolutionary development of the parallel affective response we have been describing; simple "egoistic" altruism seems adequate for that role. However, the parallel affect which evolved to foster egoistic altruism may also have made possible the existence of more truly selfless altruism as well. Although parallel affect, with its typically self-oriented negative tone, cannot provide the kind of other-oriented motivation to qualify as Batsonian altruism, a more sophisticated variant, feelings of empathic concern, can and does (Batson, 1991). Through a process to be described in the final section of this chapter, I will argue that parallel outcomes can be transformed into reactive outcomes, and specifically into empathic concern. Thus, the direct parallel response to others' distress which was evolutionarily selected for as a mechanism for egoistic altruism may be the necessary precursor to the more "sophisticated" reactive empathic responses which underlie a truly selfless altruism. In short, although evolutionary forces may have shaped the development of two capacities, parallel affect and perspective taking, which are not necessarily altruistic in nature, truly altruistic motives may nevertheless exist in humans because of the interaction of these two capacities.

How might such interactions work? One possibility is that the capacity for empathy-mediated altruism, to the degree that it indeed prompts behavior benefitting others, might serve to moderate the tendency to exploit others that accompanies Machiavellian intelligence. That is, instead of role-taking abilities being given free rein to exploit one's social partners without limit, the tendency to experience negative affect in response to others' distress may serve as a countervailing force. Humphrey (1976) noted this possibility, arguing that "the selfishness of social animals is typically tempered by what, for want of a better term, I would call sympathy" (p. 23).

The restraining role that affective sharing may have on the manipulative use of role-taking capacity prompts a further question. Does role-taking capacity have a comparable effect on affective sharing? In particular, does Machiavellian intelligence serve to reduce the amount of affectively-mediated altruism which would otherwise occur? This is a difficult question to address. On the surface it seems at least plausible that a highly developed role-taking ability, developed in the context of successfully maneuvering through the social environment, would serve to interfere with the altruism previously described, and this may in fact occur. Further reflection suggests that a more likely outcome might be a complex interaction of the two capacities, one in which the effect of a role-taking capacity would be to influence the qualitative nature of the affective response rather than simply its likelihood or strength. Thus, as noted earlier, the separate development of these two capacities might eventually lead to new emergent affective outcomes which were not necessarily selected for. The way in which innate emotional responsivity interacts with growing cognitive abilities, as it turns out, is the stuff of Martin Hoffman's comprehensive theory of empathy. We conclude this chapter with a thorough exploration of this theory.

Hoffman's Theory of Empathy: A Synthesis

Hoffman (1987) defines empathy as an "affective response more appropriate to someone else's situation than to one's own" (p. 48). As such, an empathic response need not be a close match with the affect experienced by the target, but can consist of any emotional reaction at least broadly compatible with the conditions facing the target. Hoffman's (1984; 1987) theory attempts to explain the way in which humans' capacities to react emotionally to others interact with their developing cognitive abilities to produce particular kinds of empathic responses. Because he is a developmental psychologist, Hoffman's focus has most frequently been on detailing how the outcome of this affective-cognitive interaction changes from infancy through adolescence, the time by which the most advanced cognitive skills have been acquired. His efforts have resulted in the most comprehensive attempt thus far to deal with these issues, one which incorporates a number of disparate themes. Because the theory is so multifaceted, it will be helpful to break it down a bit and consider each of the major elements in turn. Figure 2.1 displays the major elements of his model. We will start with what Hoffman sees as the six major mechanisms, or modes, by which one person comes to react affectively to the experiences of another. These six modes therefore can be considered *processes* according to the organizational model introduced in Chapter 1.

Modes of Empathic Arousal

Hoffman's first mode of empathic arousal, mentioned earlier in this chapter, is what he terms the "*primary circular reaction*" (Hoffman, 1984): the tendency for newborns to cry when they hear another infant crying. Because the response appears so soon after

AGE	MOST LIKELY MODES OF AROUSAL	COGNITIVE SENSE OF OTHERS	EMPATHIC RESPONSE
0-1 YEAR	Primary Circular Reaction Motor Mimicry Classical Conditioning Direct Association	Fusion of self and other; no clear self-other distinction	Global empathic distress; shared negative affect; unclear whether self or other is distressed
1-2 YEARS	Motor Mimicry Classical Conditioning Direct Association	Person permanence attained; internal representations of self and other	Sympathetic distress (sympathy) now possible as self-other distinction is clear; attempts to help other are often inappropriate due to lack of role-taking skill
3-10 YEARS	Motor Mimicry Classical Conditioning Direct Association Language-mediated Association Role Taking	Increasingly complex role taking develops	Increased role-taking skill leads to more sophisticated empathizing with multiple and sometimes conflicting affects; helping becomes increasingly appropriate
10-ADULT	Motor Mimicry Classical Conditioning Direct Association Language-mediated Association Role Taking	Person identity is achieved; continuity of others across situations and time	Most advanced empathizing is now possible; can look beyond situational cues to life conditions; can empathize with abstract categories

FIGURE 2.1
Hoffman's model of empathy: An affective-cognitive synthesis.

birth, and because it is evoked more strongly by others' crying than by other noxious stimuli, Hoffman argues that it may be the result of an innate releasing mechanism rather than the result of any form of learning; no conclusive proof of this assertion has yet been advanced, however. At the very least, though, this phenomenon indicates that at extremely early ages we react with distress to the distress cues of others and the primary circular reaction may therefore provide at least a rudimentary precursor of later, more full-blown empathic reactions.

The second mode of arousal, also mentioned earlier in this chapter, is *mimicry*. Hoffman's analysis suggests that empathic arousal via mimicry is a two-step process. First, the observer automatically and for the most part unconsciously imitates the target, both facially and posturally, with small mimicking movements. These movements result in internal kinesthetic cues which provide afferent feedback to the observer, and this feedback tends to create in the observer a comparable emotional reaction. As noted in Chapter 1, these two modes seem to require little cognitive processing in order to operate and thus may be considered the most primitive processes.

Classical conditioning processes constitute the third mode of empathic arousal. In this case affective reactions to others result from past situations in which the individual perceived affective cues in another person while directly experiencing the same affect. The pairing of these two events makes it more likely that subsequent exposure to such cues will evoke the affective state. Situations in which two children are exposed simultaneously to the same unpleasant stimulus would provide the conditions necessary for this mode. Each child would directly experience distress from the stimulus and at the same time witness the distress cues of the other with this combination setting the stage for later affective responses to those cues alone.

The fourth mode of arousal, *direct association,* is closely related to the third, but represents a more general application of the conditioning logic. According to Hoffman (1984), when we observe others experiencing an emotion "their facial expression, voice, posture, or any other cue in the situation that reminds us of past situations associated with our experience of that emotion may evoke the emotion in us" (p. 105). It is, therefore, not necessary for us to have ever experienced that emotion simultaneously with another person, as classical conditioning requires, only that we have previously experienced an emotion similar to the one we now observe in others. This mode is, therefore, tremendously more flexible than classical conditioning, although both are based on the same associative process. Both of these association-based modes, moreover, require similar and rather rudimentary cognitive processing. The final two modes described by Hoffman are somewhat different.

The fifth mode of arousal is *language-mediated association.* Like direct association, this one is based on the idea that an association between the target's cues and the observer's past experiences can lead to affect in the observer. The difference is that in this mode the victim's cues do not trigger associations directly, but rather symbolically through language. For example, the target might verbally label his/her emotional state ("I'm frightened") or describe the situation ("I flunked the final exam"), and the meaning symbolically expressed through these words triggers associations with comparable feelings and experiences stored semantically in the observer's memory. This mode therefore does not rely on overt expressive cues by the target, and in fact does not require the presence of the target at all. All that is necessary is for the observer to become aware in some verbal fashion of the experiences of the target. This is obviously a relatively advanced form of empathic arousal.

The most advanced form, however, is *role taking.* This mode requires a deliberate effort by observers to imagine how they would feel if faced with the circumstances affecting the target. Making this effort then produces in them an affective response paralleling that of the target, perhaps, Hoffman argues, because imagining ourselves in the target's circumstances triggers associations with actual past experiences with such circumstances. This mode therefore has some similarities to direct association and language-mediated association. Because such role-taking efforts require quite advanced cognitive skills, Hoffman believes that this mode is likely to be less frequently employed than most of the others.

It is important to note that these modes need not operate in isolation. In particular, Hoffman argues, with the exception of the primary circular reaction which is largely limited to infancy, and role taking which due to its advanced nature is infrequently used, the other four modes commonly operate in conjunction with one another. What determines which particular mode or modes will operate is the nature of the situation. The presence of strong expressive cues by the target will generally foster mimicry, the presence of clear situational cues may increase the likelihood of conditioning and/or direct association, and significant semantic content in the situation will prompt language-mediated association. Many situations contain more than one kind of cue, and thus multiple arousal modes may be activated. In any event, regardless of the particular cues present in the situation or the particular modes of arousal which are activated, the end result is the production in the observer of some form of affective response. The precise nature of this response depends, however, on the cognitive capabilities of the individual.

Cognitive Capabilities: The Cognitive Sense of Others

In one sense the cognitive capacities of the individual have already played a role in Hoffman's model through his discussion of the modes of empathic arousal. Except for mimicry and the primary circular reaction, all of the other modes require at least minimal and sometimes quite sophisticated cognitive functioning. For example, those based on associative learning involve at least some perceptual discrimination and pattern recognition (Hoffman, 1984), and the more advanced language-mediated and role-taking modes require even greater intellectual sophistication. However, the cognitive capability which has the most important and interesting impact on affective responding is what Hoffman terms the "cognitive sense of others," or the way in which we mentally represent other people, especially the relation between others and ourselves. How we mentally conceptualize other people has a crucial impact on the affective empathic reactions we have to them, and this conceptualizing is said to pass through three levels of increasing sophistication.

The first level is characterized by the acquisition of what Hoffman (1984) calls *person permanence*—the awareness that others exist as separate physical entities. For most of the first year of life children do not possess this kind of social awareness. Instead, perceptions of other people are fragmentary at best, with the child most often experiencing a self-other "fusion" in which the boundary between self and other is perceived dimly if at all. At this stage the child may be said to not even have a stable sense of self or other. By the end of the first year, however, the acquisition of person permanence has occurred, and children can conceive of another person as a stable physical entity which exists even when that person is no longer within the sensory field of the child.

Acquiring person permanence is a major step, but only the initial one. The second level is characterized by the acquisition of increasingly sophisticated role taking, or perspective taking, capacities. With person permanence, the child recognizes the permanent physical distinction between the self and others, but does not yet grasp that these separate physical entities also differ in their internal states. Children at this age, therefore, cannot accurately discern when other people think or feel differently than they themselves do. Hoffman estimates, based on the research evidence, that rudimentary role taking capacities begin to appear between the ages of 2 and 3, and then grow in sophistication throughout childhood.

Finally, by late childhood or early adolescence, a sense of *person identity* emerges. This refers to the development of a view of others as having stable identities, attitudes, experiences, and internal states, which exist beyond the immediate situation. Prior to this time, children with well-developed role-taking skills may be able to accurately infer another's internal state in any given situation by using situational and expressive cues, but they do not recognize the continuous, unchanging nature of that person's identity in other settings. With the acquisition of person identity, observers are able to "take the other's role and assess their reactions in particular situations but also generalize from these situations and construct a concept of the other's general life experience" (Hoffman, 1984, p. 111). This represents the most advanced and abstract form of cognitive awareness of others.

The Affective-Cognitive Synthesis

The importance of separately considering the production of empathic arousal and the cognitive sense of others now becomes clear. At any point during development the child's cognitive sense of others coalesces with the vicarious affect produced through the six modes to produce a distinctive empathic experience. In particular, Hoffman outlines four different levels of empathy which result from this affective-cognitive synthesis.

Global Empathy

During the first year of life, when the child has no reliable sense of the self as physically distinct from others, the empathic response to a distressed other consists of a general undifferentiated distress reaction in the observer. The self-other fusion existing at this time means that the child is in fact often unsure as to who exactly, self or other, is *experiencing* the distress. Hoffman terms this sharing of negative affect *empathic distress,* and characterizes it as passive, involuntary, and requiring only the lowest level of cognitive processing (Hoffman, 1984). However, it also provides the foundation on which more sophisticated empathic reactions will be built.

Toward the end of the first year of life, something important happens. As children begin to firmly grasp the concept of person permanence and recognize that other people are physical entities separate from the self, they begin to construct separate mental representations of self and of others. When this happens, the child's global distress reactions begin to "split," and are separately "extended to the separate image-of-self and image-of-other" (p. 112). At first the distinction between these two representations is hazy and unstable, and the child reacts to the distress of others as though "self" and "other" were simultaneously or alternately suffering. Gradually, however, as person permanence is attained, the self-other distinction becomes more firmly established and the separate distress of self and of other more reliably recognized.

Egocentric Empathy

With the acquisition of full person permanence at approximately 1 year of age, the second level of empathy begins. For the next year or so, before much meaningful role-taking capacity appears, the child is aware that others are separate physical entities but still lacks any real understanding that others differ from self with regard to internal states. Hoffman refers to this as the level of "egocentric" empathy because children often respond to distress in others by offering them inappropriate help that they, as the observers, find comforting.

More important for the present discussion, Hoffman believes that the acquisition of person permanence allows the emergence of *sympathetic distress,* a new kind of affective response to others' distress. Unlike empathic distress, which is essentially a parallel reaction mirroring that of the target, sympathetic distress is characterized by feelings of compassion for that target. It therefore qualifies as a reactive affective outcome according to the organizational model, and seems equivalent to Wispé's sympathy and Batson's definition of empathy. Hoffman carefully points out, however, that this new response in no sense takes the place of the earlier one. Empathic distress continues to result from witnessing others in pain, but the possibility now exists for a compassionate response to that other as well.

What produces this new affective reaction? Hoffman argues that it results directly from the separate cognitive representations of self and other which the child now possesses. First, he assumes generally that the experience of any unpleasant affect prompts an accompanying motive to end that aversive state. He next argues that the creation during the global empathy stage of an internal image-of-other, and the transfer to that image of some portion of the child's original global distress, consequently results in a corresponding new motive to end the suffering associated with the image-of-other. Thus, the child can now be said to possess two distinct

motives to the observed distress in others: a relatively egoistic desire to reduce one's own distress and a more truly altruistic desire
to reduce the distress of others. At this "egocentric" level of empathy, of course, in the absence of meaningful role-taking skills, attempts to aid the other may be counter-productive, as noted earlier.
That begins to change with the next level of empathy.

Empathy for Another's Feelings

Beginning at approximately 2–3 years of age, and continuing through
late childhood, the child acquires increasingly sophisticated role-
taking abilities. The effect on empathic responding is to make children more able to interpret the wide variety of cues, expressive and
situational, available in social settings. Armed with their more
highly developed role-taking capacity, they are able to make finer
distinctions among the many affective reactions they witness in others, and can even empathize simultaneously with several, possibly
conflicting, emotions. The rapid development of language skills during this time reinforces this process, allowing more complex sym-
bolic cues to be used as well. The help offered to a distressed other
is now more effective because the child is better able to accurately
understand what aid is most appropriate to the other's situation. Although Hoffman does not make the point explicitly, it also seems
plausible that the occurrence of sympathetic distress generally increases during this time, occurring as the self-other distinction becomes increasingly established through the child's more frequent
and skillful shifting of perspective from self to other and back
again.

Empathy for Another's General Condition

The final level of empathy, emerging in late childhood or early adolescence, results from the acquisition of person identity. As the individual develops an awareness of others as persons with stable
histories and identities, it becomes possible to consider more
chronic aspects of the target's life and not be as affected by the
cues available in specific situations. One example that Hoffman offers is that of seeing a laughing child who does not know he has an
incurable disease. A child observer who has not achieved person
identity will tend to focus on and react to the situational cues of
laughter, and is likely to experience a positive affective response.
An adult observer who appreciates the more chronic life condition
of the target is likely to find the situation poignantly, perhaps un-
bearably, sad. Hoffman also proposes that acquiring person identity
makes possible a more abstract kind of empathic reaction, less tied

to specific circumstances, in which an observer is empathically aroused by classes or categories of people, for example the homeless or oppressed.

Summary and Conclusion

This chapter has concerned itself with the question of capacities: the ability to engage in the cognitive process of adopting another's psychological point of view, and the capacity to experience affective reactions to the observed experiences of others. A case can be made that ancient environmental conditions exerted selective evolutionary pressures favoring the development of both capacities, although the evolutionary pressures contributing to each capacity might have had very different characters. Affective responsivity may have evolved as a mechanism for producing self-sacrificing behavior, while role taking might have evolved to allow more successful competition with one's primate peers.

Hoffman's developmental theory of empathy suggests some of the ways in which these two capacities may combine to produce distinct subjective reactions to the observation of distress in others. At the youngest ages, primitive and somewhat ''generic'' feelings of shared distress are the most likely to occur; with increasing age and cognitive sophistication, part of this empathic distress is transformed into other-oriented feelings of sympathy and compassion for the distressed other. Thus, the more advanced the level of role-taking capacity, the more reactive and less parallel the affective responses become.

There is no guarantee, however, that individuals will fully utilize the capacities, either cognitive or affective, which they possess. That is, simply being in possession of an advanced role-taking skill is not enough to ensure its use in everyday social settings, and the ability to respond to another with feelings of sympathy and compassion is not always employed when faced with an unfortunate other. Some people seem to consistently make heavy use of their capacities and others do not. There are, in short, reliable individual differences in the tendency to engage in empathy-related processes and to experience empathic outcomes. These differences in dispositional empathic tendencies are the subject of the next two chapters.

3

Assessment of Individual Differences in Empathy

The first level of analysis in considering the question of empathy's origins, addressed in the previous chapter, is that of empathic *capacities*. The next level of analysis concerns the stable individual differences which exist in the tendency to utilize those capacities. As we shall see, it is not always easy to draw a clear distinction between capacity and tendency when examining specific individual difference measures. To the extent possible, however, the primary focus of this chapter will be on assessing differences in empathic tendencies rather than abilities, with an emphasis on those instruments developed for use with adults. Although we will review a number of methods for assessing individual differences in empathy-related constructs, the review will not be a comprehensive one. The interested reader is directed to more complete descriptions of the measures and their psychometric characteristics provided by

Ford (1979), Enright and Lapsley (1980), Krebs and Russell (1981), Chlopan, McCain, Carbonell, and Hagen, (1985), and Mehrabian, Young, and Sato (1988).

Following this overview of the various techniques for assessing individual differences in empathy, Chapter 4 will offer a consideration of the possible origins of these individual differences—specifically the role of inherited predispositions and childhood environmental factors. Although the sequence of these two chapters may appear somewhat awkward, discussing methods before substance, it turns out to be quite advantageous to consider in some detail the various ways of measuring empathy before examining the research which employs these measures.

The organizational model defines individual differences in empathy as the observer's dispositional likelihood, during any given empathy episode, of engaging in some empathy-related *process* or experiencing some empathy-related *outcome*. We will use this definition to help structure our examination of the existing individual difference measures of empathy. In particular, these measures can be seen as generally falling into one of three categories. Some measures have assessed the process we have labelled **role taking,** the tendency of individuals to entertain the perceptual, cognitive, or affective perspective of others. Other measures have largely focused on what we have termed **non-affective outcomes,** such as accuracy in social judgments, which are likely to result from such perspective taking. Finally, some measures have tapped the tendency to experience **affective outcomes** to the observed experiences of others. Each of these categories of measures will be addressed in turn. Because the measures developed for use with children and adults have evolved from separate traditions and take very different forms, these measures will be considered separately, starting with those developed for use with younger respondents.

Measures of Role Taking: Children

Careful reviewers of role-taking measures (Enright & Lapsley, 1980; Ford, 1979; Krebs & Russell, 1981) have generally agreed that they address three distinct domains: **perceptual, cognitive,** and **affective** role taking. The three domains share the common core characteristic of an individual in each case going beyond his or her typical, largely egocentric means of perceiving the world and instead entertaining a different point of view. What distinguishes the three domains from one another is the specific content of these role-taking attempts. In perceptual role taking, the individual imagines how an object or set of objects appears to someone who occupies a different physical vantage point; in cognitive role taking the individual infers something about another's thoughts, motives, or intentions; in affective role taking, the individual infers the emotional reaction experienced by another person. Given their conceptual similarity, substantial correlations might be expected between role-taking measures from different domains, but such a pattern is not typically found. Reviews of the literature have found instead that measures tapping these domains seem largely independent of one another (Ford, 1979; Krebs & Russell, 1981).

The organizational model makes a clear distinction between the process of role taking and the non-affective outcomes of that process. As it turns out, this distinction is easier to maintain in theory than in practice. The reader may note, for example, that the three domains of role taking are defined primarily in terms of outcomes or by the kind of inference which results. Further, many methods of assessing individual differences in role taking require the respondent to provide an estimate of another's visual perspective, thoughts, or emotions; greater success is taken as evidence of greater role-taking proficiency. Obviously, however, the process of role taking is not being directly assessed; it is the *outcome* of the process (the more or less accurate estimates) which these tasks capture. Thus, while such measures are considered assessments of role taking, in terms of the model they actually assess varying combinations of role-taking process and non-affective outcomes.

Another theoretical distinction which becomes blurred in practice is the difference between role-taking tendencies and capacities, as it is often difficult to know for certain whether role-taking performance on a measure results from the possession of greater role-taking ability or simply a greater tendency to utilize existing capacity. Given that many role-taking tasks overtly, and often repeatedly, ask the child to estimate the internal states of others, it seems reasonable to assume that the child is frequently attempting to make maximum use of whatever capacities exist. If effort is indeed held constant, then it seems probable that these measures largely reflect individual differences in role-taking capacities, a conclusion further buttressed by the strong developmental increases in childhood typically found for these tasks (see Enright & Lapsley, 1980).

Perceptual Role Taking

The prototypical measure of perceptual role taking is the Three Mountains Task (Piaget & Inhelder, 1956). In this task the child sits in one of four chairs arrayed around a table, on which three moun-tain-shaped objects are arranged. The experimenter asks the child to indicate, sometimes by choosing from a set of photographs, the view of the mountains which would be seen by someone sitting in a different chair. Thus, the task requires the child to suppress his or her own visual perspective and to imagine that of another person. Numerous variations on this task have appeared over the years, all based on the same fundamental logic. In a measure devised by Flavell et al. (1968), for example, subjects are presented with an increasingly complex array of objects (rather than just the three mountains) and are required to make estimates of how the objects would appear to others in a different physical location. These mea-sures rather clearly seem to assess the successful *outcome* of per-ceptual role taking rather than the role-taking process itself.

Cognitive Role Taking

In contrast to perceptual role taking, which employs one basic meth-odology, cognitive role-taking measures fall into at least three dis-tinct categories. Each measure requires the subject to infer something about the mental state of others (their thoughts, motives, intentions) but the mechanics of doing so vary considerably. *Refer-ential communication* measures, for example, provide the subject with information not possessed by another, and then require the communication of this information to that other. Glucksberg, Krauss, and Weisberg (1966), for example, provide the subject with a view of a tower made of blocks in varying shapes and sizes, but provide no such view to the subject's partner. The subject then tells the partner, using only verbal instructions, how to build an identical tower. This measure therefore requires the individual to take into account the disparity between information available to self and to partner; better role taking is evidenced by instructions which recog-nize this disparity.

    Decentering tasks (e.g., Feffer and Gourevitch, 1960; Selman & Byrne, 1974) assess the degree to which subjects understand that different people possess differing perspectives on the same event. For instance, subjects may be presented with a picture depicting three characters and asked to tell a story from the perspective of one of the characters (Feffer and Gourevitch, 1960). The subject is later asked to tell the story twice more, once from the viewpoint of the second character, and then from the third. Scoring is based in part on the subject's ability to coordinate the perspectives represented by the three different versions. A similar task, Flavell et al.'s (1968) "apple-dog" story, presents subjects with a series of cartoons depicting a boy being chased by a dog and climbing an apple tree to escape. Certain key cartoons are then removed, changing the nature of the story, and the subjects are asked to retell the story based only on the remaining cartoons. The ability to suppress the earlier "privileged" information and to recast the story without using it is indicative of greater role taking.

Recursive role-taking measures employ a different strategy. These techniques assess the degree to which the subject recognizes that others' thoughts can include the subject as well. Flavell et al.'s (1968) "nickel-dime" task is an example of this type. Subjects are given a nickel and a dime and two upside down cups; one cup has a nickel taped to it and the other has a dime. Subjects are to cover their coins with the cups in such a way that the other person, who is allowed to pick either cup, will end up choosing the lesser-valued coin. Greater role taking is inferred from the child's rationale for his or her strategy; in particular, the degree of sophistication in the child's estimates of the other person's strategies (*"He* will think that *I* will expect *him* to . . .'') is an important factor. Thus, these measures seem to more directly assess the role-taking process than the outcome of this process.

Affective Role Taking

The logic of the affective role-taking measures is simple: subjects are asked to infer the emotional state of another person who is depicted in a potentially emotional situation. These measures do not, therefore, assess whether subjects actually experience an emotional reaction, merely their ability to infer it in others. One widely used measure in this domain is Borke's (1971, 1973) Interpersonal Perception Test. Subjects are told a series of short stories about children in emotional situations (e.g., losing a pet). They are then presented with a picture of the story's protagonist, with a blank face, and are asked to supply the correct facial expression.

Because one potential problem with such tasks is that subjects will simply project their own feelings onto the story protagonist, later versions have attempted to minimize this possibility. Rothenberg (1970), for instance, dealt with this problem by presenting young subjects with tape recordings of adults engaged in somewhat emotional interactions. In one vignette, for example, a husband informs his wife at the last minute that he has invited guests for dinner, and she becomes anxious about getting ready in time. Children are assumed to be less likely to project their own feelings into situations so unfamiliar to them. Other investigators (e.g., Kurdek & Rodgon, 1975) use stimuli in which the reaction of the story protagonist (e.g., frowning) is at odds with the situational cues (e.g., a festive birthday party). This variation is also intended to make it difficult for child-subjects to project their own feelings onto the protagonist and falsely appear to be engaging in role taking. All such measures, however, clearly assess the *outcome* of role taking (judgments about the affective states of others) rather than the role-taking process itself.

Measures of Affective Outcomes: Children

By far the most popular means of assessing affective empathy levels in children has been the picture/story method, and in particular the FASTE (Feshbach Affective Situations Test of Empathy; Feshbach & Roe, 1968). In this technique, the subject is exposed to another's affective state by means of pictures and/or stories regarding some protagonist. Rather than asking subjects to infer the emotion being experienced by the protagonist (i.e., affective role taking), this technique requires them to report their own emotional states, either verbally or by choosing a response from a set of facial expressions. Affective empathy is indicated by a match between the self-reported affect of the subject and that of the protagonist.

Although extensively used, the FASTE has also been criticized on logical and psychometric grounds (e.g., Hoffman, 1982b; Eisenberg-Berg & Lennon, 1980). Some critiques have focused on scoring issues. The original scoring procedure required that the child report an emotion exactly matching the protagonist's in order to be credited with an empathic response, a procedure which might underestimate the true level of affective sharing. As a result, modified scoring schemes (e.g., Levine & Hoffman, 1975) allowing for more general affective matches have since been developed. Others have criticized the FASTE because its brief stories might not be engaging enough to produce empathic responding in children (Eisenberg-Berg & Lennon, 1980), and because repeatedly asking the child how he or she feels might create strong demand characteristics (Eisenberg & Lennon, 1983).

More recently, Bryant (1982) has developed a self-report measure of emotional empathy, for children, based on the Mehrabian and Epstein (1972) adult measure (discussed later in this chapter). The Bryant scale consists of 22 items, adapted from the adult instrument to be more appropriate for children, which are read aloud to the respondents. One advantage of this measure is that it allows a comparison between younger and older respondents using similar measures, something that was impossible to do as long as self-report methods were restricted to adult samples.

Even more recently, individual differences in affective empathy have been measured by focusing on the somatic responses of children rather than their self-reports. Eisenberg and colleagues (Eisenberg, Fabes, Bustamante, Mathy, Miller, & Lindhold, 1988; Eisenberg, Fabes, Carlo, Speer, Switzer, Karbon & Troyer, 1993); Eisenberg, Fabes, Miller, Fultz, Shell, Mathy, & Reno, 1989; Eisenberg, Fabes, Schaller, Carlo, & Miller, 1991) have carried out several investigations in which children were videotaped while they were exposed to stimuli depicting others' distress. Their facial expressions were later reliably coded for the presence of specific emotional states such as fear, sadness, distress, and concerned-attention—a facial expression that seems to reflect sympathy and concern. These expressions have generally been found to correlate with the appropriate self-reported affect and with behavior consistent with that affect (see Eisenberg & Fabes, 1990). While such measures have the advantage of reflecting spontaneous emotional reactions relatively unaffected by demand characteristics, they have the disadvantage of being rather cumbersome, requiring video equipment and elaborate coding procedures. It is also possible that validity might suffer as children become better able to control their emotional expressions with age (Eisenberg, 1986).

Measures of Role Taking and Non-Affective Outcomes: Adults

The measures developed for use with adults differ in several ways from those reviewed thus far. First, the greater verbal skill and insight of adults has made self-report questionnaires—rather than situational tests—the primary method for assessing empathy-related constructs. Second, while several ways of assessing role taking among children have been developed, the same cannot be said regarding adults. Only a handful of such measures exist, and, as we shall see, they might all be better characterized as assessments of non-affective **outcomes** rather than measures of the role-taking process itself. Third, these measures do not make the careful distinctions among role-taking domains that are apparent with the children's measures. For example, adult measures completely ignore perceptual role taking, and tend to combine cognitive and affective role taking into one construct, sometimes referred to as **social perspective taking.**

The Chapin Social Insight Test (Chapin, 1942) was one of the earliest attempts in this tradition. The items of the test present respondents with hypothetical social situations (e.g., being disturbed by noisy neighbors) and ask them to choose, from four options, the most effective course of action. Although some evidence supports the measure's validity (see Chlopan et al., 1985), it seems clear that the test is essentially measuring something which might best be considered an outcome of cognitive/affective role taking. That is, someone skilled at or willing to engage in social role taking might choose more effective social actions as a result; however, other factors certainly affect these choices as well, making it difficult to view the test as a very clear measure of role taking at all.

A different approach was taken by Dymond (1949, 1950), who defined empathy in terms of the accurate transposition of the self into the thinking, feeling, and acting of others, and who then developed a procedure for assessing such accuracy. In this technique—the rating scale method—a group of subjects interact for some period of time, after which they fill out a series of questionnaires. The questionnaires call for each subject to provide a self-rating on a series of traits (e.g., friendly or unfriendly), a rating of each of the other group members on the same traits, an estimate of how each of the group members rated themselves, and an estimate of how each of the other group members rated the subject. Each subject's accuracy is then calculated in two ways: as the extent to which the subjects' ratings of others correspond to those others' self-ratings, and the extent to which subjects are able to successfully predict how the others view them.

Unfortunately, high levels of accuracy in this technique can result from several different factors, most of which have nothing to do with empathy (Cronbach, 1955; Hastorf & Bender, 1952). For example, if all members of a group tend to use the same region on a scale, favoring the midpoint, for example, apparent accuracy would be high even if no real ability to differentiate among individuals exists. Likewise, individuals who are able to guess the most common response of the group will appear relatively accurate if they simply make that response for every other group member. Although this may indicate some sort of cognitive skill, it does not require any ability to adopt the perspective of a particular person. Beyond this, moreover, the rating scale method quite clearly seems more a measure of non-affective outcomes than the process of role taking. While role taking might be expected to influence this outcome (accuracy), the rating scale method taps, imperfectly to be sure, only the outcome.

The most widely used contemporary measure based on a cognitive definition of empathy is no doubt Hogan's empathy (EM) scale. Hogan (1969) began the development of this measure with the following definition of empathy: "the intellectual or imaginative apprehension of another's condition without actually experiencing that person's feelings" (p. 308). This definition clearly restricts empathy to the non-affective realm and places the focus on both outcome (the comprehension of other's states) and process (role taking). From this starting point, Hogan then developed the 64-item EM scale through a somewhat elaborate process.

In brief, Hogan had expert judges describe the "highly empathic man," using the previous definition, by means of the 100-item California Q-sort (Block, 1961). The resulting composite description was used to identify, from an existing sample of people for whom Q-sorts had already been obtained, individuals high and low on empathy. Those whose Q-sort descriptions most (or least) closely matched the highly empathic "ideal" Q-sort were deemed high (or low) on empathy. Once these groups had been defined, their responses to previously completed questionnaires (e.g., MMPI, CPI) were used to select items for the EM scale. Sixty-four items were selected, largely on the basis of their ability to discriminate the high and low empathy groups.

Internal reliability of the EM scale has tended to be acceptable but not overwhelming. Hogan (1969) reported a Kuder-Richardson estimate of .71; Johnson, Cheek, and Smither (1983) reported an alpha coefficient of .69; but Cross and Sharpley (1982) found the alpha reliability to be only .61. Test-retest reliability has been more robust, with Hogan (1969) reporting a 2-month stability coefficient of .84. No doubt one aspect contributing to the relatively low internal reliability is the fact that the 64-item measure seems to contain either three (Greif & Hogan, 1973) or four (Johnson et al., 1983) relatively uncorrelated factors which Johnson et al. labelled as "Social Self-Confidence," "Even Temperedness," "Sensitivity," and "Nonconformity." At present, therefore, there is some ambiguity as to the precise nature of the EM scale. Given the nature of its component factors, and the fact that the scale is significantly associated with measures of better adjustment and social functioning (see Chlopan et al., 1985), it may be fair to conclude that it is not so much a measure of role taking as it is an assessment of "role-taking-mediated-social-skillfulness."

Measures of Affective Empathy: Adults

Just as Hogan's EM scale is the most widely used measure employing a cognitive definition of empathy, the Questionnaire Measure of Emotional Empathy (QMEE; Mehrabian & Epstein, 1972) has been the most widely utilized instrument adopting an affective definition. The QMEE was designed explicitly to assess the chronic tendency to react emotionally to the observed experiences of other people, and its items are intended to tap the likelihood of such responses in a variety of contexts. Specifically, the QMEE contains seven inter-related subscales tapping such constructs as "susceptibility to emotional contagion," "tendency to be moved by others' positive emotional experiences," and "sympathetic tendency," with the items of the scale created to specifically assess each of these constructs. Despite this, however, virtually all investigations employ only the overall score; the internal reliability of the measure is quite acceptable (split-half reliability of .84 reported by Mehrabian & Epstein, 1972), supporting the view that the items tap a single reasonably coherent construct.

In terms of the organizational model, the QMEE seems largely to assess what it purports to—affective empathy, defined as the tendency to react emotionally to the observed experiences of others. As suggested by the preceding discussion, however, a wide variety of affective outcomes are represented in this instrument, including both parallel and reactive responses. In particular, there are items which seem to tap pure empathic matching, empathic concern, empathic anger, and personal distress. Because of the broad array of affective responses contributing to high scores on this measure, it has been suggested that the instrument may tap a chronic emotional arousability to the environment in general, one that goes beyond any tendency to react specifically to affect in other people (Mehrabian et al., 1988).

Multidimensional Measures of Empathy: Adults

In addition to those instruments based on cognitive or affective definitions of empathy, one measure based explicitly on a multidimensional view of empathy has also been developed. The Interpersonal Reactivity Index (IRI; Davis, 1980, 1983b) takes as its starting point the notion that empathy consists of a set of separate but related constructs, and seeks to provide measures of dispositional tendencies in several areas. The instrument contains four seven-item subscales, each tapping a separate facet of empathy. These items appear in Table 3.1. The *perspective taking* (PT) scale measures the reported

TABLE 3.1 Davis's Interpersonal Reactivity Index

Respondents are asked to indicate the degree to which the items describe them by choosing the appropriate point on a five-point scale running from 0 (does not describe me well) to 4 (describes me very well). Items indicated by an (R) are first reversed (0=4, 1=3, 3=1, 4=0), and then responses to the items making up each subscale are separately summed. Each subscale consists of seven items; thus, scores on each subscale can range from 0 to 28. The subscales are the Fantasy (FS) scale, the Perspective Taking (PT) scale, the Empathic Concern (EC) scale, and the Personal Distress (PD) scale.

1. I daydream and fantasize, with some regularity, about things that might happen to me. (FS)
2. I often have tender, concerned feelings for people less fortunate than me. (EC)
3. I sometimes find it difficult to see things from the "other guy's" point of view. (PT) (R)
4. Sometimes I don't feel very sorry for other people when they are having problems. (EC) (R)
5. I really get involved with the feelings of the characters in a novel. (FS)
6. In emergency situations, I feel apprehensive and ill-at-ease. (PD)
7. I am usually objective when I watch a movie or play, and I don't often get completely caught up in it. (FS) (R)
8. I try to look at everybody's side of a disagreement before I make a decision. (PT)
9. When I see someone being taken advantage of, I feel kind of protective towards them. (EC)
10. I sometimes feel helpless when I am in the middle of a very emotional situation. (PD)
11. I sometimes try to understand my friends better by imagining how things look from their perspective. (PT)
12. Becoming extremely involved in a good book or movie is somewhat rare for me. (FS) (R)
13. When I see someone get hurt, I tend to remain calm. (PD) (R)
14. Other people's misfortunes do not usually disturb me a great deal. (EC) (R)
15. If I'm sure I'm right about something, I don't waste much time listening to other people's arguments. (PT) (R)
16. After seeing a play or movie, I have felt as though I were one of the characters. (FS)
17. Being in a tense emotional situation scares me. (PD)
18. When I see someone being treated unfairly, I sometimes don't feel very much pity for them. (EC) (R)
19. I am usually pretty effective in dealing with emergencies. (PD) (R)
20. I am often quite touched by things that I see happen. (EC)
21. I believe that there are two sides to every question and try to look at them both. (PT)

TABLE 3.1—Continued

22. I would describe myself as a pretty soft-hearted person. (EC)

23. When I watch a good movie, I can very easily put myself in the place of a leading character. (FS)

24. I tend to lose control during emergencies. (PD)

25. When I'm upset at someone, I usually try to "put myself in his shoes" for a while. (PT)

26. When I am reading an interesting story or novel, I imagine how *I* would feel if the events in the story were happening to me. (FS)

27. When I see someone who badly needs help in an emergency, I go to pieces. (PD)

28. Before criticizing somebody, I try to imagine how *I* would feel if I were in their place. (PT)

---

tendency to spontaneously adopt the psychological point of view of others in everyday life (''I sometimes try to understand my friends better by imagining how things look from their perspective.''). The *empathic concern* (EC) scale assesses the tendency to experience feelings of sympathy and compassion for unfortunate others (''I often have tender, concerned feelings for people less fortunate than me.''). The *personal distress* (PD) scale taps the tendency to experience distress and discomfort in response to extreme distress in others (''Being in a tense emotional situation scares me.''). The *fantasy* (FS) scale measures the tendency to imaginatively transpose oneself into fictional situations (''When I am reading an interesting story or novel, I imagine how *I* would feel if the events in the story were happening to me.''). Both the internal (alpha coefficients ranging from .70 to .78) and the test-retest (from .61 to .81 over a two-month period) reliabilities are acceptable (Davis, 1980). Davis and Franzoi (1991) also report substantial test-retest associations for the IRI scales over even longer periods (from .50 to .62 over a two-year period during adolescence).

In terms of the organizational model, the perspective taking scale seems to be the only existing adult measure which assesses the process of social role taking. The items of this scale explicitly ask about the respondent's likelihood of engaging in attempts to entertain the point of view of other people (process); they do not inquire about the purported outcome of that process (e.g., accuracy or social insight). In addition, the PT items focus exclusively on the individual's perspective-taking tendencies in different situations, and not on perspective-taking ability or capacity. The empathic concern scale seems clearly to tap the part of the model designated as affective outcomes, and in particular the tendency to respond to distress in others with the reactive response of sympathy/compassion. The personal distress scale also clearly assesses an affective outcome, but it is less clear whether the response is parallel or reactive. For situations in which the target is experiencing distress and discomfort, reactions of personal distress by the observer may be considered a parallel response. In other situations, such as when the target is experiencing sadness, distress in the observer is not a precisely parallel response, and may in such cases be considered reactive. The fantasy scale, in contrast to the other three IRI scales, is more difficult to fit into the organizational scheme. The thrust of the FS items, imagining oneself in the circumstances of another, suggests that the scale should fall under the heading of role taking. However, the fact that virtually all of these items deal with imagining oneself in the place of fictitious characters appearing in books, movies, and plays somewhat complicates this interpretation.

Sex Differences in Empathy-Related Constructs

As noted by Eisenberg and Lennon (1983), the impression long held by psychologists and the population at large is that females are more empathic, especially in the affective sense of that term, than males. Thus, one question of interest in this discussion of individual difference measures concerns the degree to which this stereotype is true. In short, *do* females score higher on these measures than males? This question has been addressed in several literature reviews, and the answers have been somewhat mixed. Much depends on the particular definition of empathy which is employed and the specific measures which are used.

Early reviews (Block, 1976; Maccoby & Jacklin, 1974) reached the conclusion that no reliable sex difference in empathy existed. However, each review used a rather broad definition of empathy, and included studies which examined emotional reactions, social sensitivity, role taking, and accuracy in person perception. As we have seen, these are conceptually distinct constructs; treating them as equivalent in a review might not be the most useful approach. Hoffman (1977) took a different tack, and distinguished between measures of empathy (defined as emotional responsiveness to another's emotional state) and measures of perceptual, cognitive, and affective role taking. When empathy was defined in this way, a consistent pattern emerged of females scoring higher than males, with no consistent sex differences emerging for any of the role-taking measures. Thus, Hoffman concluded that females are indeed more (affectively) empathic than males.

Eisenberg and Lennon (1983) approached the sex differences issue in the most comprehensive fashion to date, separately examining the evidence for several types of measures. With regard to the role-taking measures designed for use with children, Eisenberg and Lennon examined only those which assessed *affective* role taking (e.g., Borke, 1971, 1973; Rothenberg, 1970); they found, as did Hoffman, no evidence of a reliable sex difference. Slightly stronger evidence was found for the picture-story method of assessing children's affective *outcomes*. Using meta-analysis, a technique which allows the reviewer to test for statistical significance across a number of separate studies, Eisenberg and Lennon found a small but significant tendency for girls to display greater affective reactivity with this method. Unfortunately, this pattern is seriously compromised by the fact that girls only scored significantly higher than boys when the experimenter was female, and boys only scored higher when the experimenter was male. Thus, the sex of the experimenter turned out to be a critical factor in producing sex differences. Finally, Eisenberg and Lennon examined the evidence for sex differences among children on another measure of affective outcomes: the facial, gestural, and vocal reactions displayed to affective stimuli. In situations where the child did not know she/he was being observed, and thus where the self-presentational concerns were presumably lowest, no significant sex differences were ever found.

The results for the adult measures were even more varied. Women significantly surpassed men in the successful decoding of both visual and auditory cues of others, supporting the view of women as more accurate in person perception (see also Hall, 1978). With regard to the dispositional tendency to respond affectively to others, women likewise surpassed men on self-report measures of affective tendencies, primarily the QMEE. This highly reliable pattern was the strongest evidence of all for the hypothesis that women are more empathic. Complicating this pattern, however, is the fact that virtually no evidence was found that women experience any greater physiological response to emotional stimuli, and only weak evidence supported the view that their self-reported affective responses exceed men's in actual emotional situations. Thus, we are left with a puzzle. Women reliably describe themselves on personality questionnaires as more likely to react affectively to the experiences of other people, but measurements taken in specific situations reveal them to be generally no more reactive than men, either physiologically or in terms of their subjective emotional experience.

How can this pattern be explained? Eisenberg and Lennon concluded that one key factor may be the "obviousness" of the particular measure being used, that is, how easy it is for subjects to determine that empathic and/or sympathetic reactions are being measured. What makes this important are sex-role stereotypes. To acknowledge being emotional and generally sympathetic is probably viewed as a positive quality for females because it fits with the traditional female sex role, but such an acknowledgment by males may be viewed less favorably because it does not fit the traditional male sex role. Importantly, this *self-presentational* explanation applies equally well to both self-perceptions and perceptions by others. That is, women, relative to men, may wish to be perceived by others as more emotionally responsive and they may wish to perceive themselves in that way as well. Thus, when it is clear to the respondent that emotionality is being assessed, as it is on the QMEE, females may be generally more willing to endorse such items than males. When less obvious (and controllable) measures are used, such as physiological responses, no sex differences emerge.

This explanation is also consistent with the absence of significant sex differences for measures of role taking. The non-emotional ability or tendency to adopt another's perspective is not as tightly connected to gender roles as is affective reactivity. Some more recent research using the newest adult empathy measure (the IRI) also tends to support this interpretation. Scores on the clearly affective EC and PD scales have been found to display large sex differences, with females scoring higher in both college (Davis, 1980) and high school (Davis & Franzoi, 1991) populations. The less affectively-toned PT scale displays a similar but weaker pattern, in keeping with the notion that self-reports of role taking are less susceptible to gender-based self-presentational concerns.

Although most evidence is consistent with this explanation, it should be noted that some research conducted since the Eisenberg and Lennon review has reported significant sex differences in self-reported emotional reactions within specific experimental situations (e.g., Batson, Dyck, Brandt, Batson, Powell, McMaster, & Griffitt, 1988, Studies 1 and 3; Eisenberg, Fabes, Schaller, Miller, Carlo, Poulin, Shea, & Shell, 1991; Eisenberg, Schaller, Fabes, Bustamante, Mathy, Shell, & Rhodes, 1988; Smith, Keating, & Stotland, 1989), and in physiological responding as well (Eisenberg,

Fabes, Schaller, Miller et al., 1991). Thus, caution should probably be exercised before drawing final conclusions regarding the affective responsivity of men and women.

However, if the self-presentation interpretation is valid, what does this mean for our interpretation of these adult self-report measures? Obviously, it suggests that some unknown portion of the differences between men and women is due not to any "real" differences but to self-presentational concerns. By the same token, however, it follows that differences on these self-report measures among men and among women, because they are not subject to the same kind of sex-role concerns, are more likely to reflect "actual" differences in the likelihood/intensity of affective responding. In general, of course, self-presentational concerns have the potential to affect all self-report responses; however, the concerns associated with gender stereotypes may be seriously problematic only when one wishes to directly compare males and females.

4

Origins of Individual Differences in Empathy

In the last chapter we examined a variety of ways in which individual differences in empathy-related constructs are assessed in adults and children; in this chapter we will consider the origins of these differences. In doing so we shall focus on two classes of variables: inherited predispositions, generally thought to reflect a substantial biological component, and environmental influences, typically those occurring during childhood. Of the two, environmental influences have received more attention, although recent years have seen an increased interest in the role of heredity. The remainder of this chapter will examine the evidence for both of these potential influences on dispositional empathic tendencies.

Inherited Predispositions

The idea that variation in human personality has a substantial genetic component is now generally accepted. Reviews of the evidence (e.g., Goldsmith, 1983; Loehlin, Willerman, & Horn, 1988; Plomin, 1986) find consistent support for the view that personality has a substantial level of *heritability,* defined as the proportion of phenotypic variance which is explained by genetic variance. Most estimates of personality heritability are in the range of 40–50 percent, and this estimate holds over a variety of personality dimensions, including neuroticism, extraversion, anxiety, aggression, and assertiveness.

The bulk of the evidence in this area comes from studies involving twins, particularly the comparison of personality correlations between identical, or monozygotic (MZ), twins with those between fraternal, or dyzygotic (DZ), twins. Because MZ twins are identical genetically, while DZ twins have, on the average, only 50 percent of their genes in common, a higher correlation among MZ twins suggests a genetic component to the trait: the greater the difference between the MZ and DZ correlations, the greater that genetic component. This logic is based, however, on an assumption that the environmental conditions facing the MZ and DZ twins are equivalent, or specifically, that the MZ environment does not encourage more similarity between twins than the DZ environment. If the environments were to differ in this way, then it would not be clear that any MZ-DZ differences were solely the result of genetic factors. At present, evidence regarding the "equal environments" assumption is mixed. While some evidence supports it (Scarr and Carter-Saltzman, 1979; Plomin, DeFries, & McClearn, 1990), other evidence does not (Plomin, Chipuer, & Loehlin, 1990). Thus, as we consider the twin studies examining the heritability of empathy, we should recognize that this methodology might tend to overestimate the degree of heritability.

Evidence from Twin Studies

One of the first attempts to study the heritability of empathy, specifically, empathic concern, was carried out by Mathews, Batson, Horn, and Rosenman (1981). Mathews et al. employed a sample of 230 twin pairs (114 MZ; 116 DZ) all of whom had completed a battery of psychological inventories including the Adjective Check List (ACL; Gough & Heilbrun, 1980). The first step was to identify a set of adjectives from the ACL which could be employed as a measure of dispositional empathic concern. To do so, judges first selected 13 items from the ACL deemed to be reflective of empathic concern. An independent sample of college students then completed the ACL and the Mehrabian and Epstein QMEE. The correlation between the 13-item empathic concern index and the

QMEE was .47. With the validity of the empathic concern index thus supported, Mathews et al. then compared the MZ and DZ twin correlations. The MZ correlation for the 13-item index was .41 and the DZ correlation was .05, yielding a whopping heritability estimate of 72 percent.

Rushton, Fulker, Neale, Nias, and Eysenck (1986) also conducted a twin study which included two measures of interest to this discussion: the QMEE and the Nurturance scale from the Personality Research Form (Jackson, 1974). The latter measure includes such items as "I often take young people under my wing," and thus seems to tap a nurturant orientation bearing some resemblance to empathic concern. Using a sample of 296 MZ and 179 DZ sets of twins, Rushton et al. found evidence of substantial heritability on both measures. For the QMEE, the correlation was .54 for MZ pairs and .20 for DZ pairs, and for nurturance the corresponding correlations were .49 and .14. The heritability estimates resulting from these differences were 68 percent and 70 percent for the QMEE and the Nurturance scale respectively.

Most recently, Zahn-Wexler, Robinson, and Emde (1992) examined this issue in a different way. In this study, MZ and DZ twins were assessed at 14 and 20 months of age along a variety of empathy-related dimensions. During home visits and laboratory sessions, the children were exposed to a total of five empathy "probes" (episodes in which an adult feigned injury while the child's responses were recorded on videotape). Several reactions by the child were then coded, including empathic concern and self-distress. In both cases these affective states were evidenced by the facial, postural, and verbal responses of the child. For empathic concern, evidence of significant heritability was found at both 14 and 20 months (MZ correlations were .29 and .30 respectively, and DZ correlations were –.05 and .09). Self-distress displayed a similar pattern at 14 months (MZ, .25; DZ, .15), but not at 20 months (MZ, –.01; DZ, –.07). Using sophisticated model-fitting procedures, Zahn-Wexler et al. estimated the heritability of empathic concern to be 23 percent at age 14 months and 28 percent at 20 months—both estimates were significant. In contrast, the heritability of distress was estimated to be 20 percent at 14 months, and virtually zero at 20 months—neither estimate was significant.

The results of these three studies can be summarized as follows: genetic factors seem to make a substantial contribution to individual differences in affective empathy, perhaps especially to the reactive outcome labelled empathic concern. In fact, compared to the heritability estimates of 40 percent typically found for personality traits (e.g., Loehlin et al. 1988), estimates for affective empathy all hovered around 70 percent for adults (although much less for infants). As previously noted however, such estimates are likely to be inflated, perhaps substantially so (Plomin et. al., 1990); it therefore seems prudent to exercise considerable caution in the interpretation of specific heritability estimates. Even so, it still appears reasonable to conclude from this evidence that a significant portion of the phenotypic variance in dispositional affective empathy may be accounted for by genetic factors.

The Role of Temperament

If emotional responses to the experiences of other people are determined to a significant degree by hereditary factors, how exactly might this come about? One possibility is that these genetic differences in affective reactivity to others result in large part from a more global affective reactivity. That is, people who in general experience emotional reactions to environmental events more readily or intensely may simply react with greater affect to the observed experiences of others as well. In short, this explanation is based on the presence of an emotional **temperament.**

Temperament has been defined in various ways (e.g., Buss & Plomin, 1975; Campos, Barrett, Lamb, Goldsmith, & Stenberg, 1983; Rothbart & Derryberry, 1981), but at least two features relevant to this discussion can be identified in most approaches. First, temperament is thought to include important characteristics of the individual's affective responding, especially its *likelihood* and its *intensity.* Thus, differences in temperament may account for individual variation in the stimulus intensity necessary for an affective response to be elicited and in the overall strength of that response. Second, differences in temperament are assumed to result in large part from genetic, rather than environmental, factors.

Of the various approaches to temperament and personality, four have a special relevance to the question of individual differences in affective empathy. Buss and Plomin (1975) identify the four basic temperaments as emotionality, activity, sociability, and impulsivity. Of these, *emotionality* is most clearly germane to our discussion. The emotional person is characterized as being easily and intensely aroused, to the point of having an ''excess'' of affect. Importantly, Buss and Plomin see emotionality as being restricted to negative emotions—the temperamentally emotional person tends to become upset, distressed, and aroused in the face of threatening or annoying situations, but does not necessarily display reactivity to positive stimuli. In a similar vein, Eysenck's (Eysenck, 1967; Eysenck & Eysenck, 1985) construct of *neuroticism* includes the components moodiness, tension, anxiety, and emotionality, which roughly correspond to the negative reactivity captured by Buss and Plomin's emotionality. Both of these constructs appear to have a considerable genetic component (see Buss & Plomin, 1975; Eysenck & Eysenck, 1985; Plomin & Rowe, 1977).

Two other temperament-based constructs are also relevant. Larsen and Diener (1987) have identified an individual difference dimension, *affect intensity,* which characterizes people in terms of their tendency to experience strong emotional reactions. That is, given the same level of emotional stimulation, individuals high on affect intensity react more strongly than persons low on this dimension. Importantly, Larsen and Diener view affect intensity as determining the strength of all affective responses, not just the negative ones. Thus, those high on affect intensity respond more angrily to frustrating stimuli, more sadly to depressing stimuli, but also more joyfully to pleasant stimuli. Although no direct evidence exists concerning the heritability of affect intensity, it does appear that differences on this dimension appear early in life and are stable over time (Larsen & Diener, 1987).

Finally, Mehrabian (1980) has proposed a temperament theory of personality which specifically addresses the link between temperament and dispositional empathy (Mehrabian, 1977; Mehrabian et al., 1988). This theory argues that one of the fundamental temperaments is *arousability,* "the degree to which a sudden increase in information rate . . . affects an individual's pattern of arousal over time." (Mehrabian et al., 1988, p. 236). Those high in arousability therefore tend to be more affected emotionally by changes in their environments. Because affective responding to others' emotional expressions and experiences is by definition a subcategory of global arousability, it would be expected that those high in global arousability would also score highly on measures of affective empathy.

In fact, the logic explicit in Mehrabian's approach can be applied to the other temperament constructs discussed thus far. If individuals inherit a general tendency to react to the world with strong affect because they are high in emotionality, neuroticism, affect intensity, or arousability, this is likely to result in a heightened tendency to respond affectively to the emotional states in others. In fact, the evidence tends to support just such a conclusion. Several different investigations conducted for various purposes over the past fifteen years have included dispositional measures of both temperament and affective empathy. These associations appear in Table 4.1, and address the question of whether or not measures of emotional/arousable

TABLE 4.1 Correlations between Measures of Temperament and Dispositional Empathy

Temperament	QMEE	EC (IRI)	PD (IRI)	PT (IRI)
Affect Intensity[1]	—	.42***	.37***	−.01
Neuroticism	.33*[2]	.12*[3]	.42***[3]	−.05[3]
Emotionality[4]	—	.13*	.56***	−.22**
Arousability[5]	.65***	—	—	—

[1]Values in this row come from Eisenberg, Fabes, Schaller, Miller, Carlo, Poulin, Shea, & Shell (1991)
[2]This is the average correlation over three studies using Eysenck's Neuroticism Scale (Eysenck & Eysenck, 1978; Eysenck & McGurk, 1980; Mehrabian & O'Reilly, 1980)
[3]These values come from unpublished data (Davis, 1992) using the Neuroticism scale from the NEO (Costa & McCrae, 1985)
[4]Values in this row come from Davis (1983b). The temperament measure is the Fearfulness subscale from Buss & Plomin's emotionality measure
[5]The value in this row comes from Mehrabian (1977)
Note: *** p < .001 ** p < .01 * p < .05

temperament are in fact associated with individual differences in empathy. The table is incomplete, given the fact that this particular research question was not at the heart of any of the investigations. Nevertheless, several points of interest can be identified.

First, all eight of the reported associations between temperament and affective empathy were statistically significant, with an average correlation of .38. However, this may tend to underestimate the association as the two smallest correlations were between temperament measures which possess a markedly negative tone (emotionality and neuroticism) and the empathic concern scale, which does not. In contrast, these negatively-toned temperament measures displayed strong associations with the comparably negatively-toned personal distress scale. Further, the affect intensity measure, which incorporates both positive and negative affectivity, was substantially associated with both empathic concern and personal distress. The mean temperament-empathy correlation without the two low "mismatched" associations is .46. Thus, there does seem to be a reliable association between an emotional/arousable temperament and a chronic tendency to experience affective reactions to others. Second, there was very little association between temperament and role taking, as assessed by the IRI's perspective taking scale (mean $r = -.09$). Given the nature of the PT scale, this makes perfect sense. This scale measures the reported tendency to adopt the point of view of others in everyday social situations, with affective reactivity deliberately excluded from the measure.

The Heritability of Role-Taking Tendencies

This absence of an association between dispositional perspective taking and emotional temperament raises the issue of whether or not there is a meaningful genetic contribution to role taking. At the present time, however, there is only one piece of empirical evidence addressing this question. Davis, Luce, and Kraus (in press) examined the relative heritability of affective and non-affective facets of dispositional empathy by using data collected earlier by Loehlin and Nichols (1976). In their original study, Loehlin and Nichols administered extensive questionnaires to both members of over 850 adolescent twin pairs. Included in these questionnaires was a 159-item adjective checklist which contained a number of self-descriptors relevant to dispositional empathy. Most important, Loehlin and Nichols (1976) provided the separate MZ and DZ correlations for each of these 159 items in an extensive appendix to their study.

Davis et al. (in press) first had expert judges identify a set of adjectives from the full checklist which clearly reflected either perspective taking, empathic concern, or personal distress. Next, an independent sample of college students completed the full 159-item adjective checklist and the IRI, and items selected by the judges were eliminated if they did not correlate with the appropriate scale, PT, EC, or PD, of the IRI. Having thus established the validity of the remaining items on both conceptual and empirical grounds, the MZ and DZ correlations provided by Loehlin and Nichols were then compared for the items tapping each construct. These results appear in Table 4.2. Seventy-five percent of the affective items (8/10 for EC; 7/10 for PD) displayed a significant MZ/DZ difference, compared to only 42 percent (5/12) of the perspective-taking items. Further, the mean intraclass correlation for MZ twins significantly exceeded that of DZ twins for both EC and PD items, while no significant difference was found for PT. The heritability estimates based on these mean correlations were somewhat larger for the affective constructs (EC = 28 percent; PD = 32 percent) than for perspective taking (20 percent). Thus, the evidence from this study suggests a higher degree of heritability for affective reactivity than for individual differences in perspective-taking tendency.

To summarize, based on the handful of studies which have examined the question of genetic influences on empathy, the most consistent finding thus far is of significant heritability with regard to affective empathic responding. In contrast, little evidence currently exists to support the heritability of role taking. In fact, the Davis et al. (in press) reanalysis of the Loehlin and Nichols data

TABLE 4.2 Intraclass Correlation Coefficients for Monozygotic and Dizygotic Twins on Empathy-Related Adjectives in the Loehlin and Nichols (1976) Data Set

Perspective Taking	MZ	DZ	z	
Aggressive	.22	.04	2.70**	
Boastful	.07	.08	−.10	
Cooperative	.14	.06	1.17	
Critical of Others	.29	.26	.46	
Immature	.27	.19	1.20	
Impatient	.11	.11	.00	
Patient	.14	.01	1.87*	
Quarrelsome	.16	.13	.41	
Reasonable	.16	.00	2.25*	
Rude	.13	.12	.21	
Sarcastic	.36	.12	3.52***	
Sensitive	.28	.00	4.01***	
Mean *r*	.19	.09	1.44	h^2 = 20%

Empathic Concern				
Cooperative	.14	.06	1.17	
Egotistical	.22	.08	2.06*	
Emotional	.22	.07	2.18*	
Friendly	.21	.05	2.21*	
Generous	.27	.05	3.27***	
Obliging	.21	.16	.77	
Self Centered	.16	.05	1.67*	
Sensitive	.28	.00	4.01***	
Sincere	.20	.07	1.96*	
Warm	.28	.16	1.89*	
Mean *r*	.22	.08	2.02*	h^2 = 28%

Personal Distress				
Anxious	.22	.15	1.08	
Emotional	.22	.07	2.18*	
Excitable	.19	.12	.98	
Fearful	.21	.03	2.64**	
Maladjusted	.12	.00	1.66*	
Nervous	.24	.09	2.17*	
Sensitive	.28	.00	4.01***	
Stable	.30	.08	3.25***	
Tense	.13	.02	1.54	
Worrying	.25	.07	2.74**	
Mean *r*	.22	.06	2.30*	h^2 = 32%

Note: *** $p < .001$ ** $p < .01$ * $p < .05$

indicates a smaller degree of heritability for perspective taking than for either empathic concern or personal distress. This pattern suggests that variability in dispositional perspective taking does not primarily result from constitutional factors but may result from environmental forces. It is to that set of factors that we now turn.

Environmental Influences

Considerably more studies have addressed the question of environmental influences on dispositional empathy, yet the total number of investigations is not overwhelming, and many gaps in the research remain. In particular, most studies in this area, as in the area of genetic influences, have focused on measures of affective empathy. Thus, very little is currently known regarding the environmental antecedents of role taking. However, this heavy focus on affective empathy has produced at least a broad portrait of the factors important in the socialization of empathic responding. These factors typically fall into one of three categories: the affective quality of the child's relations with family (primarily parents), specific parenting and discipline techniques, and parental dispositional empathy. Let us consider each of these categories.

Affective Quality of Family Relations

The largest set of studies all address the link between an individual's empathic responding and the affective environment within that individual's family. Most of these studies have employed dispositional measures of empathy, although a few have used more situational measures, most notably ratings by peers. All of these investigations, however, share the assumption that more secure and affectionate family relationships, especially with parents, contribute to greater dispositional empathy. At least two mechanisms by which such an association might come about have been offered (e.g., Mussen and Eisenberg-Berg, 1977; Barnett, 1987). First, children whose own emotional needs are satisfied by a secure, loving bond with parents may be less preoccupied by self-oriented concerns and thus more responsive to others' needs. Second, warm and loving behavior by parents provides a model which the child may then adopt. There is, of course, no reason that both mechanisms could not be operating.

Attachment Status

Two studies have examined the empathic responses of children who differ in attachment status (Kestenbaum, Farber, & Sroufe, 1989;

Waters, Wippman, & Sroufe, 1979). In both, mother-child attachment was assessed when the child was between 12 and 18 months of age by means of the "strange situation" task (e.g., Ainsworth, Bell, & Stayton, 1971; Ainsworth & Wittig, 1969). In this task, a mother and child are placed in an unfamiliar room (the "strange situation"), and the behavior of the child monitored as the mother leaves the child first with a stranger (the experimenter) and later alone. *Securely attached* children display a desire for closeness and physical contact with the mother upon her return; *anxious-avoidant* children avoid the mother on her return (and may act more positively toward the experimenter!); *anxious-ambivalent* children seem to simultaneously desire closeness to the mother yet resist it when it occurs.

Two or three years after the strange situation task, the child's behavior was assessed in a nursery school setting. Waters et al. (1979) had independent raters observe the children for 5 weeks and provide ratings on a host of dimensions. As expected, the securely attached children significantly surpassed nonsecure children on a number of different measures of "peer competence." Most relevant to our discussion is that secure children were rated as more sympathetic to their peers' distress. In fact, the descriptor "sympathetic" was seen as more characteristic of the securely attached children than any other quality. Kestenbaum et al. (1989) had coders analyze 50 hours of videotaped play activity, and found that securely attached children surpassed anxious-avoidant (but not anxious-ambivalent) children in displaying concern and offering comfort to distressed peers. In both investigations, then, secure attachment was associated with behaviors reflecting empathic concern for others.

Parental Self-Report
Another approach has been to elicit self-reports from parents regarding their expressed affection toward the child, and then to examine the relation between such self-reports and the child's empathy. The results of these studies have been decidedly weaker. Hoffman (1975), for example, separately questioned mothers and fathers regarding a variety of parenting behaviors, including how frequently they engaged in such behaviors as praising, hugging/kissing, joking with, and smiling at their child. An "affection index" constructed from these responses was then correlated with peer ratings of the child's tendency to "care about" and "stick up" for other children. Fathers' self-reported affection was unrelated to this measure, while mothers' affection was significantly associated ($r = .29$) only for sons. Barnett, King, Howard, & Dino (1980) had mothers and fathers separately estimate, in a global way, how frequently they engaged

in "affectionate interaction" with their child, and correlated these ratings with the child's score on the FASTE. In this case, mothers' affection was unrelated to empathy, while fathers' affection was significantly associated, but *negatively* ($r = -.44$), for daughters.

In an interesting study, Koestner, Franz, & Weinberger (1990) used interviews with the mother when the child was 5 years old to assess a number of parental variables, including maternal and paternal warmth, which were then used to predict dispositional levels of empathic concern in the child 26 years later. Neither parent's warmth was associated with later empathic concern, reinforcing the pattern of weak results when using parental self-reports of affection. Interestingly, however, two other parental variables did have a substantial impact on empathic concern. The father's involvement in child care and the mother's tolerance of dependency, both perhaps reflective of "time spent" with the child at age five, were significantly and positively associated with empathic concern at age 31.

Child Self-Report

A third set of studies has assessed the affective bond between parent and child by means of the child's self-reports. These measures thus have the disadvantage of being susceptible to a particular kind of bias. Empathic children may exaggerate the quality of the affective bonds with their parents. However, they also have the advantage of providing the most direct assessment of how the social atmosphere "feels" to the key individual—the child. Perhaps for both reasons, the evidence from these studies is somewhat stronger. Eisenberg-Berg and Mussen (1978), for example, had high school students report separately the child-rearing practices of their mothers and fathers. These descriptions were then correlated with the students' scores on the QMEE. The only reliable associations were between mothers' child-rearing behavior and sons' empathy as the mothers of more emotionally empathic boys were reported to be less punitive and restrictive, and more egalitarian and affectionate. Barnett, Howard, King, and Dino (1980) had college students complete the QMEE and then report the degree to which each parent had displayed several kinds of behaviors when the respondent was 10 years old. Parents of the high empathy students were reported to have spent more time, expressed more affection, and encouraged more discussion of feelings than parents of low empathy students. This pattern held regardless of sex of parent or sex of child.

Eisenberg, Fabes, Schaller, Miller et al. (1991) have recently examined links between the adult child's reports of family cohesion and emotional expressiveness in general (rather than specific parental variables) and a variety of empathy measures. College undergraduates provided estimates of the family variables, completed the four scales of the Interpersonal Reactivity Index, and responded to two emotionally evocative stimulus films. Although family cohesion and expressivity were virtually unrelated to the dispositional empathy measures, they were related, for women only, to a number of responses to the stimulus films. Women from more cohesive families, and those from families in which positive emotions were frequently expressed, reported feeling more sympathy and sadness to one or both of the stimulus films; women from families in which "submissive" negative emotions (sorrow; crying) were frequently expressed displayed a similar pattern, but also reported more personal distress to both films. Thus, families characterized by closeness and emotional expressivity seem to produce daughters somewhat more likely to respond to others' troubles with sympathy, sadness, and occasionally distress.

Finally, Roe (1980) administered the FASTE to a sample of Greek children and later interviewed them regarding their beliefs about obedience to parents. Interview responses were then coded for the presence or absence of statements indicating a fear of physical punishment. If fear of punishment is taken to indicate a less affectionate parental relationship, a not unreasonable assumption, this study also supports the pattern emerging thus far. Greater fear of physical punishment, from either mother or father, was associated with lower FASTE scores for both boys and girls.

Abusive Families

Three studies have taken a somewhat different approach to the question of family affective bonds by assessing the empathic responding of children in whose families some form of abuse, either child or spouse, had occurred. The evidence supports the view that in such families, especially those in which the child suffers physical abuse at the hands of a parent, empathic responding by the child is diminished. Hinchey and Gavelek (1982) compared a group of preschool children from homes in which the father had physically abused the mother with a control group in which no such abuse had been reported. Both groups were administered an affective perspective-taking task modeled after Borke's (1971) procedure. As expected, children from the distressed families displayed significantly worse role-taking performance than the children in the control group.

Two studies examined children who had themselves been the victim of parental abuse, defined as repeated or severe physical injuries such as bone fractures, contusions, and burns, with neither study specifying whether the abuse had been inflicted by mother, father, or both. Straker and Jacobson (1981) compared 19 abused children with a control sample matched on age, race, and current home circumstances (e.g., foster care, in divorced homes, etc.). The abused children scored significantly lower on the FASTE than the controls. Main and George (1985) compared 10 abused children with a non-abused control group matched for degree of economic disadvantage. Empathic reactions were coded from narrative reports made of the social behavior of the children, particularly their responses to crying and/or distress in peers. The nonabused children were significantly more likely to respond with expressions of concern, sadness, and helping; in contrast, the abused children were more likely to display fear and hostility. Thus, both studies suggest that the extreme disruption in parental affection likely to result from physical abuse is associated with declines in empathic emotional responding. Such a conclusion must be tempered, of course, by the recognition that many other factors no doubt distinguish abusive and nonabusive families.

Parenting and Discipline Techniques

Another general approach has been to investigate links between empathic responding and the use of specific child-rearing techniques, especially an inductive discipline style in which the negative impact on others of the child's misbehavior is emphasized. The logic underlying this approach is that emphasizing the social consequences of the child's actions, more so than physical force and simple prohibition, leads the child to adopt an other-oriented view of the world in general. More specifically, Hoffman and Saltzstein (1967) argue that induction techniques enlist the child's "natural proclivities for empathy," in essence encouraging a tendency which the child already possesses.

Parental Self-Report

Three studies have examined this question by asking parents to directly report on their discipline techniques and then examining the association between these self-reports and the child's empathy. Hoffman and Saltzstein (1967) had both parents separately respond to six imaginary situations in which the child misbehaves by reporting their most likely disciplinary action. The three major discipline techniques assessed were: 1) *power assertion* (threats, physical punishment); 2) *love withdrawal* (turning one's back on the child, refusing to acknowledge the child), and 3) *induction* (appeals to guilt by stressing the consequences of the misbehavior for others). Of the many child variables assessed in this investigation, the one most relevant to our discussion was a rating, by school peers, of the child's tendency to care about and defend other children. For mothers, self-reported induction was positively associated, and power assertion was negatively associated, with their daughters' peer ratings; for sons, in contrast, mothers' power assertion was positively associated, love withdrawal negatively associated, and induction unrelated to peer-rated empathy. Fathers' self-reported discipline techniques had only one effect on empathy— power assertion was positively associated with sons' empathic reactions. All of these findings, however, were restricted to middle-class families. Similar findings did not emerge for lower class parents and children.

Hoffman (1975) addressed this question again using the same measure of empathy and a slightly modified means of assessing discipline techniques. In this investigation parents' responses to three imaginary situations were coded only for the technique of "victim-centered" discipline, a construct seemingly equivalent to induction. While the mothers' induction was significantly, positively associated with sons' but not daughters' empathic reputation with peers, the fathers' induction was associated with the empathy of daughters but not sons.

In an ambitious naturalistic investigation, Zahn-Waxler, Radke-Yarrow, and King (1979) trained mothers to observe and record their child's reactions to distress in others. Over a nine-month period, mothers noted their child's reactions to the distress of others as well as their own (mothers') responses to the child. The key variables for our purposes were the child's offering of help/sympathy to the distressed other and the typical kinds of discipline used by the mother. The children of mothers who frequently used strong affective explanations as a discipline technique, emphasizing the morality of good behavior, and stressing the pain and suffering caused by the transgression, more frequently offered reparations to the victim of their misbehavior and offered sympathy and help to victims they had not transgressed against. The use of physical punishment had no effect on either reparations or sympathy/helping. These findings held for both sons and daughters.

Recently, Nancy Eisenberg and colleagues have examined the impact of parental discipline in a different way by focusing not on overt empathic behavior by children but on their emotional reactions as reflected in facial expressions, self-reports, and physiological reactions. Miller, Eisenberg, Fabes, Shell, and Gular (1989), for example, had mothers listen to vignettes depicting a child causing distress or happiness to another, and then asked them how they would respond if the child was theirs. These responses were then coded into behavioral categories. Later, these mothers' children were exposed to films in which targets suffered mild physical distress, and their facial expressions of distress and concern were recorded and scored. Children whose mothers reported greater use of inductive reasoning displayed sadder facial expressions, as did children whose mothers responded to their child's misbehavior by engaging in direct prosocial behavior.

Two other studies in this series have examined the relationship between parents' discipline practices and their children's emotional responses to a distressed other. Eisenberg, Fabes, Schaller, Carlo, and Miller (1991) assessed parents' self-reported likely responses to instances in which their child acted in a hurtful way to others, and later exposed the children to a sympathy-evoking film of a little girl with spina bifida (a birth defect involving the spinal cord). The daughters of mothers who respond in more restrictive, punitive ways to hurtful behavior by their children reported feeling more sympathy for the child in the film, with the same pattern also emerging for the sons of fathers who employ such disciplinary tendencies. Parental discipline had little association with the reactions of opposite-sex children. In a later study, Eisenberg, Fabes, Carlo, Troyer, Speer, Karbon, and Switzer (1992) used the same sympathy-inducing film but focused only on mothers' disciplinary behavior. Maternal restrictiveness regarding hurtful behavior was associated with more distressed facial reactions, by daughters, to the spina bifida film; however, maternal restrictiveness was associated, for both sons and daughters, with less facial sadness to the film.

Child Self-Report
A second approach to the question of discipline techniques has been to employ children's rather than parents' reports of such practices. Three studies fall into this category, two of which have already been mentioned. Hoffman and Saltzstein (1967) assessed children's as well as parents' estimates of how the parents would respond to the six imaginary discipline situations. In contrast to the findings using parental self-reports, none of the child-reported maternal discipline techniques were related to either sons' or daughters' empathy (although combining sons and daughters produced an overall significant effect for induction). For fathers, child-reported induction was positively associated and love withdrawal negatively associated with empathy, but only for daughters. Eisenberg-Berg and Mussen

(1978) found high school boys' scores on the QMEE to be negatively related to their reports of mothers' tendencies to use more punitive forms of punishment; no such associations were found for mothers and daughters, or for fathers at all.

Dlugokinski and Firestone (1974) used an "imaginary situation" closely adapted from Hoffman and Saltzstein (1967) and had elementary and middle school children estimate the likelihood that their mothers would employ induction and power assertion techniques in those situations. Two variables indicative of empathic dispositions were then assessed: peer nominations of the "kindest and most considerate" classmates, and a self-report scale assessing other-centered life values such as "being a kind person" and "getting a job that helps other people". For both boys and girls, these measures were strongly and positively related to the child-reported likelihood of maternal induction (all r's > .45). Likelihood of maternal use of power assertion was unrelated to peer nominations, and was significantly negatively associated with endorsing other-oriented values.

Parenting Style

A final set of studies is different, in two ways, from the ones described thus far. First, they focus on specific interaction patterns occurring between parents and children which are not so neatly categorized as discipline techniques and which seem more appropriately described as components of a general parenting style. Second, in contrast to the heavy emphasis on affective empathy apparent in most of the research on socialization effects, all three studies in this set focus on some form of role taking by the child. Peterson and Skevington (1988), for example, identified a childrearing style they called "*distancing*" which is a Socratic technique in which the parent "queries, challenges, or disputes the child's viewpoint . . . to generate cognitive uncertainty" (p. 167). This typically consists of asking questions that challenge the child's point of view (e.g., "Why do *you* think I cannot play with you right now?"). Peterson and Skevington assessed this construct by asking mothers how they would react to a series of hypothetical situations, and assessed their children's cognitive role taking by means of a task similar to Flavell et al.'s (1968) "apple-dog" task. More frequent use of the distancing style by mothers was associated with better role-taking performance by their children.

Two recent studies have examined the link between children's role-taking performance and the degree to which conversation within the family tends to focus on feeling states. The logic of these investigations is that frequently focusing the child's attention on the affective states of self and others, and in particular on how they differ, may produce a greater awareness of and sensitivity to the thoughts and feelings of other people. Results have been somewhat mixed. Howe and Ross (1990) coded three-way verbal interactions occurring between mothers and their two children, one being 3 or 4 years old and the other 14 months. Of special interest was the degree to which mothers and older siblings directed references to one another about the infant's feelings and skills. Global perspective-taking performance of the older child was assessed by a battery of measures assessing perceptual, cognitive and affective role taking. The predicted association between perspective taking and the tendency for mothers and older children to talk about the infant's feeling states did not emerge, although direct verbalizations from the child to the infant were positively associated with perspective taking.

Dunn, Brown, and Beardsall (1991) also coded audiotapes of interactions between mothers and two children. The primary variable of interest was the degree to which the participants made reference to the feeling states of self or others. Approximately three and one-half years later, the affective role-taking performance of the younger sibling was assessed by means of the Rothenberg (1970) measure. As expected, the frequency with which mothers and those younger siblings made reference to feeling states was significantly and positively associated with the subsequent accurate perception of others' feeling states as indicated by Rothenberg's measure.

Parents' Dispositional Empathy

The final approach taken in this area has been to assess the dispositional empathy of both child and parent and test the association between the two. The most commonly offered explanation for any such effects is modeling, meaning that to the degree that the parents' dispositional empathy produces in them empathic reactions and behaviors, children may observe and then internalize such reactions and behaviors as their own. It is also possible for associations between parent and child empathy to result in other ways, such as through parental empathy's contribution to affective quality, its contribution to discipline techniques, or through direct genetic transmission. Studies in this area typically have not allowed any disentangling of these mechanisms.

Three studies have employed the QMEE as the measure of adult empathy and a comparable self-report measure of affective empathy by the child. Strayer and Roberts (1989) used Bryant's child version of the QMEE and found no relation, for mothers or fathers, with the empathy scores of sons or daughters. This conflicts somewhat with Strayer's (1983) investigation which found mothers' QMEE scores, but not fathers', to be significantly associated with both sons' and daughters' scores on the Bryant measure. To complicate matters further, Kalliopuska (1984) reported no correlation between mothers' QMEE scores and children's scores on a version (not Bryant's) of the QMEE adapted for use with children; fathers' empathy, in contrast, was significantly but very weakly associated ($r = .10$) with their children's empathy. It is difficult to imagine a less consistent pattern as one study found effects for mothers' empathy, one for fathers' (weakly), and one found no effects at all.

Two other studies have employed the QMEE to measure parental empathy but have used different assessment techniques for children. Barnett, King et al. (1980) assessed children's empathy using the FASTE and found that mothers' affective empathy was significantly and positively associated with the FASTE performance of daughters but not sons; in contrast, fathers' empathy was unrelated to the FASTE performance of sons and was negatively associated with that of daughters. Further analysis revealed that only one subset of children, girls with high empathy mothers and low empathy fathers, displayed elevated scores on the FASTE. Trommsdorff (1991) found that mothers' QMEE scores were strongly and positively related to childrens' empathy as assessed by their kindergarten teacher ($r = .61$); data on fathers were not collected in that study.

A final set of studies has employed measures other than the QMEE to tap parental empathy. Barnett, Howard et al. (1980) had college students complete the QMEE and then rate on 7-point scales the dispositional empathy of each parent. Parental empathy rated in this way was positively associated with the child's QMEE score regardless of sex of parent or child. A somewhat indirect measure of parental empathy was used by Hoffman (1975), who had parents rank order a set of life values. Two of these values, "showing consideration of other people's feelings" and "going out of one's way to help other people," arguably reflect an other-orientation similar to empathic concern. The fathers' willingness to endorse those values was associated with both sons' and daughters' ratings (by peers) as caring and considerate and the mothers' empathic values were so associated for daughters only.

In three recent studies Eisenberg and colleagues have examined the link between parental empathy as measured by the IRI and children's affective responses to others. Fabes, Eisenberg, and

Miller (1990) assessed mothers' dispositional empathy and then measured a variety of children's reactions to an emotionally evocative stimulus tape depicting a woman and her children who had been in a serious accident. The mothers' empathic concern and perspective taking were associated, for daughters, with fewer positive reactions (less happy), more negative reactions (more sad), and greater feelings of sympathy to the stimulus; the mothers' personal distress displayed the opposite pattern. Almost no significant relations between mothers' empathy and sons' responses to the stimulus were found. Two other studies (Eisenberg, Fabes, Schaller, Carlo, & Miller, 1991; Eisenberg et al., 1992) reported similar findings. Both found that mothers' scores on the PT and/or EC scales of the IRI were consistently associated with daughters' lower level of personal distress and heightened levels of empathic concern, as evidenced by facial expressions, to the spina bifida film mentioned earlier. Many fewer associations were found between maternal empathy and son's affective responses. Eisenberg, Fabes, Schaller, Carlo, and Miller (1991) also assessed fathers' dispositional empathy and found that paternal EC levels were associated, for sons, with less facial distress and greater dispositional empathic concern.

Summary

The literature regarding socialization influences on empathy is marked by considerable inconsistency, yet a few clear patterns emerge. The evidence is fairly strong that *close and secure family relationships* are associated with heightened affective responsivity to the experiences of others. Such associations have been found using standard laboratory assessments of attachment, reports by the children of relationship quality, and through comparisons of children from abusive and nonabusive families. The only exception to this pattern are the investigations which employed parents' self-reports of their affection toward the child; studies employing this technique displayed virtually no evidence for such a link. In phenomenological terms this may make sense. If the variable of interest is the empathic responsiveness of the child, it is the child's experience of emotional security which is logically most important. Parental report is the one methodology which most clearly excludes the child's perceptions from the assessment of relationship quality. There is also an indication that the link may be strongest between mothers and sons. In the four studies which separately examined the relationship quality-empathy link for the four "parent-child gender" combinations (Barnett, King et al., 1980; Eisenberg-Berg

& Mussen, 1978; Hoffman, 1975; Roe, 1980) the mother-son combination displayed the predicted significant associations three times; the other three combinations did so only once each, and all of these resulted from a single study (Roe, 1980).

With regard to *parental discipline,* the evidence is reasonably strong that mothers' use of an inductive style is associated with greater affective responsivity by their children. This pattern emerged for both sons and daughters, and in studies employing both parental and child reports of parental discipline. The evidence for fathers' use of induction is weaker, especially with regard to sons; no study to date has found a significant association between fathers' use of induction and sons' level of empathy. The preponderance of the evidence regarding mothers' use of power assertion, while not as strong as that for induction, nevertheless suggests that this discipline technique is associated with lower levels of affective empathy in both sons and daughters. For fathers, again, the evidence is quite weak. Of the six possible associations between paternal power assertion and child's empathy reviewed here, only one was significant, with fathers' self-reported power assertion being positively associated with sons' empathy (Hoffman & Saltzstein, 1967). Finally, two of the three studies which have examined non-discipline-related parenting strategies found significant associations with children's role-taking performance. Further research in this latter area clearly seems warranted.

Evidence regarding the effect of *parents' dispositional empathy* on children's empathy is mixed. As with the studies examining discipline techniques, the evidence is strongest for the impact of mothers' empathy levels, and in particular the effect of mothers on daughters. Some investigations have found evidence for a similar influence of fathers' empathy (e.g., Eisenberg, Fabes, Schaller, Carlo, & Miller, 1991), but the overall magnitude of the evidence is weaker than for mothers. The pattern therefore suggests a modeling effect, with daughters adopting the empathic behavioral style of their mothers.

Non-Affective Outcomes

Thus far we have been concentrating on the "left hand side" of the organizational model, focusing our attention on antecedents of empathy such as inherent capacities, socialization experiences, and individual differences in empathic tendencies. We are now ready to turn our attention to other parts of the model. The remainder of the book will focus on intrapersonal and interpersonal outcomes which have been associated with empathy over the years and which fall into the cognitive, affective, and behavioral realms. Sometimes the dividing lines between different outcomes will not be especially distinct. For the most part, however, this system will provide a useful way to organize the presentation of a considerable amount of research.

In the course of discussing various empathy-related outcomes, we will also need to consider the processes which lead to them. Thus, the "middle" of the organizational model, the empathy-related processes lying between antecedents and consequences, will also be addressed in the following chapters. As we shall see, the lines of demarcation between process and outcome are also sometimes difficult to maintain. Again, however, this distinction for the most part is useful in bringing order to the welter of investigations facing us.

In the present chapter the focus will be on **non-affective outcomes,** defined as some form of judgment, evaluation, or belief about other people. Investigations in this area fall more or less neatly into three categories: 1) those assessing the **accuracy of judgments** about others; 2) those assessing the nature of **attributional judgments** about others; and 3) those involving some form of **evaluative judgment.** Many of these investigations, especially those in the latter two categories, have induced cognitive or affective role taking through laboratory procedures such as instructional sets; others have used naturally occurring levels of observer-target familiarity as an index of empathic processing. In both cases, the primary focus has been on the situational forces which affect empathy-related processes and outcomes. A somewhat different focus has characterized the research on accuracy in person perception, and it is that topic which we first consider.

Accuracy in the Perception of Others

Two approaches can be identified in the research on empathy and accuracy. The first essentially defines the two as equivalent, meaning that empathy *is* the accurate perception of others. This approach was somewhat more common in earlier research. The other approach, which is more in keeping with the organizational model, has been to treat accurate person perception as an independent construct and to look for links between such accuracy and measures of empathic dispositions.

Empathy Defined as Accuracy

As noted in Chapter 3, measures of role taking employed with children have sometimes blurred the distinction between the process of role taking and the outcome of accurately estimating the mental or emotional states of other people. While these measures purportedly assess differences between individuals in role-taking abilities (process), what they frequently tap in actuality is an outcome—the degree to which individuals are able to accurately estimate the internal states of others (e.g., Borke, 1971; Rothenberg, 1970; Feshbach & Roe, 1968). This is more common with affective than cognitive role taking measures, since some cognitive measures actually score the reasoning by which the judgments are made and not the judgments per se, thus more clearly separating process from the outcome.

At the level of empirical measurement, this confusion between process and outcome may be to some degree inescapable. After all, how is one to measure dispositional affective role taking among children without using their estimates of the affective states of others? The strategy employed in some measures of cognitive role taking (to score the observer's reasoning as she tries to predict another's thoughts) is more difficult to apply to judgments of others' emotions. Thus, even when the conceptual distinction between the process of role taking and the outcome of accuracy is clear to the investigator, it may be quite difficult in practice to separately assess the two.

In contrast to this methodological confounding of process and outcome, a more profound conceptual confusion can be found in the early research on interpersonal accuracy. In the 1940s and 1950s the most prevalent conception of empathy, as exemplified by Dymond (1949; 1950) and Kerr and Speroff (1954), focused on the ability to accurately predict the thinking and feeling of other people by transposing oneself into the experiences of those others. This transposition and the resulting accuracy were so tightly linked that they were essentially considered one and the same, and measures of empathy within this tradition reflect this. For example, one early instrument, Kerr and Speroff's (1954) Empathy Test, assessed empathy by asking respondents to estimate such things as the national circulation of various magazines, or the popularity of different kinds of music for specified populations of people. The underlying logic was that a generalized ability to "get inside" the experiences of others will produce accurate estimates of those others' likes and dislikes. Thus, accuracy on this test was taken to be a measure of one's empathy.

Dymond's (1949; 1950) rating scale method, however, was by far the most common measure of empathy/accuracy during this time. As noted in Chapter 3, this method assessed accuracy by having subjects rate targets on a series of traits, and comparing these ratings with the targets' self-ratings on the same traits. The smaller the discrepancy between the observer's ratings and the target's own ratings, the greater the empathy of the observer. This simple and intuitively appealing measure of accuracy was employed in numerous investigations, many of which were included in Taft's (1955) review of the accuracy literature.

From the perspective of the organizational model, the problem with this kind of approach is that it confuses process and outcome. As it turned out, there were more serious problems as well. With the publication of several critiques of this method (e.g., Gage & Cronbach, 1955; Gage, Leavitt, & Stone, 1956), especially that of Cronbach (1955), things came to a rather abrupt halt. The problem was that accuracy in the rating scale method is made up of several different constructs, some of which seem to be the result of judge and/or target response sets rather than any kind of empathic transposition. To give one example, consider a target and observer who both happen to have the same response tendency, which is that they usually check the midpoint of a scale and seldom use the endpoints. This similar response style will make the observer appear more accurate because his/her rating will never be very different from the target's. This phenomenon ("Elevation" in Cronbach's terms) does not depend upon any ability to transpose oneself into the thinking or feeling of another individual, but it nevertheless contributes to an accuracy score which ostensibly reflects exactly this ability. As a result, such accuracy scores contain an unknown amount of statistical confounding. So thoroughly did these critiques discredit the rating scale method that almost all accuracy research was halted for 20 years.

With increases in methodological sophistication, however, there has been a growing realization that accuracy can be studied in ways which avoid the problems described by Cronbach (e.g., Funder, 1987; Kenny & Albright, 1987). As long as the undesirable components of accuracy can be removed from the total accuracy score, or eliminated through the use of other techniques, then it is possible to assess accuracy in a meaningful way. The result of this realization has been a growing number of studies which address interpersonal accuracy in a methodologically sound fashion. Importantly, some of those studies have also attempted to identify connections between accuracy and measures of dispositional empathy.

Empathy as an Influence on Accuracy

The studies which have investigated links between dispositional empathy and interpersonal accuracy differ from one another in a number of ways, but all share the common assumption that empathy and accuracy are two distinct constructs. Although associations might be expected between measures of empathy and success at judging other people, empathizing represents only one possible influence on such success. Thus, accuracy in predicting other's thoughts or emotions is not prima facie evidence of successful role taking, nor is inaccuracy necessarily evidence of role taking failure. Higgins, Feldman, and Ruble (1980) demonstrated this distinction empirically, with their finding that while accuracy in predicting the preferences of others increases with age, it is not the result of any reliable decline in egocentrism; egocentrism (the absence of role taking) was essentially unrelated to accuracy.

Post-Cronbach Correlational Studies

In addition to their shared assumption regarding the conceptual separation of accuracy and empathy, investigations in this area all faced the common challenge of how to assess accuracy in a way free of the biases identified by Cronbach. One solution to this problem, exemplified by the work of Borman (1977; 1979), has been to use Dymond's rating scale procedure but to isolate during analysis the theoretically critical component *differential accuracy,* or the ability of a judge to accurately distinguish among a set of targets. Borman (1979), for example, had over 140 judges view two series of eight videotapes. In each tape two males engaged in a scripted conversation between either a manager and subordinate or a recruiter and job applicant. The judges rated each of the eight managers/interviewers, using seven-point scales, on several behavioral dimensions such as their ability to create a favorable image for their company, or to create rapport with the subordinate/applicant. The criterion to which these ratings were compared was a set of parallel ratings made by "experts" (practicing industrial psychologists).

The traditional rating scale methodology would simply compute the difference between the judge's and experts' scale ratings, for each manager/interviewer on each dimension, and then sum the differences, producing the same problematic accuracy measure criticized by Cronbach. Instead, the solution of Borman (and others) was to correlate each judge's ratings of the eight managers/interviewers on each dimension with the corresponding ratings by the experts. The more successful judges were at distinguishing between better and worse managers/interviewers (as assessed by the experts), the higher the correlation and the greater the accuracy. Therefore, unlike the traditional rating scale technique accuracy cannot result from a simple similarity between judge and target response sets, because this technique rewards the ability to discern the actual rank ordering of targets within a given set. The association between accuracy defined in this way and dispositional empathy of the judges (Hogan's EM scale) was, however, nonsignificant.

An unpublished study by Bernstein, McGuire, Raskin, Ganzach, and Thiry (1988) also used this strategy. Observers were exposed to two videotapes, each of which depicted four targets discussing an involving topic, and after viewing each tape, observers rated each target on 32 traits for which the targets had earlier completed self-descriptions. Then, separately for each trait, observers' ratings of the targets were correlated with the targets' self-ratings, thus producing a measure of the ability to accurately predict variation in how the targets view themselves. The relation between observers' mean accuracy scores and dispositional empathy, as measured by the IRI, was then assessed. Scores on the perspective taking scale were significantly and positively associated with greater accuracy ($r = .33$); none of the other IRI scales were significantly associated with accuracy at all.

Non-Verbal Sensitivity

Another approach to this topic has been to define accuracy as nonverbal sensitivity, and to use instruments such as the Profile of Nonverbal Sensitivity (PONS; Rosenthal, Hall, DiMatteo, Rogers, & Archer, 1979), a measure which consists of 220 two-second auditory and/or visual segments depicting a young woman enacting a number of "everyday" life situations. A variety of situations are included, and each one is presented through multiple communication channels, such as facial, verbal, postural, and so on. Because there is always an objectively "correct" answer to the question of what situation the woman is expressing, a non-confounded measure of accuracy in decoding nonverbal cues can be obtained by simply summing the number of correct interpretations made by an observer.

Two studies conducted by Hall (1979) found no association between decoding accuracy and dispositional empathy. In the first, scores of 66 subjects on the QMEE were unrelated to success on a vocal decoding task. In the second study both the EM scale and the QMEE were administered to 36 subjects, along with three different decoding tasks tapping both audio and visual decoding skills. Neither dispositional empathy measure was significantly related to performance on any decoding task. In a later investigation, Funder and Harris (1986) administered the PONS and a battery of other measures, including the EM scale, to 64 subjects. As with Hall's (1979) investigations, accuracy as assessed by the PONS was not significantly associated with EM scores. Unlike Hall, however, Funder and Harris also computed scores for the four factors which apparently make up the EM scale (Johnson et al., 1983), and found that two of these factors, sensitivity and social self-confidence, were somewhat associated with greater accuracy (both r's $= .29$; p's $< .10$). Thus, the reported tendencies to take an active social role and to be emotionally sensitive demonstrated a slight relation to accuracy in decoding nonverbal cues. In a more recent unpublished study (Hart & Rosenthal, 1988) the PONS and a battery of measures including the IRI were administered to 43 subjects. Of the four IRI scales, only empathic concern was significantly associated with accuracy ($r = .36$). Given that Johnson et al. (1983) found empathic concern and the

EM "sensitivity" factor to be moderately associated ($r = .42$), this finding is perhaps consistent with the relation between sensitivity and accuracy found by Funder and Harris.

Finally, a study by Riggio, Tucker, and Coffaro (1989) examined associations between a different kind of nonverbal decoding task and several empathy measures. Subjects were shown 80 slides of targets' faces depicting one of six basic emotional expressions (happiness, sadness, anger, disgust, fear, and surprise) or a neutral expression. The observer's job was to indicate which of these seven expressions was being displayed with accuracy simply consisting of the total number of correct matches. Of the six dispositional empathy measures included in this study (the QMEE, the EM scale, and the four IRI scales) only the QMEE was significantly associated with accuracy, as higher scores on the QMEE were associated with more accurate judgments regarding facial expressions.

Forced-Choice Methods

Bernstein and Davis (1982) have taken a third approach to assessing accuracy: using a forced-choice methodology which requires observers to match targets with the targets' own self-descriptions. In this study observers viewed videotapes in which groups of five women discussed a hypothetical problem among themselves. Prior to engaging in these videotaped discussions, the five targets had individually and privately provided three words that "best described" themselves. After viewing the targets on tape, the observer-subjects were given the five three-word descriptions and asked to match each description to the person on the tape who had generated it, with accuracy being measured by the number of correct matches. Because no rating scales are employed in this procedure, it avoids the Cronbachian problems outlined earlier, and provides a relatively clear measure of differential accuracy.

All observers completed the IRI as part of the experimental procedure, and those scoring higher on the perspective-taking scale were more accurate, relative to those low in perspective taking, in matching targets with self-descriptions. This difference was significant in Bernstein and Davis' Study 1, which employed stimulus tapes that were approximately 10 minutes long. Interestingly, in Study 2 the length of the tape interacted with perspective-taking scores to affect accuracy. For high perspective takers, longer tapes produced greater accuracy; for low perspective takers, tape length had no effect. Thus, high perspective takers only displayed greater accuracy when they had sufficient exposure to the targets. None of the other three IRI scales displayed any association with accuracy.

Dollinger and Riger (1984), in an intriguing study, also used a forced-choice technique to assess accuracy. In that investigation observers were shown ten videotapes, each consisting of three "suspects" being administered a word-association test. The "suspects" were undergraduate students, one of whom had been told beforehand to explicitly and realistically imagine that they had found a wallet containing money, had decided to keep the money, and had then lied to the wallet's owner about finding it. Thus, one of the three suspects was told to imagine being "guilty" of a crime; the other two were not told to imagine anything at all. The word-association test which was administered to the three suspects included several words (e.g., "thief," "wallet," and "steal") which would be relevant to the guilty party but not to the other two suspects. The observers were to watch the suspects on tape and then indicate which one, from each set of suspects, was the guilty party. Neither the EM scale nor the QMEE contributed to greater accuracy on this task; in fact, higher scores on the EM scale were marginally associated with worse performance.

Naturalistic Methods

Ickes, Stinson, Bissonnette, and Garcia (1990) have recently assessed accuracy within an interesting and relatively naturalistic procedure. Mixed-sex dyads made up of unacquainted undergraduates were secretly audio- and videotaped during a six-minute period as they sat waiting for an experiment to "begin." Later each participant separately viewed the tape and systematically indicated the specific thoughts and feelings that they recalled having at specific points throughout the six-minute period. Finally, the participants individually viewed the tapes a second time, with the experimenter stopping the tape at every point where their dyad partners had reported having a specific thought or feeling, the subjects then estimating their partners' thoughts/feelings at each point. Accuracy was indexed by the frequency with which subjects were able to successfully estimate the dyad-partner's thoughts and feelings.

All subjects in this experiment had completed the IRI at an earlier point in the semester, but analyses revealed that none of the four scales were significantly associated with accuracy. In contrast, accuracy was related to several characteristics of the dyadic interaction itself. For example, the degree to which the subjects made attributions about each other was positively associated with greater accuracy, as was the degree to which they asked questions of one another. Thus, while accuracy was associated with meaningful situational variables, it displayed no reliable relation with individual differences in empathy.

In a subsequent investigation, Stinson and Ickes (1992) had male dyads, made up of strangers or friends, interact in the same procedure. Again, measures of dispositional empathy were essentially unrelated to accuracy in estimating the dyad partner's thoughts and feelings. As with the Ickes et al. (1990) study, characteristics of the dyadic encounter itself (frequency and duration of verbalizations, gazes, smiles/laughter, etc.) were associated with greater accuracy, but only for the dyads made up of strangers. In other words, male strangers were more accurate to the degree that their level of interactional involvement during the conversation was high. Although dyads made up of friends displayed higher involvement overall, and were generally more accurate, analyses suggested that it was not the involvement which produced the accuracy, but the greater wealth of knowledge about each other that the friends brought to the dyadic encounter.

In a third investigation, Marangoni, Garcia, and Ickes (1993) demonstrated that success at this task, while not associated with measures of dispositional empathy, does reflect significant individual variation. Subjects in this investigation viewed three different women talking with a therapist about personal problems (e.g., divorce), and estimated the thoughts/feelings of these targets in the same manner as the previous studies. Performance on this task was quite stable over all three tapes. Those who displayed more accuracy on the first tape tended to display comparable accuracy on the others. In addition, accuracy was enhanced by training. Some subjects received feedback following their estimates (they learned the actual thoughts and feelings that the target reported) during part of the tape. Results revealed that these "training trials" significantly improved the subsequent accuracy of those subjects receiving them.

Finally, Levenson and Ruef (1992) have also employed a naturalistic setting to study accuracy. In this study husbands and wives engaged in a series of conversations while a number of physiological measures were taken, including heart rate and skin conductivity. Afterward, each spouse viewed a videotape of the interaction and indicated continuously, using a dial, how "positive" or "negative" they felt throughout the interaction. Subsequent to this, completely independent observers also viewed the tapes and attempted to estimate, using the same apparatus, how one of the two spouses was feeling throughout the tape; the observers' physiological reactions were monitored during this procedure. Accuracy was measured by the percentage of time during each tape that the observer's rating of positive or negative affect matched the target-spouse's self-rating. Dispositional empathy of the observer (the QMEE) was found to be weakly related to accuracy, displaying a positive relationship with the accurate prediction of positive emotion for one of the two stimulus tapes. More strongly associated with accuracy was *physiological linkage,* the tendency for observer and target to experience similar physiological reactions at the same time. Thus, the more similar the observer's physiological reaction was to the target's, the more accurate the observer was in predicting the target's affect, especially the target's negative affect.

Summary

The evidence regarding the link between empathy and accuracy in person perception is summarized in Table 5.1; the overall pattern, to put it charitably, is mixed. Several investigations have reported significant associations, but the data have been so sparse, and the pattern so inconsistent from study to study, that very little confidence can be placed in the evidence thus far. If any reliable effect of dispositional empathy on accuracy is to be found, however, it may prove essential to carefully distinguish between different kinds of accuracy. For example, accuracy at distinguishing among a group of targets in terms of stable characteristics such as personality traits (Bernstein et al., 1988) or self-descriptions (Bernstein & Davis, 1982), was associated to some degree with perspective taking (IRI's PT scale). Accuracy at decoding the meaning of another's specific expressive cues has been associated with empathic concern (Hart & Rosenthal, 1988), with the QMEE (Riggio et al., 1989), and with the component of the Hogan scale tapping sensitivity (Funder & Harris, 1986) which are all measures of affective reactivity. Finally, no measure of dispositional empathy has been associated with a third form of accuracy, the ability to infer another's specific thoughts and feelings (Ickes et al., 1990; Marangoni et al., 1993; Stinson & Ickes, 1992). This pattern, based on a small number of studies is, of course, highly speculative; however, the possibility that accuracy in different domains (traits, feelings, thoughts) might be associated with different empathic dispositions seems worth exploring.

No matter which kind of accuracy is being assessed, however, real limits may exist regarding the degree to which it can be predicted from individual characteristics such as dispositional empathy (Kenny & Albright, 1987). One reason for this is that accuracy in person perception may largely be an emergent phenomenon, resulting from the particular verbal and nonverbal interactions which take place during specific social encounters. This would suggest that the best predictors of accuracy may not be stable individual tendencies

TABLE 5.1 Associations between Dispositional Empathy Measures and Measures of Interpersonal Accuracy

	EM Scale	QMEE	PT (IRI)	EC (IRI)	PD (IRI)	FS (IRI)
Correlational						
Borman (1975)	ns	—	—	—	—	—
Bernstein et al. (1988)	—	—	.33*	ns	ns	ns
Non-verbal Decoding						
Hall (1979; audio)	—	ns	—	—	—	—
Hall (1979; audio + visual)	ns	ns	—	—	—	—
Funder and Harris (1986)	ns[1]	—	—	—	—	—
Hart and Rosenthal (1988)	—	—	ns	.36*	ns	ns
Riggio et al. (1989)	ns	.29*	ns	ns	ns	ns
Forced-choice						
Bernstein and Davis (1982)	—	—	.20*[2]	ns	ns	ns
Dollinger and Riger (1984)	-.24+	ns	—	—	—	—
Naturalistic						
Ickes et al. (1990)	—	—	ns	ns	ns	ns
Stinson and Ickes (1992)	—	—	ns	ns	ns	ns[3]
Levenson and Ruef (1992)	—	.38*[4]	—	—	—	—

[1] Although findings for the full EM scale were nonsignificant, scores on two factors making up the scale, "sensitivity" and "social self-confidence," were marginally associated with greater accuracy

[2] This value is an effect size calculated from the analysis of variance reported in Study 1

[3] Higher scores on the FS scale were significantly associated with greater accuracy for the stranger-dyads only

[4] This significant association with accuracy was only found for positive emotions

Note: * p < .05 + p < .10 ns = nonsignificant

but the reactions and judgments occurring within a particular situational context. Some support for this can be found in the work of Ickes and colleagues (Ickes et al., 1990; Stinson & Ickes, 1992), in which specific features of the dyad's encounter, such as the tendency to ask questions of one another, and overall level of involvement, were associated with greater accuracy while IRI scores were not. Levenson and Ruef's (1992) finding that physiological linkage between observer and target most strongly predicted observer accuracy is also consistent with the view that emergent properties of the interaction, rather than static properties of the observer, may be especially important. A second, related, factor is that if empathy measures largely assess tendencies rather than abilities, strong situational forces which prompt attempts at accuracy may engage the empathizing abilities that everyone possesses and overwhelm the effect of any dispositional differences in empathic tendencies.

Another possibility is that while considerable individual variation in accuracy exists (e.g., Marangoni et al., 1993), observers typically lack any realistic awareness of just how accurate (or inaccurate) they are. Ickes (in press) terms this a lack of "metaknowledge" by observers regarding their empathic accuracy, and suggests that it may account for the extremely limited success thus far in finding personality correlates of accuracy. In short, if people don't know how accurate they are, then measures which ask them to report on their abilities will not be of much use. In any event, the picture that currently emerges of empathy's relation to accuracy is a cloudy one. While further research seems warranted, at present the prospect of discovering reliable empathy effects does not seem especially strong.

Attributions Regarding Other People

In contrast to the rather meager evidence for its influence on interpersonal accuracy, notably stronger associations have been found between empathy and another non-affective outcome: the attributional judgments that observers make about targets. In addition to the fact that these two sets of investigations focus on different outcomes, there is a large methodological difference between them as well. While empathy-accuracy effects were studied exclusively by means of dispositional empathy measures, the attribution research has almost as exclusively relied on situational manipulations. The technique used most frequently is to employ instructional sets designed to prompt or inhibit role taking by observers. The dependent variable in these investigations is almost always the kind of causal attribution that the observers offer for the target's behavior.

Instructional Sets and Causal Attributions

The initial impetus for most of the studies in this area came from the finding that actors and observers typically differ in the causal attributions they offer, with actors tending to stress the importance of situational forces and observers tending to stress the importance of the actor's dispositions (e.g., Jones & Nisbett, 1971; Nisbett, Caputo, Legant, & Maracek, 1973). For example, imagine a college student who signs up for an astronomy class which meets at 8:00 a.m. An observer might well conclude that this choice is the result of dispositional characteristics of the student, such as a strong interest in astronomy. The student, on the other hand, is generally more likely to see this decision as primarily resulting from situational factors; perhaps this was the only course still open when the student registered. This difference between actor (target) and observer in terms of how they explain the target's behavior is often called the *actor-observer difference* (Jones & Nisbett, 1971).

One explanation for this pattern is that actors and observers base their divergent attributions on different kinds and amounts of information, with observers usually possessing less information about the actor's past behavior. Another explanation is that actors and observers possess similar information but process it differently, perhaps by focusing on different aspects of identical information pools. In an important experiment, Storms (1973) demonstrated that the usual actor-observer pattern could be reversed by exposing actors and observers to the visual perspective of the other person. After actors saw a videotape taken from the observer's perspective, and observers saw one taken from the actor's perspective, both parties tended to make attributions more typical of the video perspective they had seen. These findings reinforced the information-processing explanation of the actor-observer difference, and set the stage for the following series of studies.

The prototypical investigation in this area was conducted by Regan and Totten (1975), who reasoned that if reversing the visual perspective of actors and observers could change their attributional patterns, then reversing the psychological perspectives might do the same. To explore this possibility, they had female undergraduates watch an unscripted "get acquainted" conversation between two female students with one of these two women (Margaret) designated as the target. Afterward the participants were asked to rate Margaret on four dimensions (friendliness, talkativeness, nervousness, and dominance), and to indicate for each dimension the degree to which that behavior was caused by her personal characteristics and the degree to which it was caused by characteristics of the situation.

Prior to viewing the conversation, all subjects were given a written instructional set modeled after those used by Stotland (1969). Those in the "empathic set" condition were told to do the following:

> " . . . empathize with Margaret . . . Imagine how Margaret feels as she engages in the conversation . . . picture to yourself just how she feels in the situation . . . Think about her reaction to the information she is receiving from the conversation . . . visualize how it feels to Margaret to be in this conversation . . ."

Clearly the intent of these instructions is to urge the observer to engage in *affective role taking* by imagining the emotional reactions of the target. Regan and Totten's reasoning was that such role taking would prompt the observer to process the available information in a more "actor-like" way, specifically by focusing attention on situational rather than dispositional factors. Other subjects received the "observer set," instructions designed not to prompt affective role taking. These participants were instructed simply to pay close attention to the target's behavior, and carefully observe her actions.

As predicted, those who received the "observer set" reacted as observers typically do, and attributed Margaret's behavior more to dispositional than situational causes, while those receiving the "empathy set" reversed that pattern, and attributed the behavior more to situational factors. This general finding has been successfully replicated by researchers employing different stimulus materials, instructional sets, and attributional measures (Archer, Foushee, Davis, & Aderman, 1979; Betancourt, 1990a; Galper, 1976; Taylor & Atchitoff, 1974; Wegner & Finstuen, 1977). Thus, the evidence seems fairly clear that instructions to engage in affective role taking tend to produce in observers attributional patterns which de-emphasize actors' dispositions and emphasize situational forces.

A slightly different approach has been less frequently employed in this area. Instead of utilizing the typical actor-observer difference, Gould and Sigall (1977) took as their point of departure a different attributional phenomenon: the tendency for actors to make more dispositional attributions when they succeed and more situational ones when they fail (e.g., Streufert & Streufert, 1969; Wolosin, Sherman, & Till, 1973). For example, a student might well conclude that a low exam score is primarily the result of situational factors (an unusually difficult test, or an unexpected last-minute emergency interfering with test preparation) but that a high score is the result of dispositional factors such as high intelligence or motivation. Gould and Sigall reasoned that this pattern, which ostensibly results from an actor's desire to enhance or defend self-esteem, might also be created in observers if they can be led to view the world as the actors do. Thus, Gould and Sigall had female students view an 8-minute videotape depicting a male and female student engaged in a "get acquainted" conversation. Prior to this they received written instructions, similar to those of Regan and Totten (1975), directing them to either empathize with or carefully observe the male on the tape.

Subjects were also given false feedback concerning the kind of impression the male had made on the female with half being led to believe that he had made quite a good impression and the other half the opposite. Finally, all subjects were asked to indicate on a single 11-point scale the degree to which this outcome was due to the male's dispositional factors (1), or factors in the situation (11). As expected, the attributions of those who received the "observe" instructions were not affected by the male's outcome; in contrast, women instructed to engage in affective role taking made more dispositional attributions when the male succeeded than when he failed, mirroring the self-serving pattern typically found in actors. Using highly similar procedures and an identical instructional set, Melburg, Rosenfeld, Riess, and Tedeschi (1984) replicated this finding. It should be noted, however, that in a separate condition the effect was weakened to nonsignificance by a fairly small change in the empathy instructions. Thus, the robustness of this particular finding is open to question. In sum, however, the evidence fairly consistently supports the view that affective role-taking instructions lead observers to offer causal attributions which resemble those typically found among actors.

Observer-Target Relationship and Attributions

Pre-Existing Observer-Target Relationships
Another set of investigations has examined the impact on observer attributions of the relationship existing between the target and observer. The logic of these investigations is that observers who are more similar to the target, who like the target more, or who have known the target longer/better will generally make attributions for the target which are more "actor-like." One way to explain such findings, if they occur, is in terms of empathy. Being similar to

another person, or having that person as a close friend, may be expected to increase sensitivity to his/her experiences. If so, then the process underlying the instructional set findings (affective role taking) may also lead observers to process information about similar or familiar targets in a more "actor-like" way and produce more "actor-like" attributions.

This is not the only way to explain such effects, however. Taylor and Koivumaki (1976), in one of the earliest efforts in this area, began with a different assumption, derived from Jones and Nisbett (1971), that attributions regarding familiar targets will be more situational because observers are aware of those targets' cross-situational behavioral variability. Thus, just as we emphasize the effect of situations on our own behavior because we are aware of how our behavior varies across situations, so too will we reach such conclusions regarding people we know well. Taylor and Koivumaki tested this notion by having subjects make attributions for a variety of hypothetical behaviors said to be performed by self, spouse, a friend, and an acquaintance. Instead of the expected pattern, that subjects would stress situational attributions for self and dispositional factors for others, they found that positive behaviors were increasingly attributed to dispositional factors as one moved from acquaintance to friend to spouse to self; negative behaviors were attributed more and more to situational factors across that same continuum. Thus, the closer or better known the target, the more flattering the attributions that were offered. This pattern is thus more consistent with the view that attributions are influenced by some affective link between target and observer than with the notion that greater knowledge about close others was responsible. Had greater knowledge about other's behavior variability been the key variable, an across-the-board tendency to make situational attributions for well-known others should have been found.

Similar findings resulted from a study by Regan, Strauss, and Fazio (1974; Experiment 2), in which subjects provided the names of liked and disliked acquaintances, and at a later point in the semester were asked to make attributions for an act of helping supposedly committed by one of those persons. In this experiment, which required subjects to offer explanations for what they thought were actual behaviors, attributions were clearly affected by liking. Respondents were much more likely to explain liked acquaintances' prosocial actions in terms of their dispositions and disliked acquaintances' in terms of situational forces.

A more recent position advanced by Sande, Goethals, and Radloff (1988) holds that there is a more subtle reason that actors generally stress situational causes for their behavior. According to this view, actors routinely see themselves as possessing not few but many traits—more, in fact, than they think others possess. Further, they see themselves as possessing contradictory traits (e.g., skeptical and trusting), either of which can manifest itself depending upon the situation. In short, because they see themselves as possessing a wide repertoire of characteristics, people tend to believe that they are more multifaceted than others. The tendency in previous studies for actors to attribute their behavior to the situation may therefore reflect their belief that these situations simply make one of their many dispositions more appropriate (Sande et al., 1988). If this is true, then subjects should be expected to report that they, and others whom they know well, possess contradictory sets of traits.

As part of a series of studies, Sande et al. (1988) had subjects indicate whether one, the other, or both traits in contradictory trait pairs (e.g., serious-carefree, quiet-talkative) were possessed by several targets: the self, a liked and well-known other, a disliked well-known other, a liked acquaintance, and a disliked acquaintance. Two results are of special interest. First, as expected, subjects reported possessing a greater number of contradictory traits than any other target; the difference between the self and the liked well-known other was not significant, however, indicating that subjects viewed the self and a well-known and liked other as equally multifaceted. Second, liking for the target had a powerful effect. For both well-known others and casual acquaintances the liked target in each category was seen as much more multifaceted than the disliked target. Aron, Aron, Tudor, and Nelson (1991) have also used the Sande et al. procedure and reported similar results. The self was seen as most multifaceted, followed by best friend and then by a friendly acquaintance. Thus, as with the Taylor and Koivumaki study, the evidence suggests that something other than simple familiarity with the target is at work; instead, affect toward the targets seems to play a role in the trait ascriptions made to them.

Manipulated Observer-Target Relationships
All of the studies discussed thus far have examined attributions made within the context of pre-existing relationships. However, at least two studies have manipulated the relationship between observer and target and examined the resulting attributional judgments. Regan et al. (1974; Experiment 1) manipulated liking for a female confederate by having subjects: 1) see her acting rudely and then learning via a bogus attitude scale that she was dissimilar to

them; or 2) see her acting pleasantly and then learning that she was similar to them. The subjects later saw her perform well or poorly on an experimental task and offered attributions for that performance. As expected, more dispositional attributions were made to the liked target who performed well and the disliked target who performed poorly.

More recently, Houston (1990) manipulated similarity between observer and target in a more sophisticated way, by using Higgins' (1987) self-discrepancy model. According to this model, people possess cognitive representations corresponding to an *actual self,* an *ideal self* (containing one's hopes and aspirations), and an *ought self* (consisting of duties and obligations). Specific kinds of emotional distress are said to result from the specific kind of self-discrepancy one experiences, either between the actual and ideal selves, or between the actual and ought selves. Houston (1990) reasoned that observer-target similarity could be created, and greater role taking therefore result, by manipulating the degree to which they share the same kind of self-discrepancies.

By pre-testing a large number of students early in a semester, Houston was able to identify individuals who possessed specific patterns of self-discrepancies (e.g., high in actual/ideal discrepancy but low in actual/ought discrepancy). These subjects later read transcripts of an interview with a target who was portrayed as possessing certain kinds of self-discrepancies and experiencing the attendant emotional reactions. The self-discrepancies of these fictitious targets matched to varying degrees the actual self-discrepancies of the observers. As expected, when observers were asked to indicate how much the target's difficulties were attributable to dispositional or situational factors, they offered more situational attributions for similar targets, those with whom they shared a particular kind of self-discrepancy, and more dispositional attributions for dissimilar targets.

Summary

Evidence in this area suggests two conclusions. First, instructions to adopt the affective perspective of a target reliably produce attributions for that target's behavior which are more "actor-like," especially in their emphasis on situational factors; and second, greater liking for a target, whether naturally occurring or created via manipulation, is also associated with more "actor-like" attributions, especially the tendency to give targets attributional "credit" for positive outcomes. What is somewhat unclear at this time is the precise nature of the mechanism which produces these effects.

Evaluative Judgments of Others

The final class of non-affective outcomes remaining is the evaluative judgments made about targets by observers. This category includes observers' liking for the target, attitudes toward the target, and tolerance for the target. These judgments differ from the attributional judgments reviewed earlier in several ways, including the fact that evaluative judgments tend to be more global in nature than causal attributions.

Liking for Individual Others

Some of the earliest evidence regarding a link between empathy-related processes and evaluative judgments came from a series of studies which evolved from investigations into the "just world hypothesis" (Lerner & Simmons, 1966). This hypothesis holds that we need to believe that individuals receive the outcomes they deserve. Such a belief allows us to view the world as stable and predictable, and because stability is so valued, the belief in a just world is not easily surrendered. When exposed to the apparent injustice of an innocent person suffering, therefore, one response of observers is to judge the victim more harshly. This derogation of the victim makes the world again seem just, and re-establishes predictability (Lerner & Miller, 1978).

Following the initial demonstration that such derogation actually occurs (Lerner & Simmons, 1966), Aderman, Brehm, and Katz (1974) argued that the instructions given to observers in the Lerner and Simmons investigation might have served to inhibit empathizing with the target. These instructions, to "observe closely the emotional state of the worker and to watch for cues which indicate her state of arousal," do in fact resemble the "control" instructions frequently used in laboratory studies (e.g. Regan & Totten, 1975; Gould & Sigall, 1977). According to this logic, then, derogation may have occurred not because of a need to believe that victims deserve their fate, but simply because the natural tendency to empathize with a victim was stifled.

To examine this idea, Aderman et al. had undergraduate women view a female target participate in a learning experiment during which she appeared to receive 20 painful shocks. Prior to this, participants received one of three instructional sets: 1) the original Lerner and Simmons set; 2) a "watch her" set typical of those used in empathy investigations; or 3) an "imagine self" set. In this set, subjects were instructed to "imagine how you yourself would feel . . . picture to yourself just how you would feel . . . concentrate on yourself in that experience. . . . " Thus, unlike the instructions typically used in the attribution research, which explicitly urge the observer to take on the affective role of the target and imagine the other's feelings, these instructions urge observers to imaginatively place themselves in the situation and experience the resulting affective reactions. It may therefore be thought of as a transposition instruction rather than an affective role-taking instruction.

Derogation of the target was assessed in the Lerner and Simmons fashion by comparing the way observers rated themselves on a series of nine bipolar adjective scales at the beginning of the experiment with how they rated the target on the same scales at the end. Consistent with expectations, subjects receiving either the original Lerner and Simmons instructions or the "watch her" instructions derogated the target, rating her lower than they had earlier rated themselves. In contrast, the "imagine self" subjects showed no derogation, and actually rated the target slightly more positively then they had earlier rated themselves. Thus, the Lerner and Simmons instructions did produce effects identical to those produced by the empathy-inhibiting "observe" instructions, suggesting that the just world findings may have been influenced to some degree by the inhibition of empathizing with the victim. Subsequent studies (Brehm & Aderman, 1977; Brehm, Fletcher, & West, 1981, Experiment 1) have supported these results, finding that imagine-self instructions, relative to "watch him" instructions, do reduce derogation of victims.

Evidence for the effect of empathy-related processes on evaluative judgments has also come from investigations outside of this Brehm-Aderman series. Turner and Berkowitz (1972) employed "imagine-self" instructions before exposing subjects to an excerpt from a boxing film. Relative to those not receiving such instructions, those who imagined themselves in the place of the victorious fighter were significantly more convinced that he "should" have won, a belief which may be taken as a positive evaluation of the target. Batson, Duncan, Ackerman, Buckley, and Birch (1981; Experiment 1) manipulated perceived similarity between observers and a target receiving electric shocks. The similar target was rated as more attractive and likeable, although not more intelligent, friendly, or cooperative.

Interestingly, three studies have found no effect of empathy instructions on evaluative judgments of the target, and all employed the affective role-taking instructions rather than "imagine self" instructions. Toi and Batson (1982) presented subjects with affective role-taking or "listen objectively" instructions prior to playing an audiotape which described the plight of a college student who had recently been in an auto accident. Later ratings of the student's likability were not affected by instructional set. Dovidio, Allen, and Schroeder (1990), and Eisenberg, Fabes, Schaller, Miller et al. (1991) used highly similar instructional sets and both found that a needy target was perceived as no more likable by empathizing than by nonempathizing subjects.

Tolerance for Outgroups

In addition to the studies which have examined the impact of empathy-related processes on liking for individual targets, two investigations have examined the impact of dispositional empathic tendencies on tolerant attitudes toward stigmatized social groups. These studies therefore examine an evaluative judgment made by observers regarding some class of targets. Underwood and Briggs (1980) studied this issue in an interesting way. Following the seizure, in 1979, of the American embassy in Iran, Underwood and Briggs administered questionnaires to University of Texas undergraduates inquiring about their feelings of punitiveness toward Iran and Iranians (e.g., ''I think all Iranian students in this country should be deported''). Those scoring high on the IRI's PT scale were significantly less likely to offer harsh and punitive evaluations of Iran, and they were also more likely to assign the United States some share of the responsibility for the circumstances leading up to the seizure.

Sheehan, Lennon, and McDevitt (1989) examined the impact of dispositional empathy on attitudes toward a very different set of stigmatized outgroups: homosexuals and AIDS sufferers. Over 350 college students were administered questionnaires tapping the respondents' potential reactions to both groups. Specific items assessed such things as a willingness to interact with members of each group, and the desirability of restricting the civil rights of such persons. In addition, the IRI was administered to all subjects. As expected, higher scores on both the PT and EC scales were significantly associated with more favorable attitudes toward both homosexuals and AIDS sufferers; no results regarding the PD and FS scales were reported. Thus, as in the Underwood and Briggs study, dispositional empathy was associated with more tolerant attitudes towards a stigmatized target group.

Summary

A number of studies support the view that empathizing produces a more positive evaluation of the target; however, most of these studies employed the particular empathy induction technique of imagine-self instructions. The three studies employing affective role-taking instructions (Dovidio et al., 1990; Eisenberg, Fabes, Schaller, Miller et al., 1991; Toi & Batson, 1982) all failed to find any effect of instructions on liking for the target. Given the relatively small number of studies involved, this pattern might simply be coincidence. Nevertheless, it suggests that "imagine-self" and role taking instructions are not always equivalent, and may in fact produce different kinds of evaluative reactions to needy or distressed others. Investigations directly comparing the two forms of instructions could prove most informative.

Affective Outcomes

In light of the emphasis on affective definitions of empathy in recent years, it is not surprising that a substantially greater volume of contemporary research has focused on affective rather than cognitive outcomes. Several factors have contributed to this emphasis on emotion, including a vigorous recent interest in the question of altruism (e.g., Batson, 1991; Cialdini, Baumann, & Kendrick, 1981; Eisenberg & Miller, 1987), especially the role played by observers' affective reactions in motivating helping behavior. Although this particular question will be addressed in the next chapter, a number of studies devoted to the issue have also examined causal antecedents of affective outcomes, and much of that research will be considered here. Because a number of recent investigations have addressed this topic, it is possible to draw reasonably definitive conclusions about some questions in this domain, especially regarding the links between particular empathy-related processes and particular affective outcomes.

Following the organizational model, this chapter shall focus on the two broad classes of affective outcomes: parallel and reactive. The first part of the chapter will consider the nature of emotional responses falling within each class, and will discuss possible relations between these outcomes and empathy-related processes. The second part of the chapter will examine the empirical evidence bearing on these relations. Finally, we will evaluate the degree to which this empirical evidence supports the hypothesized relations. First, however, let us turn our attention to the nature of empathic affective responding and the processes likely to influence these responses.

Parallel and Reactive Responding

As noted in Chapter 1, parallel empathy occurs when observers experience affective states which match or reproduce the target's affect (Staub, 1987). Experiencing fear when faced with a frightened target, or happiness when exposed to a joyous one, would be examples of this type of reaction. In actuality, almost all empirical work has involved distressed targets only, so that studies of parallel reactions routinely involve the induction of some sort of unpleasant emotion.

In contrast, reactive affective responses go beyond a simple matching of affect and consist of the observers' emotional reaction *to* the target's affect. In other words, they are responses experienced by the observer but typically not by the target. These reactions can be viewed as more developmentally advanced than parallel responses (Staub, 1987), perhaps requiring a greater degree of cognitive activity by the observer (Eisenberg, Shea et al., 1991). A variety of emotions can fall into this category. Staub (1987), for example, specifically mentions feelings of sympathy/compassion, feelings of guilt, and feelings of anger at seeing a target suffering unjustly as examples of reactive affect.

One tricky definitional issue is where one "draws the line" between parallel and reactive outcomes. For example, if a target is experiencing anger, what reaction in an observer constitutes a parallel response and what constitutes a reactive one? Clearly, an observer who feels anger is experiencing a parallel affective outcome; so too, it seems, is one who experiences emotions highly similar to the target in *tone* and *intensity* (e.g., extreme irritation or frustration). Affective responses which differ markedly from the target's (e.g., sadness or joy rather than anger) would qualify as reactive outcomes. Thus, the key defining feature is the degree of *similarity* between the affect of target and observer. Of course, defining parallel and reactive outcomes in this way means that the same affective state in the observer (e.g., sadness) can be either parallel or reactive, depending on the target's emotion (for example, sadness vs. fear).

In practical terms, however, only one construct clearly falling within the reactive domain has attracted much empirical attention, and that is the feeling of compassion for others which have been variously labelled sympathy (Eisenberg & Strayer, 1987; Wispé, 1986), empathy (Batson et al., 1987), and empathic concern (Davis, 1980; 1983b). Prompted by the theoretical contributions of Hoffman (1984; 1987) and the theoretical/empirical work of Batson (e.g., Batson et al. 1981; Batson, Batson, Slingsby, Harrell, Peekna, & Todd, 1991), a number of recent investigations have examined causes and consequences of this affective state.

Accompanying the empirical interest in empathic concern over the past decade and a half has been a comparable surge of interest in another affective state, *personal distress,* a self-oriented response characterized by feelings of anxiety and unease to distressed targets. One reason for the simultaneous increase in attention given to these two emotional states is clear. Batson's work on altruism has frequently drawn direct comparisons between the contrasting motivational properties said to accompany feelings of empathic concern and personal distress. As a result, many studies focusing on motives for helping behavior have simultaneously examined both affective states. In this chapter, the evidence regarding personal distress will be placed, along with empathic concern, under the reactive outcome category. It should be noted, however, that doing so will disturb somewhat the tidy taxonomy we have been employing. The specific problem is that personal distress does not seem to fit very easily into the reactive category just described; more generally, it does not fit very easily anywhere.

The root of this classification difficulty lies partially in a basic confusion which exists regarding the essential nature, either self-oriented or other-oriented, of parallel outcomes. Staub (1987), for example, describes parallel affective reactions as predominantly self-oriented, and contrasts them with other-oriented reactive responses. Consistent with this view, he places the clearly self-oriented personal distress reactions in the parallel outcomes category. In contrast, Eisenberg, Shea et al. (1991) view parallel responses (which they label simply "empathy") as neither self- nor other-oriented. Because parallel outcomes are "content-free," consisting simply of responses matching the target's own, it is impossible to predict in advance the precise nature of a parallel response. Thus, Eisenberg et al. view parallel responses as essentially neutral with regard to self/other orientation, and are reluctant to place the clearly self-oriented feelings of personal distress in that neutral category. Instead, they distinguish personal distress from both parallel and reactive outcomes, effectively assigning distress reactions a status all their own. If Staub places personal distress in the parallel category, and Eisenberg et al. leave it outside the categorization scheme entirely, why have I placed it in the reactive outcome category?

That is a good question. My reasoning is that in some cases, perhaps many, personal distress is clearly reactive because it is not a direct reproduction of the target's affect, but a discriminably different (although similarly-valenced) affective state. Consider, for example, an observer who experiences personal distress after seeing a target who is blind, retarded, or confined to a wheelchair. Assuming that the target is not at the time displaying obvious distress, these feelings of personal distress in the observer cannot be considered parallel responses; they are instead reactions to the other's condition. Therefore, observer distress in these cases seems clearly reactive, although it is obviously not other-oriented in the sense that empathic concern is.

In other settings, of course, observer personal distress seems much closer to a parallel affective reaction. When the target is facing an acute threat and displaying distress/anxiety cues, similar reactions by the observer would seem to qualify as both a parallel outcome and as personal distress. Thus, distress reactions may qualify as either parallel or reactive depending upon the situation. In fact, personal distress might be viewed as falling between parallel outcomes and empathic concern on a continuum reflecting the sophistication of affective responses. Thus, personal distress may be considered more complex than purely parallel responses because it represents, at least sometimes, a crude transformation of the target's emotional experience into a different affective state in the observer. It may be considered less complex than empathic concern because the affective tone remains strongly negative and the focus remains largely self-centered. However, based on the fact that personal distress is at least sometimes clearly distinguishable from affective matching, I have chosen to define it here as a reactive affective response, recognizing nevertheless that this will sometimes be an awkward fit.

Causal Antecedents of Affective Responding

According to the organizational model, affective responses are the result of personal factors, situational factors, and more proximally, a variety of empathy-related processes varying in their level of cognitive sophistication. To understand the links between these constructs and particular affective responses, it will be useful to briefly review the positions of the three contemporary theorists who have been most explicit regarding the causes of affective responses to distress in others: Martin Hoffman, Dan Batson, and Nancy Eisenberg. While addressing the same fundamental domain, all three approaches have unique emphases which give them distinctive "flavors." One goal of this brief review will be to identify areas of commonality among them.

Three Approaches: Hoffman, Batson, and Eisenberg

Hoffman's (1984; 1987) work, described in some detail in Chapter 2, needs only a brief recapitulation here. Hoffman notes six different modes by which affect in a target comes to create affect in an observer. Two of these, motor mimicry and primary circular reactions, are relatively primitive, operating in a largely automatic fashion without significant higher-order cognitive functioning. Two other modes, classical conditioning and direct association, are more advanced, requiring at least modest cognitive sophistication. The final two modes are more advanced still. Language-mediated association refers to the process by which information about the target activates comparable feelings and experiences (stored semantically in the observer's memory) producing affective responses in that observer. Role taking, the most advanced mode, requires a deliberate effort by observers to imagine how they would feel if faced with the circumstances affecting the target.

The precise nature of the resulting affective response depends on the observer's level of cognitive development, especially the sophistication of his or her "cognitive sense of others." Prior to the development of a reliable sense of self as distinct from others, exposure to a distressed target produces a global reaction in which the observer cannot in fact distinguish the self's distress from that of the target. With the acquisition of person permanence and more sophisticated role-taking capacities, observers begin to experience separate forms of distress for the self and other, and eventually come to experience genuinely compassionate feelings for distressed targets. Because all forms of affective responding fundamentally depend on an initial arousal in the observer, it seems fair to say that in Hoffman's view all affective responses, parallel or reactive, would generally be intensified by the operation of all six modes of arousal, with the precise nature of the affect dependent upon the cognitive sophistication of the observer. Likewise it seems reasonable to conclude that Hoffman sees greater role-taking by observers as likely to produce more other-oriented feelings.

Such a conclusion would certainly be compatible with Batson's theoretical position as well. Although his chief focus has been on the question of altruism, and particularly the different motivations for helping that result from feelings of personal distress and empathic concern, Batson (1991) has explicitly considered the antecedent conditions likely to produce each of these affective states. With regard to personal distress, Batson cites Piliavin, Dovidio, Gaertner, and Clark's (1981) position that such feelings are made more likely or intense by perceived "we-ness," similarity, and attraction between observer and target. In contrast, sympathy/compassion for the target is said to result primarily from attempts by the observer to take the target's perspective. Such a perspective-taking "mind-set" may result from explicit instructions, prior experience in similar situations, or feelings of attachment between target and observer. Batson's position therefore implies that the factors which lead directly to personal distress (similarity, attraction) will frequently contribute indirectly to empathic concern as well, through their effects on role taking.

Recently, Eisenberg and colleagues (Eisenberg, Shea et al., 1991) have addressed the causes and consequences of affective responses to target distress, and have offered some interesting speculations regarding the ways in which parallel and reactive responses are related. They begin, as did Hoffman, by distinguishing between different modes of arousal. Eisenberg et al. focus on cognitive modes of arousal and describe two processes, conditioning/direct association and labeling, which roughly correspond to some of the lower modes of arousal identified by Hoffman, and which are said to operate largely automatically and without conscious direction by the observer. The more advanced cognitive processes involve role taking and *elaborated cognitive networks*. In the latter process observers note target-related cues, access previously stored chunks of relevant knowledge, and then incorporate such pre-stored information into their responses. Therefore, it seems to bear some relation to Hoffman's mode of language-mediated association.

The other part of Eisenberg, Shea et al.'s (1991) analysis focuses on the relations among various forms of affective responding. The single most crucial assumption they make is that observing a distressed target typically leads first to the parallel reaction of affective matching which is then followed by a response of empathic concern or personal distress. As a rule, the immediate parallel response is transformed through some form of cognitive activity. Cognitions focusing on the other's feelings and needs produce empathic concern, while those focusing on one's own arousal produce personal distress. Eisenberg, Shea et al. further speculate that the more primitive forms of cognitive processing generally tend to produce parallel responding and/or personal distress, but are not likely in and of themselves to create empathic concern. Sophisticated processes such as role taking and elaborated networking, on the other hand, can generate empathic concern as well as personal distress and parallel responses.

Theoretical Propositions

From these three approaches it is possible to derive two propositions to guide our examination of the empirical evidence in this area:

1. *Each of the six modes of empathic arousal will tend to produce greater affective responding of both types: parallel and reactive.* This proposition can be inferred from Hoffman's theory because of his argument that specific emotional reactions are the result of an affect-cognition synthesis, one in which the arousal resulting from various processes combines with the cognitive development of the individual to produce particular affective responses. Regardless of the mode, then, greater arousal generally produces stronger affective reactions. In a similar fashion, Eisenberg, Shea et al.'s contention that reactive affect usually stems from an initial parallel response means that anything increasing the intensity of that parallel response, and this would include all six empathy-related processes, also indirectly increases the intensity of any subsequent reactive affect.

2. *Although tending in general to produce affect of all types, adopting the perspective of the target is the process especially likely to produce empathic concern.* This proposition is couched in developmental terms by Hoffman, who argues that our increasingly sophisticated mental representations of other people, including an advanced role-taking capability, underlie our capacity to experience sympathy and compassion for others. Batson makes the point more explicitly, arguing that attempts to take the perspective of the target are crucial for generating empathic concern as opposed to personal distress. While Eisenberg, Shea et al. argue that perspective taking can lead to any affective response, it likewise seems clear that they view higher order cognitive activity, such as perspective taking, as the key mechanism for transforming parallel affect into empathic concern.

These two propositions, derived from the work of the major contemporary empathy theorists, provide us with a framework for interpreting the many empirical investigations in this area. The remainder of this chapter will consider the evidence regarding causal antecedents of parallel and reactive outcomes, with an eye toward noting how well the evidence supports these theoretical propositions. To begin, let us consider the most fundamental emotional response of the observer—parallel affective outcomes.

Parallel Outcomes

A substantial number of investigations have examined potential influences on parallel responses. As it turns out, however, two of the six empathy-related processes, motor mimicry and role taking, have received most of this attention, with a few studies also examining links between parallel outcomes and the two antecedent factors of individual differences in dispositional empathy and degree of observer-target similarity. Let us first discuss the work on motor mimicry.

Motor Mimicry

One way in which a target's emotion might come to be experienced by the observer is through **motor mimicry,** the tendency for the observer to mimic the facial and body cues of the target. This process has long been considered a likely candidate to explain affective sharing. Lipps (1926) and Titchener (1909) both identified mimicry as the key mechanism underlying empathy, and it is one of the six empathic modes identified by Hoffman (1984). Before concluding that it is a viable mechanism, however, two conditions must be met. First, witnessing affective cues (e.g., facial expressions) in others must actually lead to the generation of parallel cues in observers, and second, this cue production by observers must then produce in them some change in physiological and/or subjective states.

Several investigations have addressed the first link in this inferential chain. In a pair of studies, Vaughan and Lanzetta (1980) had observers watch a target who was ostensibly receiving intermittent shocks while performing a memory task. Observers' physiological arousal was measured, as was the activity of facial muscles in the orbicularis oculi (surrounding the eye) and masseter (jaw) sites; activity at each of these locations is typically associated with the facial expression of pain. In both studies for orbicularis oculi, and one study for masseter, increased muscle activity in observers was found on those trials when the target apparently received a shock.

When the target grimaced, the observer's facial activity tended to match it. In both studies, however, this effect was significant only during the early trials, with the increased facial activity disappearing by the end of the study. In a later investigation, McHugo, Lanzetta, Sullivan, Masters, and Englis (1985) had observers view still images of President Ronald Reagan displaying happiness, fear, and anger. They found increased corrugator supercilii (brow) activity to the threat displays, and more zygomatic (cheek) activity to the happiness displays. Both patterns correspond to the muscle activity typically found in targets expressing those emotions.

Facial mimicry is also affected by the nature of the observer-target relationship. Englis, Vaughan, and Lanzetta (1982) had observers and targets play a simulated "investments" game, during which observers witnessed the targets displaying smiles (following rewards) or grimaces (following shocks). Some observers (Symmetry condition), were rewarded when the target smiled and received shocks when the target grimaced. For other observers (Asymmetry condition) these contingencies were reversed. Target smiles co-occurred with observer shocks, and target grimaces with observer rewards. As did Vaughan and Lanzetta (1980), Englis et al. found that orbicularis oculi activity in observers matched that of targets, but only in the symmetry condition. In fact, when the rewards and shocks of targets and observers were asymmetric, observer facial activity was *counter-empathic;* that is, the observers came to grimace in response to the target's smiles. In a later study, Lanzetta and Englis (1989) obtained similar effects when observers merely expected to cooperate or compete with the target. Observers displayed facial mimicry when they expected to cooperate with the target, and counter- empathic facial activity when they expected to compete.

It thus appears that in many, though not all, circumstances observers react to observed facial affect with matching facial activity of their own. What then of the proposition that one's facial activity affects one's own emotional reactions? This proposition, known as the *facial feedback hypothesis* (e.g., Buck, 1980; Izard, 1977), is currently supported by a substantial body of evidence (see Adelmann & Zajonc, 1989, for a review). A number of studies have found that whether subjects are instructed to deliberately simulate facial expressions representing specific emotions (e.g., Laird, 1974), or merely to suppress or exaggerate naturally occurring facial expressions (e.g., Zuckerman, Klorman, Larrance, & Spiegel, 1981), these variations in facial expression reliably affect autonomic responses such as heart rate, blood volume, and skin conductance as well as self-ratings of subjectively experienced affect. Although disagreement exists regarding the mechanism producing these effects (Adelmann & Zajonc, 1989; Fiske & Taylor, 1991; Strack, Martin, & Stepper, 1988), the evidence seems reasonably clear that facial expressions can significantly affect the emotional state of the individual.

In an investigation which spans both elements of the motor mimicry hypothesis, Vaughan and Lanzetta (1981) had observers view a target who was apparently receiving intermittent shocks, and monitored the activity of their orbicularis oculi and masseter muscles. In addition, subjects were instructed either to inhibit their naturally occurring facial expressions as they watched the target, to amplify those expressions, or received no instructions. Consistent with the facial feedback hypothesis and the motor mimicry explanation, observers who exaggerated their natural facial expressions displayed greater skin conductance and faster heart rate than observers receiving no instructions. Those inhibiting their facial expressions displayed a decreased heart rate, but no change in skin conductance. Taken as a whole, then, the accumulated evidence supports the idea that observers frequently mimic the facial expressions of targets, especially ones toward whom a cooperative orientation exists, and that this mimicry influences the observers' autonomic activity and subjective experience of emotion.

It should be noted, however, that motor mimicry may have other functions as well. Bavelas and her colleagues (Bavelas, Black, Lemery, MacInnis, & Mullett, 1986; Bavelas, Black, Lemery & Mullett, 1986; 1987), for example, have argued that mimicry's purpose is largely communicative, a means by which observers express to targets that they are aware of and in fact are experiencing the target's affective state. According to this view, then, mimicry is not simply the automatic external manifestation of an observer's feeling state, but is instead part of an independent and parallel communicative process.

In support of this position, Bavelas et al. (1987) present evidence that mimicry is more frequent and pronounced when observers are aware that the targets will perceive the mimicked expressions, a pattern consistent with the view that the purpose of mimicry is to direct an affective message to the target. This is an interesting and novel perspective, but it is not necessarily inconsistent with the other evidence reviewed thus far. It is certainly possible for mimicry to have evolved as a largely communicative act as Bavelas argues, and nevertheless to also have the effect of producing in observers the affective state they are attempting to communicate. It is also possible that the evolutionary development of mimicry may be ''overdetermined''. Two separate evolutionary advantages, one resulting from group members sharing affect and the other from group members effectively communicating that this sharing had occurred, may have combined to encourage development of the single mechanism of motor mimicry.

Role Taking

A number of investigations have found that observers will experience parallel affective responses when they step outside their usual perspective on events and entertain the perspective of the target. In practical terms, role taking has typically been manipulated by providing observers with instructional sets explicitly directing them to adopt the psychological perspective of the target. Two variants of these instructions, both initially developed by Stotland (1969), have been commonly employed: *imagine-self* and *imagine-the-other* instructional sets. Subjects receiving *imagine-self* instructions are typically asked to:

> "imagine how you yourself would feel . . . picture to yourself just how you would feel . . . concentrate on yourself in that experience . . . in your mind's eye, you are to visualize how it would feel . . ." (Stotland, 1969, p. 292).

Those receiving *imagine-the-other* instructions are asked to:

> "imagine how [the other person] feels . . . picture to yourself just how he feels . . . concentrate on him in that experience . . . in your mind's eye, you are to visualize how it feels to him . . . " (Stotland, 1969, p. 292).

The imagine-the-other instructions are essentially the same as the affective role-taking instructions employed in the attribution studies described in Chapter 5. Most investigations employing either of these instructional sets also include a "control" set which directs the observer to simply observe the target carefully, noting and remembering audio or visual details with as much clarity as possible.

Four studies have compared the parallel responses of observers receiving imagine-self instructions with those receiving control instructions. Stotland (1969) exposed observers to a target undergoing a diathermy (heat) treatment described as either painful or pleasurable. Observers instructed to imagine themselves in the target's place exhibited greater palmar sweating than control subjects when the treatment was thought to be painful, and also reported feeling more tense and nervous. Aderman (1972) found that imagine-self observers reported feeling more unhappy and resentful after listening to a tape in which the target failed to receive help from another person. Aderman et al. (1974) similarly found that observers who imagined themselves in the place of a target receiving electric shocks reported feeling more angry and defiant. In each case, subjects instructed to place themselves imaginatively in the position of a distressed other reported emotions paralleling the likely reactions of the targets themselves. The one exception to this pattern is an investigation by Brehm, Powell, and Coke (1984) using much younger respondents. First-grade children who were instructed to pretend that what happened to the target had actually happened to them were no more likely than control subjects to report feeling bad or sad after hearing about a same-age target who was unable to have a birthday party.

Four studies have examined the impact of imagine-the-other instructions on parallel responding. Stotland (1969) found that while the imagine-self instructions produced increased palmar sweating and self-reports of anxiety, imagine-the-other instructions had no such effect; they did, however, lead to increased vasoconstriction (restriction of blood flow in the fingers). Miller (1987) had observers view a target performing several embarrassing tasks (e.g., singing the "Star Spangled Banner"). Those observers who were instructed to imagine the feelings of the target not only estimated the target's embarrassment as higher, but also displayed heightened skin conductance and greater self-reported feelings of embarrassment as well. Batson, Batson, Griffitt, Barrientos, Brandt, Sprengelmeyer, and Bayly (1989, Study 3) provided observers with imagine-the-other or control instructions and then exposed them to an audiotaped depiction of a female college student trying to support her family following the death of her parents. Those attempting to imagine the other's feelings reported more sadness than did the control subjects. Davis, Hull, Young, and Warren (1987) exposed observers to excerpts from two movies depicting tense and depressing subject matter, *Who's Afraid of Virginia Woolf* and *Brian's Song*, and found no significant main effect of instructions on self- reported emotional reactions. There was, however, an interactive effect of instructional set and the subjects' dispositional tendency to engage in perspective taking. The affective responses of subjects scoring high on the IRI's PT scale were influenced by the instructional set, with those receiving the imagine-the-other instructions reporting affective reactions more congruent with those in the film (e.g., decreased happiness); those low in dispositional perspective taking were unaffected by the instructional set.

Individual Differences

In addition to those studies which have addressed the impact of mimicry and role taking on parallel reactions, some investigations have examined the impact of personal and situational antecedents as well. Evidence from two studies, for example, indicates that empathic tendencies of the individual can affect the likelihood of experiencing parallel affective outcomes. Wiesenfeld, Whitman, and Malatesta (1984) found women who were very extreme scorers on the QMEE (upper and lower 5 percent of the distribution) to differ in their physiological and subjective reactions to silent videotapes of smiling and crying infants. High QMEE scorers displayed significantly greater increases in heart rate and skin conductance to both types of infant displays. The other study, the Davis et al. (1987) investigation, found scores on the PT scale of the IRI to interact with imagine-the-other instructions in affecting parallel reactions. In that same investigation, however, dispositional empathic concern was found to directly influence observers' affective responses. Following exposure to the movie excerpts, those observers scoring high on the IRI's EC scale reported greater feelings of hostility, anxiety, and depression, affective states generally consistent with the affective tone of the stimuli.

Similarity between Observer and Target

Finally, several studies have examined the effect on parallel outcomes of an antecedent situational factor: similarity between target and observer. Interpreting the precise meaning of these investigations is somewhat problematic, however, since similarity may have an impact on most of the empathy-related processes identified by Hoffman (1984) and Eisenberg, Shea et al. (1991). Motor mimicry, for example, might be intensified when observer and target are similar. Greater observer-target similarity of experience or background might increase the likelihood that associative processes such as conditioning and labeling would operate, and even the most advanced processes such as role taking might be facilitated by perceived similarity between observer and target. Because of this, the meaning of any reliable association between similarity and affective responding will be subject to differing interpretations.

Perhaps the earliest of these investigations was conducted by Stotland and Dunn (1963), who manipulated perceived similarity by leading observers to believe that they and the target (a confederate) had previously worked on the same or different experimental tasks. Observers then watched the target perform a new task and publicly receive either good or bad feedback regarding task performance. When observers believed themselves to be similar to the target, their self-reported anxiety matched the ostensible state of the target, namely, greater anxiety when the target performed poorly. In the dissimilar condition, target performance had no effect on observers' anxiety. Contrary to prediction, however, physiological arousal (palmar sweating) was unaffected by similarity.

Subsequent investigations have generally supported the similarity-parallel outcome association. Stotland (1969; Stotland et al., 1971) has conducted several studies indicating that similarity produces increased physiological arousal (palmar sweating). It should be noted, however, that these findings were often more reliable among some observers than others, most notably later-borns and females. Krebs (1975) manipulated observer-target similarity by informing observers that they had been deliberately paired with a target whose personality test scores were either highly similar or dissimilar to their own. Some observers then saw the target apparently receive either electric shocks or money during 18 "conditioning trials," while the remaining observers were led to believe that no such rewards or punishments were involved. As expected, observers who believed they were similar to the target displayed heightened skin conductance and vasoconstriction when the target appeared to receive shocks. They also reported feeling worse during the procedure.

Not all investigations have supported the notion that similarity produces parallel affect. Marks, Penner, and Stone (1982, Experiment 1), for example, found that observers who believed they were similar to targets in academic interests and personality were no more likely to report feeling anxious as they watched the targets receive electric shocks. In an interesting study, Gruen and Mendelsohn (1986) exposed undergraduate observers to one of two films, one depicting a young woman whose boyfriend is leaving her (rejection film) and the other depicting a young woman having disagreements with her parents over her desire to move away from home (conflict film). Afterwards, the observers completed an emotion checklist which included items directly corresponding to the emotion experienced by the woman in the film.

Similarity or dissimilarity to the target was defined as the degree to which the observers' own personality traits, as assessed by the Adjective Check List (ACL; Gough & Heilbrun, 1980) corresponded to the reactions displayed by the target in the film. For the rejection film, observers with higher scores on the ACL's succorance and abasement scales, denoting a tendency to feel inferior and victimized, were considered more similar. For the conflict film, observers with higher scores on the achievement, dominance, and self-confidence scales were considered more similar to the independence-seeking target. Similarity defined in this way had only a weak effect on parallel affect. Greater similarity was somewhat associated with more affective matching for the rejection film, but was weakly associated with less matching for the conflict film.

Reactive Outcomes

Empathic Concern

In recent years, several investigations by Eisenberg and her colleagues have attempted to identify facial or physiological changes corresponding to the state of empathic concern (e.g., Eisenberg, Fabes et al., 1989; Eisenberg, Fabes, Schaller, Miller et al., 1991; Eisenberg, Schaller et al., 1988). These studies, some of which were described in Chapter 3, have been generally successful. However, the overwhelming majority of investigations examining this affective state have employed the methodology of observers' self-reports. In particular, most studies have assessed empathic concern by means of a set of adjectives (e.g., *sympathetic, moved, compassionate,* and *tender*) originally developed by Batson and colleagues (e.g., Coke, Batson, & McDavis, 1978; Toi & Batson, 1982). Considerable evidence supports the psychometric adequacy of this measure (see Batson et al., 1987), and its relation to overt behavior (see next chapter). Unless otherwise noted, then, all of the research cited below employed some subset of these empathic concern items.

Most of the investigations examining empathic concern's antecedents have focused on **role taking,** and have used instructions to induce a role-taking set toward the target. Moreover, virtually all of the studies have employed the imagine-the-other instructional set. Following delivery of the instructional set, subjects in these studies were typically exposed to a target in some distress. One frequently used target is "Katie Banks," originally introduced by Coke et al. (1978). In this paradigm subjects listen to an audiotape, ostensibly a newscast from a campus radio station, in which the plight of a young college student, Katie, is described. Following the recent death of her parents, Katie is struggling to support her younger brother and sister while finishing school. The tape includes an emotional interview with Katie in which she voices her fear that she might have to give up the children for adoption. After listening to this tape, participants typically complete a questionnaire containing the empathic concern items. Other commonly used paradigms have exposed observers to targets who were injured in an auto accident (e.g., Toi & Batson, 1982), who were experiencing college-related stress (e.g., Batson, Batson et al., 1991, Study 2), who needed volunteers for a research project (e.g., Coke et al., 1978), and who were receiving painful electric shocks (e.g., Batson, Bolen, Cross, & Neuringer-Benefiel, 1986; Batson, O'Quin, Fultz, Vanderplas, & Isen, 1983).

The vast majority of these investigations, whether using "Katie Banks" or some other target, have found imagine-the-other instructions to produce significantly greater feelings of sympathy for the target than control instructions. Of the 16 studies which have used this set, 13 (81 percent) found a significant effect of instructions on empathic concern (Batson, Batson, et al., 1989; Batson, Batson, et al., 1991; Batson et al., 1988; Betancourt, 1990a; Cialdini, Schaller, Houlihan, Arps, Fultz, & Beaman, 1987; Davis, 1983a; Dovidio et al., 1990; Fultz, Batson, Fortenbach, McCarthy, & Varney, 1986; Fultz & Cialdini, 1986; Miller, 1987; Schaller & Cialdini, 1988; Schroeder, Dovidio, Sibicky, Mathews, & Allen, 1988; Toi & Batson, 1982). Only three investigations failed to find such an effect (Eisenberg, Fabes, Schaller, Miller et al., 1991; Smith et al., 1989; Wise, 1985).

Two studies have manipulated observer-target similarity and assessed the resulting degree of empathic concern. The Gruen and Mendelsohn (1986) investigation, in which similarity was indexed by the degree to which observer personality matched the filmed target's reactions, was described in some detail in the earlier discussion of parallel outcomes. For both the rejection and conflict films in that study greater observer-target similarity was associated with more self-reported feelings of compassion. The Houston (1990) study, also described in Chapter 5, operationalized observer-target similarity in terms of Higgins' (1987) self-discrepancy model. Observers and targets were considered similar if the observer's chronic self-discrepancies matched the kind of situational self-discrepancy the target was portrayed as having. As with the Gruen and Mendelsohn study, greater similarity was associated with heightened feelings of sympathy and compassion for the target.

Finally, most of the remaining investigations of empathic concern have focused at least in part on the impact of dispositional empathic tendencies, primarily using the IRI for this purpose. Five studies (Batson et al., 1986; Davis, 1983a; Eisenberg, Fabes, Schaller, Miller et al., 1991; Eisenberg, Miller, Schaller, Fabes, Fultz, Shell, & Shea, 1989; Wise, 1985) have assessed observers' standing on some or all of the IRI's four scales and have also exposed them to a distressed target. The clearest associations between dispositional empathy and sympathy for the target have emerged for the perspective taking (PT) and empathic concern (EC) scales. Both measures were significantly associated with self-reported sympathy in 4 of 5 studies, with mean r's across all five studies of .22 (PT) and .29 (EC). The personal distress scale was less consistently associated. Of the four investigations employing it, two found significant positive associations with sympathy and one found a significant negative relation, with a mean r over the four studies of exactly .00. The fantasy scale was also used in four studies, and was significantly related to sympathy in two of them (mean r of .15). It should be noted that one of these studies (Wise, 1985) also employed the EM scale and found it unrelated to empathic concern, while another (Eisenberg, Miller, et al., 1989) also administered the QMEE and found it to be significantly positively associated.

Personal Distress

In contrast to investigations of empathic concern, which all evolved from a single research tradition, evidence regarding the causal antecedents of personal distress falls into two distinct categories. The first is made up of studies, discussed earlier, which largely focused on parallel outcomes. As previously noted, in cases where targets are experiencing anxiety, fear, and distress, comparable reactions by the observer are difficult to interpret. They obviously qualify as parallel reactions, but the specific nature of this affect also qualifies as personal distress. Thus, some studies which found similarity (e.g., Stotland & Dunn, 1963; Krebs, 1975) or role taking (e.g., Stotland, 1969) to produce greater anxiety and distress in response to distressed targets will be considered in this section as well.

A second set of studies was conducted more recently. Because contemporary theorizing has so frequently focused on the contrasting motivational properties of empathic concern and personal distress, virtually every study explicitly addressing the antecedents of personal distress has simultaneously examined empathic concern as well. Thus, many investigations reviewed in the previous section on empathic concern also address the issue of personal distress. One consequence of this is that virtually the same experimental procedures and targets have been employed in investigations of both affective states. For example, situational personal distress is typically assessed via a questionnaire instrument initially developed by Batson and colleagues (Coke et al., 1978; Toi & Batson, 1982), and similar to the one used to assess empathic concern. While the empathic concern index contains such items as "tender" and "sympathetic," personal distress is reflected by such descriptors as *worried, upset, disturbed,* and *distressed.* As with the empathic concern index, considerable evidence (see Batson et al., 1987) supports its psychometric adequacy. Although empathic concern and personal distress, as measured by these self-report items, have usually been clearly discriminable from one another, it should be noted that a few investigations (e.g., Batson et al., 1988; Eisenberg, Fabes, et al., 1989) have found self-reports of personal distress to also reflect, to some degree, feelings of empathic concern.

As with empathic concern, most studies in this area employed role-taking instructional sets, and all of these used some version of the imagine-the-other instructions. In contrast to the pattern found for empathic concern, however, the effect of these instructions on feelings of personal distress is not quite as reliable. Six of 12 studies found that imagine-the-other instructions led to a significant increase in personal distress (Betancourt, 1990a; Cialdini et al., 1987; Dovidio et al., 1990; Fultz & Cialdini, 1986; Schaller & Cialdini, 1988; Schroeder et al., 1988), while another six did not (Davis, 1983a; Eisenberg, Fabes, Schaller, Miller et al., 1991; Fultz et al., 1986; Smith et al., 1989; Toi & Batson, 1982; Wise, 1985). Thus, while imagine-the-other instructions produced heightened empathic concern in over 80 percent of the investigations, it had such an effect on personal distress only 50 percent of the time. Because studies in which the instructional set fails to influence affective outcomes are probably less likely to be published, however, these "success rates" may actually be lower, to some unknown degree, for both types of affect.

Evidence regarding the effect of similarity on personal distress is also somewhat inconsistent. Of the earlier studies, Stotland and Dunn (1963) and Krebs (1975) found similarity to be associated with greater reactions of anxiety and distress to a distressed target. Marks et al. (1982), however, found no such effect. More recently, Houston (1990) found that while similarity reliably produced stronger feelings of empathic concern, this pattern did not hold for personal distress. Observers who shared the target's same specific self-discrepancy were no more likely to feel personal distress than those who did not.

Finally, the same five studies which employed the IRI scales as predictors of empathic concern also examined their links with personal distress. Dispositional perspective taking and empathic concern were significantly related to personal distress in three of five instances, with mean r's over all five studies of .21 and .18, respectively. Dispositional personal distress and fantasy were significantly associated with reported distress in two of four instances, with respective mean r's of .16 and .15. The study (Wise, 1985) which employed the EM scale found it to be unrelated to self-reported distress, while the investigation (Eisenberg, Miller et al., 1989) which used the QMEE found it to be significantly and positively related.

Evaluating the Theoretical Propositions

How well do these empirical findings jibe with the theoretical propositions outlined earlier? Taken as a whole, the level of support is reasonably strong, although there are exceptions to this pattern. Let us examine the key propositions.

1. *Each mode of empathic arousal will tend to produce both parallel and reactive affective responding.* This proposition accords fairly well with the accumulated evidence. With regard to parallel affect, at least some evidence supports the links with mimicry (e.g., Vaughan & Lanzetta, 1980; 1981; McHugo et al., 1985) and perspective taking (e.g., Aderman et al., 1974; Stotland, 1969); thus, both primitive and advanced processes display some association with parallel responding. The situational antecedent of observer-target similarity (Krebs, 1975; Stotland, 1969) also displayed a significant effect on parallel outcomes. The reactive outcomes of empathic concern and personal distress also are affected to some degree by perspective-taking instructions and by similarity; in both cases, however, the evidence is stronger for empathic concern than for personal distress. As previously noted, moreover, it is difficult to know the precise mechanism by which similarity influences affective responses. Thus, the degree to which less advanced processes may be affecting reactive empathy is presently unknown. One thing clearly missing from this picture is any systematic investigation of reactive affect using an induction technique other than instructional set. Although a handful of studies have examined reactive outcomes as a function of observer-target similarity and empathic predispositions, the majority have limited their study of causal antecedents to role taking.

More generally, this review reveals an almost total absence of investigations directly focusing on the actual processes underlying affective outcomes. For example, while theorists agree that an important role in producing empathic affect is played by largely automatic associative processes, such processes have almost completely escaped empirical attention, and little is known about their operation.

Likewise, while numerous studies have used instructional sets to induce role taking, virtually nothing is known about what *precisely* happens when people respond to such instructions. How, for instance, does one actually go about imagining the other's feelings, or imagining oneself in the other's situation? Do observers even distinguish between these two imaginative acts, or do the imagine-the-other and imagine-self instructions actually produce in observers exactly the same kind of cerebrations? These will not be easy questions to answer, but they are certainly not impossible. The success in recent years of research examining links between cognitive structures and affective reactions (see Fiske & Taylor, 1991) suggests that the time is ripe for employing theory and methodology from the field of social cognition in our efforts to understand the cognitive processing associated with affective outcomes.

2. *Adopting the perspective of the target is the process especially likely to produce empathic concern.* Viewed in one way, this proposition is reasonably well supported by the data. The imagine-the-other instructional set produced significantly greater empathic concern in 13 of 16 investigations, while producing comparable increases in personal distress in 6 of 12 instances. Consistent with theoretical expectations, then, this form of role taking was more likely to produce sympathy than distress. The few studies employing these instructions and assessing parallel affect yielded somewhat inconsistent findings. Two studies (Miller, 1987; Batson, Batson et al., 1989, Study 3) reported greater affective matching, while two others (Davis et al., 1987; Stotland, 1969) reported weak or inconsistent findings. Thus, affective role-taking instructions do appear to be somewhat more reliably associated with empathic concern than with any other emotional response. The other major instructional set, imagine-self instructions, has been infrequently employed in examinations of affective responding. Only four studies of parallel affect used these instructions, and three reported greater affective matching as a result. Regarding reactive affect, only one study (Brehm et al., 1984) employed imagine-self instructions and failed to find an effect on self-reported empathic concern.

Viewed in a different way, however, the evidence regarding this proposition is inconclusive. While the role taking/empathic concern link does appear robust, the notion that empathic concern typically requires this advanced form of processing is difficult to evaluate, largely because so few attempts have been made to induce such affect by any other means. The sparse evidence available thus far (Gruen & Mendelsohn, 1986; Houston, 1990) suggests that observer-target similarity may also exert a reliable effect on empathic concern. It is, of course, quite possible that one effect of such similarity is to induce more perspective taking activity by the observer. If so, then this might account for the effects of similarity on empathic concern. Without some evidence that this is the case, however, it is also possible that similarity is inducing empathic concern through less cognitively advanced processes, and as noted earlier, these are precisely the processes about which so little is known. Because of this uncertainty, then, it seems too early to conclude that perspective taking is uniquely important for the experience of empathic concern.

This difficulty in interpreting the similarity research also points to a more general issue which complicates our understanding of the link between empathic processes and affective outcomes, and that is the interactive nature of these processes. While most investigations of affective responses focus on a single causal variable such as similarity, or role taking, or mimicry, it seems highly likely that manipulating any one process will affect other processes as well. It has already been demonstrated, for example, that prior experience with a target can reverse the usual motor mimicry pattern, and produce observer smiles in response to target pain or observer grimaces in response to target joy (Englis et al., 1982; Lanzetta & Englis, 1989). It does not seem unreasonable to expect that perceived similarity, or role-taking efforts, can likewise affect the mimicry process. It also seems likely that reciprocal relationships may exist between perceptions of similarity and role-taking efforts, with greater perceived similarity prompting more role taking, and greater role taking producing perceptions of greater similarity. Thus, while it is possible to distinguish among the various empathy-related processes on conceptual grounds, in "real life" they may resist such clear separation.

Summary

Painted in broad strokes, the emergent picture regarding affective empathic outcomes includes the following features. The existence of parallel affective outcomes, a rough matching between the affect of the target and observer, seems well-established. One mechanism probably contributing to this phenomenon is a mimicking by the observer of the target's facial cues, which then contributes to the experience of affect consistent with those facial expressions. Similarity between observer and target also seems to make parallel responses more likely, although this evidence is not entirely consistent. Instructional sets designed to induce perspective taking seem to make affective sharing more likely, with the evidence perhaps a bit stronger for the imagine-self than imagine-the-other set. Although it seems reasonable that reliable individual differences exist in the tendency to experience parallel affect, the empirical evidence is so far sparse and sketchy.

With regard to reactive outcomes, instructional sets to imagine-the-other are quite reliably associated with feeling sympathy and compassion for the target, and somewhat less reliably associated with personal feelings of anxiety and distress. The very small number of studies which have manipulated similarity suggest that greater observer-target similarity leads to more sympathy, but it is not clear that a similar effect exists for personal distress. Finally, several investigations have found dispositional perspective taking and empathic concern to be associated with feelings of both sympathy and distress in response to a distressed target. Dispositional personal distress has also displayed significant associations with situational feelings of distress.

Altruism and Helping Behavior

The two previous chapters have focused on the intrapersonal outcomes of empathy-related processes: observers' affective and nonaffective responses to (usually) distressed targets. These responses are intrapersonal because they occur largely within the observer, and in and of themselves need not be manifested in observable behavior. The next three chapters, in contrast, will focus on *interpersonal* outcomes, which are so named because they consist of overt behaviors directed toward other people. In keeping with the logic of the organizational model, the intrapersonal outcomes discussed thus far are seen as playing a major role in determining the overt interpersonal behaviors.

The specific focus of this chapter will be on altruism and helping behavior—actions carried out by one individual which benefit another person. Such behavior has attracted considerable interest from social scientists for over a century (e.g., Comte, 1851/1875; McDougall, 1908; Hartshorne & May, 1928; Macauley & Berkowitz, 1970; Latané & Darley, 1970; Eisenberg, 1986; Batson, 1991), and a variety of theoretical approaches have been taken in attempting to understand it. It is important to note, then, that in only some of these approaches do empathy-related processes and outcomes play an important role. Consequently, this chapter will by no means attempt a comprehensive survey of theory and research related to altruism/helping behavior, but will focus solely on those approaches which give a meaningful role to the empathy-related constructs we have identified thus far. As we shall see, however, this will still cover quite a lot of ground. More comprehensive treatments of issues related to altruism/helping can be found in a variety of sources, including Krebs (1970), Macauley and Berkowitz (1970), Wispé (1978), Staub (1978, 1979), Eisenberg and Mussen (1989), and Rushton and Sorrentino (1981).

Definitions: Helping and Altruism

Before going further, it is necessary to more carefully define the terms altruism and helping behavior. One approach to this problem has been to essentially treat these two terms as interchangeable, with both of them referring to actions taken by one person which, at some cost to the self, improve the welfare of another by either reducing negative states and/or increasing positive states for that other. This approach defines an act as altruism/helping solely on the basis of its outcome, with no emphasis placed on the motivation underlying the helping act. Thus, it does not matter whether one helps another out of an unselfish desire to provide aid, to escape the distress which results from seeing another in distress, to avoid the guilt that would result from not helping, to gain the social rewards that result from acting in socially approved ways, or even to share in the joy that the distressed target may be expected to experience. As noted in Chapter 2, this ''amotivational'' conception of altruism/ helping underlies sociobiological treatments like those of Dawkins (1976), Trivers (1971), and Wilson (1975).

Another approach has been to distinguish between helping behavior and altruism according to the kind of motivation which prompts the act. There are, in fact, at least two versions of this approach. The first reserves the term altruism for those helping acts which do not seem to be motivated by desire for an external reward or desire to avoid some external punishment (e.g., Eisenberg & Mussen, 1989; Staub, 1978; Cialdini et al., 1981). Thus, helping carried out to gain social approval or material rewards, or to avoid social sanctions for failing to help, would not qualify as altruism; it would simply be helping behavior. Any helping which did not appear to be the result of external motivation, however, is altruistic, and this includes helping acts carried out in order to gain internally administered rewards such as feelings of pride, or to avoid internally administered punishments such as feelings of guilt and shame. Because such motives involve efforts by the helper to maximize his or her own well-being as the ultimate goal, with the helping act serving essentially as a means to this end, this definition would still encompass some helping acts which arguably are motivated by largely selfish concerns. We may characterize it, then, as a weak version of altruism.

In contrast, a strong version of altruism can also be identified. In this version, the term altruism is reserved only for those helping acts carried out solely for the purpose of increasing the welfare of the other. According to this position, helping which is carried out to avoid some internal punishment like guilt, or to gain some internal reward like pride, is fundamentally egoistic in nature, and cannot be considered truly altruistic. The strongest proponent of this definition of altruism is Batson (1991), who argues that other writers who have offered somewhat similar arguments (e.g., Hoffman, 1975, 1982a; Krebs, 1975) have failed to explicitly exclude all potentially egoistic motivations from their definitions.

In part because of the difficulty in teasing apart egoistic and altruistic motivations for overt acts of helping, and in part because of the strong behaviorist tradition in contemporary psychology (see Batson, 1991), the dominant view for some time has been that all helping acts are fundamentally egoistic. That is, despite any surface indications that a helping act is intended simply to aid the victim, this view maintains that all helping ultimately results from a desire to increase the welfare of the helper rather than the victim. Thus altruism, if it exists, is only of the weak form, carried out to gain or avoid internally administered rewards and sanctions. The most notable exception to this view is the work of Batson (e.g., Batson et al., 1981; Batson et al., 1983; Fultz et al., 1986), which will be considered later in this chapter.

Although the foregoing discussion of the different definitions of altruism may give the impression that research in this area has been organized and orderly, this would not be entirely accurate. In much of the earlier research investigating links between empathy and altruism/ helping, these distinctions were not much considered, and the terms altruism and helping behavior were frequently used more or less interchangeably. More recent theorizing and research has increasingly focused on questions of motivation, however, with the result that more sophisticated theoretical accounts and empirical techniques have evolved. Two excellent reviews of the literature, Underwood and Moore (1982) and Eisenberg and Miller (1987), have summarized the evidence linking empathy and altruism/helping, and both reviews concluded that reliable associations exist between helping behavior and empathy-related constructs. Underwood and Moore, for example, concluded that perceptual and cognitive role-taking capacity among children was significantly associated with helping behavior. Eisenberg and Miller concluded that most empathy-related constructs (e.g., self-reported individual differences, self-reported situational affective responses, physiological responses, similarity) were significantly and positively associated with helping behavior. The one exception to this pattern are the studies employing picture-story measures of empathy which revealed essentially no reliable connection between empathy and helping.

The remainder of this chapter will examine the evidence regarding connections between altruism/helping and the empathy-related constructs of affective reactions, non-affective judgments, role-taking processes, situational factors, and personality traits. We will begin with those constructs "closest" to helping in the organizational model, the intrapersonal outcomes, and then consider those increasingly more distant. The first topic to be considered, then, and the one which has been most vigorously investigated in recent years, is the link between affective outcomes and helping.

Affective Outcomes and Helping

The idea that affective reactions in an observer are causally linked with subsequent helping is central to a number of historical (e.g., Smith, 1975/1976; McDougall, 1908) and contemporary (e.g., Hoffman, 1982a; Batson, 1991; Eisenberg, 1986) explanations of helping, and has sparked considerable research. From our limited standpoint, however, research in this area is relevant only to the degree that the observer's affect is *empathically* aroused, resulting from the observation of the needy target and not from some other source. Thus, some approaches to the question of how affect and helping are related are largely irrelevant to our concerns.

One example of such an approach is the work linking feelings of guilt to subsequent helping. In general, research indicates that those who are presumably experiencing stronger feelings of guilt tend to offer more help to needy targets (e.g., Freedman, 1970;

Regan, Williams, & Sparling, 1972). This research falls largely outside the scope of our discussion, however, because guilt is not a vicarious emotion, as empathic affective outcomes are, but is an example of what Eisenberg (1986) refers to as a "self-evaluative" emotion: an affective state which results from an observer comparing his or her behavior to some relevant value or standard. In the case of guilt, the individual evaluates the self negatively because of a failure to live up to some standard of correct behavior. Although such feelings may prompt helping behavior, they are not affective reactions experienced solely as a result of observing others' experiences. A substantial self-evaluative component also exists.

Another example is the body of evidence concerning the effect of positive affect/good mood on helping. A consistent pattern has emerged indicating that individuals experiencing positive mood states are more helpful than those not experiencing such moods (e.g., Isen, 1970; Isen, Shalker, Clark, & Karp, 1978). While it is possible that observing another's pleasure will induce parallel feelings in the observer, and consequently make helping more likely, virtually no investigations in this literature have induced positive mood in such a way, preferring instead to induce affect in the observer directly. Moreover, since situations in which happy targets are in need of help from an observer seem relatively uncommon, the role of positive affect in producing helping does not lend itself especially well to a meaningful empathy analysis. The role of negative affect, in contrast, obviously does. In fact, the hypothesized link between negative affect and helping has been explained in several different ways.

Reduction of Aversive Arousal

Perhaps the most straightforward explanation of how negative affect prompts the observer to help the target is that the negative affect is experienced as an unpleasant state of arousal, and helping is simply an instrumental response which reduces this undesirable state. Because the ultimate goal in such a sequence is to improve the well-being of the observer, such helping seems clearly egoistic in Batson's (1991) sense of the term. Early evidence consistent with this view was provided by Weiss, Boyer, Lombardo, and Stich (1973) and Weiss, Buchanan, Altstatt, and Lombardo (1971). In these studies observers watched a same-sex target perform a complex task while simultaneously receiving a continuous and obviously painful shock. The observers were periodically prompted by signal lights to provide evaluative ratings of the target using a series of "report buttons" on a panel in front of them. For the experimental group, pressing these buttons stopped the electric shock for 10 seconds, providing the target with relief from the painful stimulus, but for the control group, pressing the buttons had no effect on the shock. Consistent with the idea that witnessing pain in others produces an unpleasant state of arousal in the observer, the experimental observers became increasingly quick to press the report buttons, in effect displaying the learning curve typically found when more traditional reinforcers (such as escape from one's own shock) are employed. Control subjects, whose button pushing had no effect on the target's welfare, showed no such change.

The contemporary theoretical position most fully reflecting this view is probably the *arousal: cost-reward model* of Piliavin et al., (1981). According to this model, witnessing the distress of another person is often physiologically arousing, and if this arousal is strong enough it is perceived as aversive. If the arousal is strong enough to prompt a behavioral response, the observer will choose the response which most quickly reduces this unpleasant affect while incurring the fewest possible net costs. Frequently, the behavioral option fitting this description will be to help the target; however, if an equally effective option for reducing arousal is less costly than helping, no helping will result. Thus, greater arousal in response to the target will sometimes increase helping behavior, but the motivation in such cases will be clearly egoistic. A number of studies have supported various elements of this model, specifically that exposure to distressed targets increases observer arousal and that greater arousal can be associated with faster helping (e.g., Gaertner & Dovidio, 1977; Gaertner, Dovidio, & Johnson, 1979; Piliavin et al., 1981).

In terms of the organizational model, what kind of affective response does this approach address? For the most part the arousal: cost-reward model seems concerned with parallel outcomes—the tendency for observers to experience negative emotional states which roughly correspond to those of the victim. For example, experimental scenarios employed in testing this model have involved the target taking a nasty fall while standing on a chair or ladder, or having a stack of chairs collapse on her. The measure of arousal employed in these investigations is typically an increase in heart rate or skin conductivity (see Piliavin et al., 1981, for a review of this research). Because increases in heart rate and skin conductivity are not generally associated with other-oriented responses, but with self-oriented distress reactions which seem congruent with feelings of pain, fear, and arousal (Eisenberg, Fabes et al., 1988; Eisenberg,

Fabes, Schaller, Miller et al., 1991; Eisenberg, Schaller et al., 1988), the physiological responses in these experiments seem likely to reflect the experience of parallel affect.

Negative State Relief

A different way to conceptualize the link between negative empathic affect and helping behavior is offered by the *negative state relief (NSR) model* (Cialdini, Darby, & Vincent, 1973; Cialdini & Kenrick, 1976). Like the arousal: cost-reward model, the NSR model sees the helping act as essentially egoistic, its ultimate purpose being to increase the welfare of the helper rather than the recipient. The means by which this comes about, however, is somewhat different. According to the NSR model, helping another person—*any* other person—is a behavior which generally improves the helper's mood. The reason for this is that such actions are typically valued and praised by others (which is rewarding), and through repeated association over time the helping act itself comes to be rewarding. Therefore, when experiencing an unpleasant mood, one way to alleviate the problem is to provide help to another person. The helping act is in effect a way to manage one's own affective state.

Although the NSR model can apply to situations in which no empathic affect is present (for example, when negative affect is induced not through exposure to a needy target but through some other technique), it is also clearly relevant to the prototypical empathy situation in which an observer witnesses a needy target. According to the NSR logic, exposure to such a target produces in the observer an unpleasant affective state, which the observer then seeks to eliminate through the pleasure-producing effects of a helping act. In contrast to the arousal: cost-reward model, the purpose of helping is not simply to reduce unpleasant arousal by removing the cause of the arousal, but is to overcome or "cancel out" unpleasant affect by carrying out a pleasure-producing act. The fundamental tenets of the NSR model have received support from a number of studies (e.g., Cialdini et al., 1973; Cialdini & Kenrick, 1976; Kenrick, Baumann, & Cialdini, 1979), although some questions remain regarding the model's overall level of empirical support (Carlson & Miller, 1987).

In addition to differing from the arousal: cost-reward model with regard to the mechanism linking affect and helping, the NSR model also differs in terms of the nature of the affective response said to prompt the helping act. While the arousal: cost-reward model focuses on unpleasantly high levels of physiological arousal, with clear distress/anxiety connotations, the NSR model argues that the emotional state which leads to helping is a depressed mood state characterized by feelings of sadness and dejection. In fact, Cialdini et al. (1987) have argued specifically that intense, distress-oriented reactions such as anger and agitation are not typically reduced by the instrumental use of helping behaviors, and thus are unlikely to consistently produce greater helping. In terms of the organizational model, this raises a ticklish question. Is the state of sadness identified by the NSR model a parallel or reactive response? It seems likely that it might qualify as both, in much the same manner as personal distress (see Chapter 6). When exposed to a target clearly experiencing dejection and despair, the observer's feelings of sadness constitute a parallel response; when exposed to targets experiencing more vigorous negative affects, such as fear, frustration, or anger, sadness in the observer seems more reactive. In fact, the quiet, "down" affective tone of sadness seems generally similar to that of empathic concern.

"True" Altruistic Motivation

The two approaches discussed thus far offer somewhat different explanations for the mechanism by which negative affect produces helping; however, they both share the fundamental assumption that this helping is egoistic in nature. Without denying that empathically induced affect can lead to helping behavior through the essentially egoistic means described thus far, Batson (1987; 1991) has argued that at least some helping is not egoistic at all, but is in fact intended solely to benefit the needy target. Such helping would therefore qualify as "true" altruism under the strong definition of that term outlined earlier. Moreover, the source of such true altruism is said to be the reactive emotional response of empathic concern. Because this approach is perhaps the most comprehensive contemporary attempt to understand the relation between empathically produced affect and helping behavior, we will examine it in some detail.

Batson's Model
Batson (1987; 1991) has argued that there are three different paths by which observer affect may lead to helping, each of which begins with observing another person in need. In the first of these, the *reinforcement path,* simply observing the needy target is not enough to produce help. The observer must also believe that helping will lead to the receipt of some kind of reinforcement or the avoiding of

some kind of punishment. Reinforcements might include material reward, social approval, or increased self-esteem, whereas punishments for not helping might include social disapproval or guilt. In each case, the costs and benefits of helping are weighed, and a helping decision made, with the ultimate goal of increasing the welfare of the helper—a clearly egoistic path. The NSR model is an example of the kind of helping occurring on this path, where the sight of a distressed other produces an affective state (sadness) which can be alleviated through the rewarding properties of helping.

In the second approach, the *arousal reduction path,* observing the needy target produces in the observer an unpleasant state of arousal characterized by feelings of personal distress and anxiety. The magnitude of this aversive arousal is determined by such factors as the severity and salience of the target's plight. The greater the observer's personal distress, the greater the motivation to have it reduced. As with the first path, the observer then weighs the costs and benefits of helping or not helping, and makes the decision. One especially important factor in this path is how easy or difficult it is for the observer to simply escape the situation without helping, and thus avoid the sight of the distressed target which is the source of the unpleasant arousal. If reduction of aversive arousal is the observer's primary motivation, and if it is easy to escape the situation without helping, then greater levels of personal distress may very well lead not to helping but to escape. The arousal: cost reward model seems fundamentally to be an example of such "Path 2" helping, although as Batson (1991, p. 81) notes, it has elements of "Path 1" as well.

In the third approach, the *empathy-altruism path,* something very different happens. Observers again witness a needy target, but in this case they view the target in a particular way by adopting the target's perspective and imagining the target's thoughts and feelings. Such perspective taking may result from specific instructions to do so, or from the feelings of closeness or similarity already existing between observer and target. Regardless of its source, adopting the perspective of the needy target is said to produce in the observer the feelings of compassion and tenderness we have labelled empathic concern.

Batson's contention is that this emotional response (which he terms ''empathy'') is the source of a truly altruistic motivation. The stronger the feelings of compassion for the target, the greater is the motivation to reduce the target's need. This is similar to Hoffman's (1984; 1987) position that sympathetic distress for other people produces a true other-oriented desire to alleviate their distress rather than one's own. According to Batson's reasoning, observers experiencing empathic concern are driven to improve the welfare of the target rather than the self. Thus, unlike Path 2, the ease or difficulty of escape from the situation is of no consequence to the observer. Because escaping the situation will not satisfy the Path 3 motive to reduce the target's distress, it will typically not be a viable option for observers experiencing high levels of sympathy for the target. Thus, in contrast to the egoistic helping resulting from the first two paths, Path 3 helping is truly altruistic.

Although these three motivational paths can be clearly differentiated at the conceptual level, Batson (1991) notes that it is likely that they will at least sometimes operate simultaneously. It seems quite possible, for example, that in response to an emergency an observer will experience some degree of unpleasant personal distress, some level of sympathy for the target, and have some expectation that intervening in the emergency will lead to social rewards. Some situations, such as extremely gory accidents, may be especially likely to produce feelings of personal distress; others, such as witnessing the suffering of innocent children, may be especially likely to engender empathic concern. In many cases, however, it seems probable that multiple paths may be "activated." If observers in such situations offer help, how can we know whether the motivation for the act is egoistic or altruistic? The short answer is that we can't. In any single situation, the presence of several different motives makes it impossible to know for sure which motive "really" prompted the behavior. To answer questions of this sort, it is necessary to examine the phenomenon in the more controlled environment of the laboratory, and that is what Batson and his colleagues have done in an impressive series of investigations.

Early Evidence For "True" Altruism
In a set of studies conducted early in this series (Batson et al., 1981; Batson et al., 1983; Toi & Batson, 1982), Batson and colleagues attempted to demonstrate the existence of "Path 3" helping by constructing an experimental design which contrasts the effects of a truly altruistic motivation with those of an egoistic arousal reduction (Path 2) motivation. To do so, they made use of the hypothesized difference in importance to these motivations of the ease or difficulty of escape.

For example, consider an observer, Roseanne, who is experiencing a high degree of personal distress while in the presence of Dan, a needy target. Roseanne's high level of aversive arousal creates in her a motivation to reduce it. If physically escaping from the situation is difficult for some reason, then this high level of arousal

TABLE 7.1 Batson's Experimental Design: The Effect of Empathic Emotion and Ease of Escape on Helping Behavior

		Predominant Emotional Reaction	
		Personal Distress	*Empathic Concern*
Ease or Difficulty of Escape	*Easy*	Escape	Help
	Difficult	Help	Help

will probably lead her to help as a means of eliminating the source of the arousal; on the other hand, if escape from the situation is easy, then she may well choose that option instead. The behavior resulting from this egoistic motivation depends, therefore, on the ease or difficulty of escape. In contrast, consider a situation in which Roseanne is predominantly experiencing empathic concern for Dan. In this case the ease or difficulty of escape is irrelevant to Roseanne's goal of reducing Dan's distress. As a result, she is likely to help whether escape is easy or difficult. If this logic is correct, and feelings of personal distress and empathic concern really do produce, respectively, egoistic and altruistic motivational states, then an experiment producing the four conditions displayed in Table 7.1 should produce levels of helping which conform to the 1 vs. 3 (personal distress/easy escape vs. all other combinations) pattern depicted there.

This is precisely the pattern which has emerged in five separate studies (Batson et al., 1981; Batson et al., 1983; Toi & Batson, 1982). In each of these investigations a comparison was made between subjects predominantly experiencing empathic concern and those predominantly experiencing personal distress. In some cases these emotional reactions were produced through experimental manipulations (e.g., instructional set, observer-target similarity) and in others the predominant emotional response was simply assessed via self-report questionnaire. In every instance the subjects who were experiencing empathic concern provided relatively high levels of help (from 58 percent to 91 percent, with an average of 75 percent), regardless of ease or difficulty of escape. Subjects who were primarily experiencing personal distress displayed the predicted sensitivity to the ease of escape manipulation; when escape was difficult they helped at the same level as those experiencing empathic concern (from 64 percent to 89 percent; average = 79 percent), but when escape was easy the level of helping dropped dramatically (from 18 percent to 40 percent; average = 30 percent). Importantly, this pattern held up over a variety of different need situations (e.g., target receiving electric shocks, target was in an auto accident). Based on these investigations, a convincing case can be made that empathic concern and personal distress are two distinctly different affective reactions, and that the motivation associated with personal distress is clearly egoistic in nature. As Batson (1991) notes, however, despite this consistent pattern, it is not clear from these early studies that the motivation associated with empathic concern is truly altruistic.

Alternative Explanations For The "True" Altruism Findings
The problem is that while these initial studies essentially make a prima facie case for altruistic (Path 3) helping as opposed to arousal-reducing (Path 2) helping, they do not rule out the possibility that this apparently altruistic behavior actually results from some form of reinforcement (Path 1). How would this work? Recall that reinforcement-based helping is based on the idea that the observers expect helping to lead to some form of reward or to avoid some form of punishment. It is possible to explain away the apparently altruistic helping discussed thus far if it is assumed that through socialization we learn that there are specific rewards (and punishments) associated with helping (or failing to help) people toward whom we are experiencing empathic concern. That is, we may learn that when we feel compassion toward another and then act on that compassion we may expect special rewards such as pride and praise, or that when we fail to help in such circumstances there are special punishments such as guilt and loss of social status.

If feelings of empathic concern routinely produce such expectations in us, then the help that results may not be altruistic at all. Instead, the link between empathic concern and helping may simply reflect our attempts to acquire the rewards and avoid the punishments associated with these feelings of sympathy. More specifically, the finding in the early studies that observers experiencing empathic concern tended to help even when it was easy to escape may simply mean that physical escape is irrelevant to receiving the rewards and avoiding the punishments associated with feelings of sympathy. It is easy to imagine, for example, that observers, if they anticipate guilt feelings for failing to help targets for whom they feel sympathy, may very well help even if it is easy to escape the situation. Guilt, after all, is self-administered and such feelings may well occur outside the physical presence of the target. Thus, while helping under conditions of easy escape can effectively rule out the arousal reduction path, it does not necessarily eliminate the reinforcement path.

In fact, Cialdini et al. (1987) have proposed that the apparently altruistic helping in Batson's early studies is actually the result of egoistic reinforcement-seeking by the empathizing observers, and that the results are more simply explained in terms of the NSR model. Specifically, they argue that variables (such as perspective-taking instructions) which produce empathic concern may also cause increased sadness in the observer, that the increased sadness leads to greater helping, and that the ultimate purpose of the helping is to improve the mood of the observer/helper. Thus, as Batson (1991) notes, this position does not claim that there are special rewards associated with helping those for whom we feel sympathy, but does argue that people feeling empathic concern will frequently experience sadness as well, and thus have a special need for the rewards that result from helping. Thus, the NSR explanation does seem to qualify as an example of the Path 1 alternative explanation for apparently altruistic helping.

Cialdini et al. (1987) report the results of two studies which provide some support for their position. In the first, they used perspective-taking instructions to induce an empathic set (and presumably empathic concern) in some observers. For some of these empathizing observers, moreover, they provided a mood-enhancing experience (receiving praise or money) before the observers got the opportunity to help the target. If the logic of the NSR model is correct, and the motivation of the empathizing observers is primarily to enhance their own mood, then the introduction of a mood-enhancing experience should reduce the need for further mood management and thus reduce the likelihood of help. The results of the study generally supported this prediction. In a second study they again used instructions to induce an empathic set, but before allowing observers the opportunity to help, information was presented to some of them indicating that a drug they had previously taken (actually a placebo) would have the effect of "fixing" their mood, making it resistant to change, for the next 30 minutes. If the logic of the NSR model is correct, and empathizing observers help in order to boost their own mood, then the "mood-fixing" manipulation should have the effect of reducing help for those observers. That is in fact the pattern which was found.

However, subsequent research addressing this question has produced somewhat equivocal results. Schroeder et al. (1988), for example, used a mood-fixing paradigm quite similar to Cialdini et al.'s, but obtained results supporting Batson's altruism position more strongly than the NSR position. Schaller and Cialdini (1988) conducted a near-replication of Cialdini et al.'s (1987) mood-fixing procedure, but replaced the observers' expectation that their moods would remain fixed with an expectation that a mood-enhancing experience (listening to comedy routines) would soon be administered. The expectation that one's mood was about to be elevated should have the effect of reducing the need for any mood-elevating helping. The results, while somewhat equivocal, tended to support the NSR position. Finally, Batson et al. (1989) used a similar procedure in two investigations and found clear evidence in favor of the altruism position. In both investigations, observers experiencing empathic concern offered more help to the target regardless of whether or not they anticipated a mood-enhancing experience.

Taken as a whole, the evidence thus far probably favors the altruism rather than the NSR explanation. There is, however, one further potential problem with the altruism position: the possibility that empathic concern is associated not with a greater need for the mood-enhancing power of helping, but with a greater fear of self-induced punishment. It is quite plausible, after all, that failing to help someone for whom you are feeling compassion will result in feelings of guilt. The anticipation of that guilt may therefore produce an egoistic motivation to avoid this self-censure by helping. As the reader may well imagine, this possibility could prove quite tricky to evaluate. If feelings of empathic concern inevitably trigger anticipatory guilt over not helping, how is it possible to ever tell the difference between altruistic (sympathy-based) helping and egoistic (guilt-based) helping? One answer, in Batson's view, is to create a situation in which the observers feel justified in not helping. If a plausible reason for not helping can be provided, then observers will not feel as guilty if they choose that option. Thus, if providing such a justification reduces helping among those observers experiencing empathic concern, this will suggest that it is the anticipation of guilt which produces helping, and such a pattern would therefore be evidence of egoistic, Path 1, helping.

Batson et al. (1988) conducted three studies addressing this possibility. The central problem in each study was how to make observers feel that a decision not to help is justified, and therefore eliminate guilt as a motivating force. In one study (Batson et al., 1988, Study 2) justification was manipulated by leading some observers to believe that most people in this situation had previously chosen not to help, and leading others to believe that most others had helped. Learning that most people do not offer help was assumed to reduce the likelihood that observers would anticipate feeling guilty if they decided likewise. Consistent with the altruism position, providing this justification did not reduce helping among those experiencing empathic concern. Similar patterns were found in two other studies using slightly different justification procedures.

Evaluation Of The "True" Altruism Position

The accumulated evidence testing Batson's empathy-altruism hypothesis is quite impressive. It seems clear that feelings of empathic concern are often distinct from the feelings of personal distress which frequently accompany them, and that the two states are differently related to helping. Personal distress is associated with a largely egoistic desire to reduce one's own unpleasant arousal, while empathic concern is not. Further, empathic concern appears to motivate helping even when the possibility is eliminated that such helping will lead to positive affective outcomes (Batson et al., 1989) or will allow the avoidance of negative ones (Batson et al., 1988). This series of studies has provided a strong foundation for the position that some helping is the result of a genuinely non-selfish motive to aid another in need.

This view is not universally shared, of course. Batson's position has been criticized on several grounds, both theoretical and methodological (e.g., Krebs, 1991; Hornstein, 1991; Wallach & Wallach, 1991). However, the careful, systematic approach he has taken to this issue, coupled with his very consistent findings, has resulted in a largely convincing body of evidence. The most vulnerable point in this formulation may be the evidence which bears on the possibility that anticipatory guilt underlies the effects of empathic concern on helping. All of the experimental procedures designed to reduce the observers' belief that failing to help would lead to guilt were based to some degree on leading them to believe that not helping was a common response. As predicted, providing such "cover" to the observers did not reduce the association between empathic concern and helping. While this may be because guilt is not in fact mediating the empathic concern-helping relationship, it may also be because the "cover" does not really provide a fully effective escape from guilt.

It seems plausible, for example, that someone anticipating guilt for a failure to help may not be completely protected by learning that others have previously chosen not to help. After all, the behavior of others is essentially irrelevant to the morality of one's own actions, and the fact that others have not helped may not make it morally acceptable for the observer to choose this option. Efforts to instill moral values in children frequently emphasize the fact that the behavior of others is no justification for one's own transgressions ("Just because your friends did it doesn't make it right"). If this reasoning is correct, and the guilt "cover" does not actually eliminate the anticipation of self-punishment for a failure to help, then the investigations using this procedure may not provide adequate tests of the guilt hypothesis. This is, admittedly, a difficult methodological problem to solve. It may in fact prove impossible to design experimental procedures which can conclusively rule out such an explanation. The evidence collected thus far, however, has already gone much farther toward establishing the existence of a truly altruistic motivation than most might have imagined, and the possibility of a convincing experimental demonstration of a "guilt-free" empathy-altruism link cannot be dismissed.

Non-Affective Outcomes and Helping

While the dominant approach in recent years has clearly been to emphasize the role of emotion in determining helping behavior, the role of non-affective outcomes, the other class of constructs most proximal to helping in the organizational model, has not been ignored. Research in this area has explored the possibility that empathy-related processes such as role taking can influence non-affective outcomes, which in turn can influence helping behavior. In particular, the one form of cognitive judgment concerning targets which has been demonstrated to result from empathy-related processes and which has been implicated in the offering of help is causal attributions.

The first to explicitly make a case for the role of attributions in the helping process were probably Ickes and Kidd (1976). These investigators took as their starting point a handful of studies which had previously found that observers offer more help to targets whose neediness results from external forces such as bad luck, and less help to those whose neediness results from internal causes, such as the target's own bad decisions (e.g., Berkowitz, 1969; Schopler & Mathews, 1965). Ickes and Kidd argued that this internal/external dimension was in all probability confounded with the more important dimension of intentionality, or the degree to which the target's neediness resulted from intended or unintended actions. Specifically, observers would be more likely to help someone whose behavior unintentionally led to a need state, because this would imply that the person was not responsible for it. Regardless of the specific

dimension of causality accounting for the effect, internality or intentionality, the results of these early studies suggested that attributional
judgments about a target play a significant role in mediating helping.

More recent attempts to explore attribution's role in helping
have relied heavily on Weiner's (1972; 1986) typology of attributions, which holds that there are three fundamental dimensions of
causality: 1) locus (whether the cause is internal or external to the
target), 2) stability (whether the cause is perceived as temporary or
permanent), and 3) controllability (whether or not the cause is subject to influence by the target). The third dimension, controllability,
corresponds to the intentionality dimension emphasized by Ickes
and Kidd (1976). In a series of studies Weiner and others have explored the relations among these causal dimensions, empathy-related
emotional states, and helping.

The basic paradigm used in these investigations is rather
straightforward. Subjects are typically presented with a written scenario describing a situation in which another person is in need of
help. For example, one commonly used scenario (Weiner, 1980a;
Reisenzein, 1986) describes the collapse of a fellow-passenger on
the subway. Information in the scenario provides a manipulation of
the likely cause of the target's plight, in most cases by simply varying the degree to which the target's need appears to be controllable
or not. In the subway scenario, for example, the cause of the pas-
senger's collapse is typically either drunkenness (a controllable
cause) or illness (an uncontrollable one). Respondents are then
called upon to estimate the degree to which targets had control over
their outcomes, and to indicate their (the observers') likely emotional responses if faced with this situation. In most cases the two
affective dimensions assessed are feelings of pity/compassion on the
one hand, and feelings of anger/irritation on the other (Betancourt,
1990a; Schmidt & Weiner, 1988; Reisenzein, 1986). Finally, respondents indicate the likelihood that they would help the target if
faced with this situation.

Six different investigations have employed this basic paradigm
(Weiner, 1980a, 1980b; Reisenzein, 1986; Betancourt, 1990a; Meyer
& Mulherin, 1980; Schmidt & Weiner, 1988), and have reported a
highly consistent pattern of results. First, the more that observers
feel the target's need is under the target's control, the more anger
and less sympathy they feel toward that target. Second, the greater
the observers' anger, and the lower their sympathy, the less likely
they are to believe that they would offer help. Third, in most cases
the substantial effect of controllability attributions on helping disap-
pears completely when the effects of the affective reactions are

statistically controlled. That is, the effect of attributions on helping does not appear to be a direct one at all, but seems instead to be mediated almost entirely by the emotional responses of anger and sympathy.

Three points should be made concerning these results. First, the fact that virtually all of the association between controllability attributions and helping is due to the mediating role of affective responses underscores the value of focusing on affect as the primary determinant of helping. It also emphasizes the importance of specifying a link between affective and non-affective outcomes in the organizational model. These results clearly indicate that some forms of cognitive judgments regarding targets can influence the affective domain as well. Second, however, virtually all of these studies have used a simulation technique in which observers are not confronted with real targets at all, but are asked to estimate what their cognitive, emotional, and behavioral responses would be if the situations were real. Despite the consistency of the results, doubts can therefore be raised regarding the generalizability of these findings to non-simulated situations. Third, the studies described thus far also have one shortcoming, as far as the organizational model is concerned. The dimension of causality which seems most powerfully implicated in affecting helping (controllability) is not the dimension examined in the earlier studies of empathy and attribution. In those studies (e.g., Regan & Totten, 1975; Gould & Sigall, 1977) perspective-taking instructions were reliably associated with the locus dimension (dispositional vs. situational), but none of them examined the issue of controllability.

A recent pair of investigations by Betancourt (1990a) have addressed some of these concerns. In the first experiment the usual scenario study was employed, but the observers were told that it was a ''real-life story'' about a student on campus who was having academic difficulties as a result of numerous absences. The controllability of these absences was manipulated by varying the reason given for them with the reasons ranging from quite controllable (the target went out of town with friends for fun) to quite uncontrollable (the target was hospitalized and unable to read for two weeks). Observers were asked to provide the usual assessments of target's controllability, their own affective state, and their estimated likelihood of helping the target. In a slight deviation from the usual procedure, Betancourt explicitly assessed the emotional states of empathic concern and personal distress using the adjectives typically employed by Batson.

In a more important departure from usual procedure, Betancourt also provided observers with one of two instructional sets, either imagine-the-other or control instructions, prior to reading the scenario. Thus, it is possible in this investigation to examine whether or not taking the perspective of the target influences the particular dimension of causality, controllability, previously implicated in the helping process. As expected, instructional set had a highly reliable impact on judgments of controllability, with those observers who imagined the target's perspective reporting that target to have significantly lower levels of control. As in previous research, greater perceptions of target controllability were associated with lower levels of sympathy for the target, and lower levels of sympathy were in turn associated with lower estimated likelihood of helping. In contrast to previous work, however, perceptions of target controllability had a significant direct effect on helping independent of the mediating influence of affective response.

This study therefore demonstrated that the empathic process of role taking can influence observers' judgments about the specific dimension of causality, controllability, which seems most important in influencing affective responding. In the second study, Betancourt used the same general paradigm, but provided observers with an opportunity to actually help the individual in the scenario. After receiving an instructional set, reading the scenario manipulating the apparent controllability of the target's academic difficulties, and responding to the attributional and emotional reaction questions, the observers were then unexpectedly given the opportunity to help the target by meeting with him/her to go over notes, answer questions, and so forth. Again, perspective-taking instructions significantly influenced controllability attributions, these attributions significantly affected empathic concern, and empathic concern significantly affected actual offers of help. This investigation therefore provides at least some indication that the attribution/affect/helping path so consistently evident in the simulation studies may operate for real-world helping opportunities as well.

Perspective Taking And Helping

The evidence reviewed thus far indicates that both affective and non-affective intrapersonal outcomes significantly influence helping behavior. Let us now turn our attention to the impact on helping of empathy-related processes. As it turns out, the link between helping and only one such process, role taking, has received any empirical attention. Eisenberg and Miller (1987), in their review of the empathy-altruism literature, found a modest but significant association between perspective-taking instructions and helping. Since the time of that review, a number of other studies (e.g., Batson et al., 1989; Batson et al., 1991; Cialdini et al., 1987; Dovidio et al., 1990; Smith et al., 1989) have used such instructions to investigate helping, and have also generally found significant effects of instructions on helping. Taken as a whole, this pattern generally supports the view that instructions to imagine the affective state of a target frequently trigger a process which ends in the offering of help to that target.

What mediates this effect of instructional set on helping? Four studies have explicitly tested the notion that perspective taking influences helping solely through its effect on intrapersonal outcomes. In three investigations (Dovidio et al., 1990; Shelton & Rogers, 1981; Toi & Batson, 1982, Experiment 2) it was found that after controlling for the effect of empathically produced emotion (usually empathic concern), a significant effect of instructional set on helping was reduced to nonsignificance. Smith et al. (1989) conducted a similar analysis, but found that instructions still had a significant effect on helping even after controlling for affect. Thus, the evidence from these few attempts to directly address this issue suggests that the effect of role-taking instructions on helping are frequently mediated to a substantial degree by the affective responses created by the instructions; it may be premature, however, to conclude from this evidence that the *entire* effect of manipulated perspective taking on helping can be accounted for in this way.

Observer/Target Similarity and Helping

The only characteristic of the situation that has received attention as a possible influence on helping is the degree of observer-target similarity. Eisenberg and Miller (1987) located nine tests of this hypothesis, reported in five publications, which manipulated similarity along a variety of dimensions, including race, interests, and personality characteristics. In general, similarity was positively associated with helping; as Eisenberg and Miller noted, however, this pattern is strengthened if the studies manipulating race similarity are excluded, as those investigations were notably unsuccessful. In addition to the studies reviewed by Eisenberg and Miller, I have been able to identify only one other (Marks et al., 1982), an investigation in which no effect of similarity (in interests/personality) on helping was found.

How are these results to be interpreted? As discussed in Chapter 6, it seems probable that observer-target similarity triggers multiple empathy-related processes, with resulting effects on both affective and non-affective outcomes. Thus, perceptions of similarity can produce helping through a variety of pathways. Evidence reviewed in earlier chapters indicates that greater similarity is associated with observers making more actor-like attributions (Houston, 1990), experiencing more empathic concern (Gruen & Mendelsohn, 1986; Houston, 1990), and perhaps more parallel affective outcomes as well (Stotland, 1969; Krebs, 1975), any of which can serve as mediators of the similarity-helping link. However, given the generally powerful relationships between affective outcomes and helping, it seems likely that emotional reactions to the target are a primary means by which similarity influences helping.

Individual Differences

Individual Differences and Helping Behavior

The conventional wisdom for a considerable period of time was that evidence for the influence of personality on helping was weak or non-existent. Rushton (1981), for example, cited several influential researchers and theorists (e.g., Krebs, 1978; Latané & Darley, 1970; Mussen & Eisenberg-Berg, 1977) who viewed the search for such evidence with varying degrees of pessimism, with Gergen, Gergen, and Meter's (1972, p. 113) characterization of this research as ''a quagmire of evanescent relations among variables, conflicting findings, and low order correlation coefficients'' perhaps being the most colorful.

At least two factors may have contributed to this conclusion. First, as Clary and his colleagues (Clary & Orenstein, 1991; Clary & Snyder, 1991) have noted, most investigations have studied personality's impact on spontaneous helping, limited acts of help which occur in response to clear situational conditions, often in a laboratory setting. Such situations probably restrict the role of personality factors, however, because situational forces may more powerfully affect the quick decision to help or not that these situations typically demand. In contrast, dispositional factors may play a larger role in affecting helping which occurs nonspontaneously, when helpers have the chance to think about, and seek out, helping opportunities. Second, Rushton has argued that this pessimism has also been in large part due to a misreading of the evidence, most notably that collected during the massive Hartshorne and May (1928; Hartshorne, May, & Maller, 1929; Hartshorne, May, & Shuttleworth, 1930) studies of children's honesty and altruism. It was Rushton's position that when proper analysis procedures are employed the evidence quite strongly supports the notion of a general ''trait'' of altruism, using the term in the weak form described earlier.

Evidence from the reviews by Underwood and Moore (1982) and Eisenberg and Miller (1987) generally supports this more optimistic conclusion, although more strongly for adults than for children. For example, the associations between helping behavior and individual differences in perceptual and social role-taking, reviewed by Underwood and Moore (1982), were quite reliable, while the evidence regarding affective reactivity and helping was weaker and less consistent. Eisenberg and Miller's (1987) review of the research using picture-story indices of affective responsivity in fact revealed virtually no effect on helping at all. On the other hand, research carried out principally with adult subjects, in which self-report questionnaires were used to assess affective responsivity, displayed much stronger relations with helping.

At least two factors may be contributing to this pattern. First, it may be due to weaknesses in the picture-story indices. It has been suggested that these measures are not evocative or realistic enough to engage the subject, and that they may be especially susceptible to experimental demand characteristics (Eisenberg & Lennon, 1983). Consequently, these measures may simply not provide a valid indicator of affective responsivity, in which case the lack of a relation with helping is not surprising. Second, the pattern may result from the fact that these particular measures are used only in studies involving fairly young subjects. The weak results may therefore be due not to the measures but to the age of the respondents. As Eisenberg and Miller (1987) point out, the integration of affective and behavioral reactions tends to increase with age. Adults have greater capabilities for interpreting their affective responses and effectively acting on them, and this may account for the weak link between dispositional affect and helping found among children.

Evidence from Eisenberg and Miller's (1987) review may provide more support for the first explanation than the second. When reviewing the 36 studies which used self-report measures of dispositional affective empathy (primarily the QMEE, the Bryant measure, and the IRI), they found a substantial relationship between empathy and helping. Because 27 of these studies (75 percent) employed subjects of high school age or older and the remainder used younger subjects, it is possible to compare the size of the empathy-helping association, using comparable measures of dispositional empathy, in younger and older subjects. However, an inspection of these two clusters of studies reveals virtually no difference between them, supporting the view that it is not so much the age of the respondents but the method of empathy assessment which is critical. Thus, the evidence suggests that when younger respondents are given measures other than the picture-story indices, they demonstrate an association with helping comparable to that of adults.

Individual Differences and "True" Altruism

The evidence seems to point toward the conclusion that individual differences in empathy-related constructs, both cognitive and affective, are reliably associated with helping. In recent years the question has also been raised as to whether there is any evidence for a link between personality and the strong version of altruism (helping which results completely from non-egoistic motives). This question was addressed first by Batson et al. (1986), who proposed using the same experimental paradigm to investigate altruistic personality that had been successfully used to investigate the question of altruistic motives generally. In brief, Batson et al. argued that evidence for a truly altruistic personality must necessarily include evidence that persons possessing such a personality help under conditions of easy escape. That is, those with a genuinely altruistic personality must help even when it is possible to escape the distressed victim.

Batson et al. (1986) tested this notion by placing subjects in an experimental situation which had already been successfully employed (Batson et al., 1983) to demonstrate the existence of altruistic motivation. In this paradigm observers have the opportunity to trade places with another subject who is receiving electric shocks and experiencing considerable distress. Agreeing to trade places and receive the other's shocks constitutes the measure of help. Subjects in the easy escape condition are able to leave the experiment immediately if they decline to help while those in the difficult escape condition must remain and watch the other subject receive more shocks. Given the logic of the Batson paradigm, agreeing to help in the easy escape condition can be considered evidence of an altruistic motivation while help in the difficult escape condition cannot.

At a time prior to the experimental session several personality measures, including the IRI, were completed by all subjects. Contrary to the pattern expected if dispositional empathy were reflective of truly altruistic motivation, none of the four IRI scales were significantly related to helping in the easy escape condition; the perspective taking scale had the highest, albeit nonsignificant, association (.21). In contrast, scores on the empathic concern scale were significantly associated with helping in the difficult escape condition, a pattern consistent with the view that this measure taps an egoistic rather than altruistic motivation. This picture is somewhat clouded, however, by the fact that situational feelings of empathic concern, which Batson routinely finds to be significantly associated with helping under conditions of easy escape, failed to display such a pattern in this investigation. Instead, situational empathic concern was significantly associated with helping when escape was difficult but not when it was easy, a pattern identical to that of dispositional empathic concern, and indicative of an egoistic motivation.

Eisenberg, Miller et al. (1989) next examined this question by presenting all subjects with an easy escape situation. They were exposed to a videotape depicting a woman whose children had been injured in a car accident, and they later had the opportunity to volunteer their time to help her and her children. All subjects were led to believe that they would have no contact with the family if they chose not to help, and that the experimenter would be unaware of their decision. To address the possibility that those with high scores on "altruistic" personality dimensions such as dispositional empathy might help out of a fear of negative social evaluation, subjects completed the IRI, the QMEE, and several measures tapping the motivation to act in socially desirable ways. Consistent with the view that dispositional empathy possesses a truly altruistic component, scores on the IRI's PT and EC scales were significantly associated with helping, as were scores on the QMEE. This can be taken as evidence of altruistic personality, Eisenberg et al. argued, because the situation facing all the subjects was one in which escape was easy. Importantly, these relations between dispositional empathy and helping remained even after the effects of a concern for social desirability were statistically controlled.

Although consistent with the position that dispositional empathy contributes to an altruistic personality, these results are not definitive. Batson (1991) in particular has noted possible flaws in the design, especially the possibility that the situation was not really an easy escape situation. Specifically, he argued that the cost to the subjects of helping might have been so low that a failure to help would lead to guilt, at least among some subjects, and in particular among those who portray themselves on questionnaires as being highly empathic. If so, then the helping by those high on dispositional empathy could be egoistic. Without a manipulation of ease of escape, it is impossible to evaluate Eisenberg, Miller et al.'s (1989) assumption that escape truly was easy.

Carlo, Eisenberg, Troyer, Switzer, and Speer (1991) therefore placed female subjects in a situation in which ease of escape was manipulated, as was the evocativeness of the target's need. Subjects were exposed to an ostensible fellow subject (actually a confederate) who began to experience distress while reading short vignettes about cases of personal assault. It soon became apparent that the fellow subject had been the victim of an assault several months previously. In the high evocative condition, the target's distress (agitation, tears) was very clear, while in the low evocative condition it was more subtly portrayed. Similar to the Batson paradigm mentioned earlier, subjects were given a chance to trade places with the target. In the easy escape condition they would no longer watch the target if they refused to help, and in the difficult escape condition they would continue to watch her read the remaining 13 vignettes.

Consistent with predictions, Carlo et al. found that a composite index of altruistic personality (two of whose four component parts were the IRI's PT and EC scales) was significantly associated with helping, but only when the target's distress was highly evocative and escape was easy. As in the Eisenberg, Miller et al. (1989) investigation, the effects of social desirability concerns were statistically controlled in this analysis. Importantly, the state measure of empathic concern displayed the same pattern, an association with helping only under conditions of high evocativeness and easy escape, reinforcing the conclusion that helping under these conditions reflects altruistic motivation. Neither the dispositional index nor the state measure of empathic concern was associated with help in either of the difficult escape conditions. While this pattern is consistent with the notion of an altruistic personality, it must be noted that the effect was especially pronounced among female subjects, while the association between the dispositional index and helping in the high evocative/easy escape condition did not reach statistical significance for males.

What are we to make of this? In contrast to the general issue of altruistic motivation, which has been addressed in at least 25 different studies (Batson, 1991), the question of altruistic personality has received much less attention. Consequently it seems too early to offer definitive conclusions. The contradictory findings which have emerged to date suggest that while there may be personality characteristics capable of displaying altruistic associations with helping, there may be as yet unrecognized moderating conditions as well. The Carlo et al. investigation may provide a step in the right direction by focusing attention on the particular situational conditions (e.g., evocativeness of target need) necessary for the manifestation of altruistic personality effects.

A related issue recently raised by Smith (1992) concerns the role of dispositional empathy in affecting one's willingness to enter emotionally evocative situations in the first place. Smith found that high scorers on the IRI's EC scale were significantly more likely to enter situations in which the experience of sympathy for another was likely, but only if they would have some control over the situation (e.g., the opportunity to offer help to the target). This suggests that those high in dispositional empathic concern may more frequently put themselves in proximity to needy others, under the proper circumstances, than those low on this trait.

Finally, it may prove useful to further explore the mechanisms by which altruistic personality, if it exists, comes to produce helping. The most logical possibility is that altruistic individual differences operate through the situational affective response (empathic concern) already demonstrated to have an altruistic character. Thus, the chain of dispositional empathy/situational empathic concern/helping seems plausible. Interestingly, both Eisenberg, Miller et al. (1989) and Carlo et al. (1991) examined this question. In the former study, evidence indicated that while dispositional empathic concern and perspective taking had such indirect effects (mediated by situational empathic concern) on helping, they also had direct effects as well. The latter study also found the dispositional index to have a direct effect on helping in the high evocative/easy escape condition even after controlling for the mediating effect of situational empathic concern. It thus appears from these initial studies that additional mediating variables must be identified in order to fully account for the effect of "altruistic" personality traits on helping.

Summary and Conclusion

What can we conclude from this rather lengthy chapter? First and foremost, it seems clear that empathically induced affective states have reliable effects on helping behavior, and that a broad distinction can be drawn between two ways that this happens. Experiencing parallel affect and/or personal distress to a needy target can produce helping for largely egoistic reasons (e.g, Piliavin et al., 1981; Cialdini et al., 1973), and experiencing empathic concern can produce helping through apparently altruistic ones (e.g., Batson et al., 1981). Although some questions regarding possible alternative explanations still remain, the evidence at present tends to support Batson's view that the motivation associated with empathic concern has a truly altruistic component.

A second conclusion concerns the impact of role taking and attributional judgments on helping. In general, viewing the target's neediness as due to factors under his/her control reduces the likelihood of help being offered. This effect is virtually entirely mediated, however, by the affective reactions of anger and/or sympathy which accompany such attributions. Similarly, situational role taking (induced by instructional sets) tends to be associated with greater helping, although in three of the four investigations examining the question, these effects were found to be mediated by the empathically produced emotion resulting from these instructions. Thus, the primacy of affect as a determinant of helping is evident in both cases.

Finally, individual differences in empathic tendencies seem to be reliably associated with helping, especially for adults and especially when using self-report measures rather than picture-story indices. Evidence from two studies (Eisenberg, Miller et al., 1989; Carlo et al., 1991) suggests that at least some portion of the personality-helping relation might reflect "true" altruism, but the evidence for this is still preliminary. It also appears from these two studies that the "altruistic" effect of individual differences on helping is not completely mediated by situational empathic concern. Thus, the altruistic personality, if it exists, may influence helping directly or through some as yet unspecified construct.

Aggression and Antisocial Behavior

This chapter addresses a second major category of interpersonal outcomes: aggressive or antisocial behavior directed toward another person. In a way, this is the ''flip side'' of the previous chapter's focus on altruism and helping behavior. Rather than examining empathy's role in promoting helpful behaviors, this chapter considers empathy's contribution to preventing or diminishing harmful ones. One difference between these two topics is that considerably less attention has been devoted to the empathy-aggression connection, especially in recent years, than has been given to the empathy-helping issue. Further, as we shall see, this research has overwhelmingly focused on the association between aggressive actions and dispositional empathy, with very little direct attention given to the role played by empathy-related processes or intrapersonal outcomes.

Thus, in terms of the organizational model, most of the research has examined the link between two elements, dispositions and interpersonal outcomes, which are the most distant from one another in the causal chain. One effect that this might be expected to have is to generally weaken the observed association between empathy and aggression, since the most proximal causes of behavior, the cognitive and affective reactions occurring within the situation itself, have been largely ignored.

Theoretical Links between Aggression and Empathy

Cognitive Links

At least two mechanisms by which empathy can inhibit aggressive activity have been proposed—one focusing on cognitive, role-taking activity and the other on affective reactivity. In brief, the cognitive approach argues that an ability or willingness to adopt the perspective of others, especially within a potential conflict situation, leads to a greater understanding of and tolerance for that other's position, in turn making hostile and aggressive reactions toward that other less likely (Feshbach, 1978). Thus, persons with greater perspective-taking skills, or those who are induced in some way to engage in perspective taking, may act in less aggressive ways.

To understand how this might work, consider a situation in which David acts in a way that is potentially threatening to Jay, perhaps by insulting Jay's intelligence or heritage. If the insult is provocative enough, and no extenuating circumstances can explain it, then an aggressive response by Jay may result. If, on the other hand, perspective-taking efforts lead Jay to conclude that David's remark was misinterpreted, unintentional, or the result of situational forces beyond his control, then a greater willingness to tolerate the behavior and refrain from aggression may result. In essence, perspective taking may produce an attributional analysis of the behavior which is more actor-like in its emphasis on situational or uncontrollable factors, and which therefore assigns less blame and responsibility to the transgressor. As noted in Chapter 5, perspective-taking inductions, at least under some circumstances, do appear to have such an effect on attributions for others' behavior.

Richardson and colleagues (Richardson, Hammock, Smith, Gardner, & Signo, 1992) have recently offered a similar argument, and have expanded on it by borrowing from Zillmann's (1988; 1990) work on the interaction between cognition and excitation in producing aggressive behavior. Zillmann (1988) has argued that cognitive appraisal processes, which typically serve to inhibit aggression, generally operate most effectively at intermediate levels of arousal. At high levels of arousal in particular, cognitive activity is usually of very limited effectiveness in inhibiting aggression, and at such times well-learned aggressive behaviors are likely to occur in response to provocation. Richardson et al. (1992) argue that this analysis applies specifically to perspective taking as well, because social perspective taking is a particular form of cognitive activity which generally tends to inhibit aggression. Thus, perspective-taking's inhibitory effect may be most likely to operate at low to moderate levels of arousal, whereas under conditions of high arousal this effect will be disrupted, and aggression more likely as a result.

Affective Links

The affective explanation for empathy's hypothesized inhibitory effect on aggression takes two forms. One view is that observing the victim of one's own aggression, especially his or her pain and distress cues, leads to a sharing of the victim's distress. To escape this vicarious distress, the aggressor stops or reduces the aggression (N. Feshbach, 1978; S. Feshbach, 1964). In terms of the organizational model, this affective response seems to qualify as either a parallel outcome or reactive personal distress. In operation, there is also a noticeable resemblance between this process and the "arousal reduction path" to helping behavior (Batson, 1991) described in the previous chapter. The second affective approach argues that the victim's distress cues sometimes lead aggressors to experience the reactive emotional response of empathic concern, and the resulting motive to increase the victim's welfare prompts the cessation of the aggression (Miller & Eisenberg, 1988).

There are some potential difficulties with these analyses, however. One problem which applies to both affective explanations is that under some circumstances victim pain cues might have a reinforcing effect on aggression rather than an inhibiting one. To understand this, it is useful to consider the difference between *instrumental aggression*—actions carried out to attain some non-aggressive goal—and *angry aggression,* carried out for the purpose of causing harm to another (Baron, 1977). During instances of angry aggression, aggressive behaviors may in fact be strengthened by witnessing the desired outcome of victim pain and distress. In a related vein, one's reinforcement history can sometimes lead the distress and pain of others (which might result, for example, after one has successfully overcome a threatening attacker) to become associated with some reinforcing state (for example, relief at the removal of the threat), and such distress cues may therefore acquire a secondary reinforcing power of their own (e.g., Bandura, 1973; Feshbach, 1964). In such cases victim pain cues might make aggression more likely.

Another potential problem applies specifically to the "shared distress" explanation. Research has indicated that in many circumstances the presence of negative affect tends to produce higher levels of aggression (e.g., Berkowitz, 1984; Baron & Ransberger, 1978). Because of this, it is possible that parallel distress reactions in response to a target's suffering, a clearly negative form of affect, might under some circumstances increase aggression rather than reduce it. The empathic concern mechanism, of course, is not as subject to this latter complication. The specific prosocial motive which characterizes empathic concern is less clearly negative in tone and is more clearly related to actions, such as halting an aggressive act, intended to better the other's welfare.

In any event, and despite these potential complications, the crucial prediction of the affective empathy explanation is that aggressors will experience some affective reaction in response to the victim's distress, and this reaction will prompt an inhibition of the aggression. In fact, the available evidence regarding the link between victim distress cues and aggression supports this view. In general, the presence of such cues inhibits further aggression, although this tendency is by no means universal. Considerable research indicates that when individuals have not been previously provoked, the targets' pain and distress cues reliably reduce the magnitude of aggression toward them (e.g., Buss, 1966a, 1966b; Baron, 1971a, 1971b; Geen, 1970; Milgram, 1965). When the potential aggressor has been previously insulted or otherwise provoked by the target, the presence of distress cues sometimes reduces aggression (e.g., Baron, 1971a, 1971b; Geen, 1970) and sometimes does not (e.g., Baron, 1974; Feshbach, Stiles, & Bitter, 1967). In fact, under some conditions victim cues can actually increase aggression (Baron, 1979).

What accounts for this inconsistency under conditions of provocation? One answer may lie in the distinction between instrumental and angry aggression outlined earlier. When one has been strongly provoked by another, the resulting aggression may well be directed toward the goal of inflicting suffering on the provoker. At those times the distress of the victim may take on a reinforcing quality. If the provocation produces less extreme levels of anger, however, distress cues may sometimes retain their aggression-inhibiting power. It may also be that at high arousal levels such as those accompanying strong provocation, the addition of empathically produced distress increases the overall level of negative affect enough to prompt further aggression. In any event, while affective feedback from the target by no means guarantees a reduction in aggression, the bulk of the evidence suggests that such cues do frequently have a meaningful inhibitory impact on aggression, as the affective empathy analysis suggests.

The remainder of this chapter will examine the evidence bearing on the hypothesized connections between cognitive and affective facets of empathy and aggressive/antisocial behavior. The organizational model will again guide this discussion as we first examine those constructs closest to aggressive behavior in the model, and then consider the evidence for more distant constructs. As we shall see, the overwhelming majority of studies have focused on the association between aggression and dispositional empathy. Relatively little research has examined the most proximal intrapersonal outcomes, either affective or non-affective.

Non-Affective Outcomes and Aggression

As suggested earlier, the non-affective outcomes most likely to play a substantial role in affecting aggressive behavior are the causal attributions that an observer-aggressor makes for a target-victim's behavior. As Betancourt (1990b) and Ferguson and Rule (1983) have noted, an extensive body of literature currently supports the conclusion that attributional processes significantly affect the occurrence and magnitude of aggression. A common approach in this literature has been to expose subjects to an insulting provocation carried out by a confederate, to provide varying degrees of mitigating information which could explain the rude behavior (e.g., the confederate is worried about a midterm exam), and then allow the subject the opportunity to aggress against the confederate. The typical finding is that when mitigating information is provided which makes the confederate's insults seem less the result of internal-controllable causes, and more the result of external-uncontrollable ones, the aggression delivered to that confederate decreases (e.g., Kremer & Stephens, 1983; Rule, Dyck, and Nesdale, 1978; Zillmann, Bryant, Cantor, & Day, 1975). An important influence on the size of this effect, however, is the point in the sequence at which the subject receives the mitigating information. When the information is received prior to the provocation the mitigating effect is significantly stronger than when that information is received later (Johnson & Rule, 1986; Kremer & Stephens, 1983; Zillmann & Cantor, 1976).

Similar findings have emerged from other investigations in which the subject competes against a confederate in a "reaction time" task. In these studies the observer's attributions about the target are manipulated not by providing mitigation for provocations, but through leading the observer to believe that the confederate's level of aggression during the task was unusually high compared to most players' (e.g., Dyck & Rule, 1978), or by making the confederate appear increasingly aggressive throughout the task (e.g., Greenwell & Dengerink, 1973). Both manipulations make the confederate's behavior appear more internal-intentional, and both have the effect of increasing the retaliatory aggression directed toward those confederates. Thus, manipulations designed to affect aggressors' causal attributions regarding target-victims' behavior generally have a substantial effect on aggression.

Given this pattern of results, and the fact that empathy manipulations in previous research have generally made observers more likely to see targets' behaviors as situationally determined and less controllable, it seems quite plausible that empathizing with a potential target of aggression may in fact produce an attributional set which reduces the likelihood or intensity of subsequent aggression. Such a pattern would be consistent with the theoretical positions of Feshbach (1964) and Richardson et al. (1992). Unfortunately, virtually no direct tests of this hypothesis have been carried out. That is, no studies have been conducted in which empathy-related processes such as perspective taking have been manipulated in order to influence attributions toward the potential target of aggression. Thus, while prior research has separately documented the perspective taking/attribution and attribution/aggression links, no research has yet demonstrated the perspective taking/attribution/ aggression sequence in its entirety.

In fact, demonstrating this sequence may turn out to be a challenge. It may prove quite difficult, for example, to induce empathic sets in aggressors within the context of an aggression experiment, especially if any form of prior provocation has been carried out. That is, the effect of perspective-taking instructions may prove too fragile to operate when powerful negative affective responses toward the target already exist, or when high levels of general arousal are present (Zillmann, 1988). Because the previous demonstrations of empathy instructions affecting attributions took place in relatively non-arousing settings (e.g., Gould & Sigall, 1977; Regan & Totten, 1975), it cannot be assumed that such instructional effects will necessarily occur in aggressive contexts.

Affective Outcomes and Aggression

Traditional treatments of the link between affective responses and aggressive behavior have not typically considered the possible inhibitory role of empathy. For example, the prototypical explanation of affect-based aggression, the *frustration-aggression* hypothesis (Dollard, Doob, Miller, Mowrer, & Sears, 1939), argues that having one's goals thwarted (frustration) prompts one to engage in aggressive acts. More recent modifications to the hypothesis have argued that frustration has this effect because it specifically produces anger (Berkowitz, 1962; 1978), or negative affect more generally (Berkowitz, 1989), and that such affective states induce a readiness to aggress under the proper circumstances. In fact, considerable evidence indicates that negative affect resulting from a variety of sources (e.g., frustration, heat, noise) can make aggression more likely (for a review, see Baron, 1977, and Berkowitz, 1982). However, the clear focus of most theory and research along these lines has been on negative affect which is produced in the potential aggressor by the environment in general, or by the provoking actions of the potential victim in particular—*not* on the affect created by empathizing with the potential victim's feelings.

At least two factors probably contribute to this state of affairs. The first is the heavy theoretical emphasis in aggression research on the emotional reaction of anger. Because the association between anger and aggression is considered to be so strong (Averill, 1982; Rule & Nesdale, 1976), attempts to link aggression with affect have understandably focused on this particular emotional response. However, feeling anger toward a target is not an affective response which fits easily with traditional empathy analyses, most of which emphasize feelings of distress or compassion for a distressed target. Thus, the affective response most strongly associated with aggression is one which has been rarely examined in empathy investigations. The second contributing factor, directly related to the first, is the reliance in many studies on producing aggression through provocation. It is an article of faith in much research that aggression is more likely, and in fact, may only occur, if the aggressor is provoked in some fashion by the eventual victim of the aggression. Thus, in many experimental situations matters are arranged so that the subject is provoked, either physically or verbally, by the victim-to-be. Given the unavoidable awkwardness involved in trying to induce an empathic set toward someone who has just insulted or aggressed against you, it is perhaps understandable that research has so seldom attempted to examine empathically produced emotions (such as empathic concern) and aggression within the same experimental design.

For all these reasons, virtually no research has manipulated situational emotional reactions toward an aggression victim through the induction of empathy-related processes. As noted above, there does seem to be a clear link between anger and aggression (see Ferguson & Rule, 1983, for a review), but that anger is never created via empathy-related processes. If it is assumed, however, that such processes (e.g., perspective taking) can reduce feelings of anger toward a target, then the already established link between anger and aggression can be seen as consistent with the organizational model.

It is difficult to tell how justified this assumption is. The studies reviewed in the previous chapter (e.g., Weiner, 1980a; Schmidt & Weiner, 1988), which examined the relations among attributions, affective reactions, and helping, offer hints that it might in fact be valid. In several of these studies, attributions regarding the controllability of a target's actions were associated with feelings of anger. The more controllable the target's behavior, the more anger in the observer. In two investigations, moreover, Betancourt (1990a) found perspective-taking instructions to significantly affect such controllability attributions, although anger was not assessed in those studies. Taken together, these studies suggest that perspective taking may reduce observers' anger toward a target by producing fewer attributions of controllability regarding that target.

In fact, Ferguson and Rule (1983) have offered an attributional analysis of anger and aggression which is quite compatible with this position. Although not concerned with the role of empathy per se, Ferguson and Rule argue that in many cases the observer's attributions for a transgressor's actions, especially attributions involving the intentionality of the act and the foreseeability of the act's outcomes, will have a substantial impact on the anger experienced as a result. Generally speaking, the more intentional the act is seen to be, and the more foreseeable the consequences, the greater the anger. The greater the anger, the stronger the aggressive response. Thus, Ferguson and Rule suggest a mediating role for feelings of anger, with attributional effects on aggression largely dependent on the intervening level of anger.

Ferguson and Rule (1983) review a considerable number of studies whose results are at least broadly compatible with this "attribution-anger-aggression" sequence, although virtually none were conducted specifically to test it. Recently, however, Betancourt and Blair (1992) carried out such a specific test. In this study, subjects read a vignette describing a situation in which a male college student shattered the windshield of another student's car with a rock. Some subjects were led to believe the act was deliberate and others were led to believe it was not. Subjects were then asked to offer their attributions for the incident (controllability and intentionality), their emotional reactions toward the perpetrator (anger, sympathy), and to estimate how aggressive their own behavior toward the perpetrator would be. As expected, attributions of greater controllability were associated with more anger and less sympathy for the perpetrator, feelings of anger were strongly and positively associated with greater aggression, and feelings of sympathy were negatively related almost as strongly.

What are we to conclude, therefore, about affective outcomes and aggression? One important fact to consider is that many of the relevant studies are limited in important ways. Some are simulations, some do not assess key constructs, and in some the target was not actually aggressing against anyone, least of all the observer. Thus, whether or not empathy-related processes actually have a direct impact on attributions, anger, and aggression in real-world settings is still open to debate. However, if it is assumed that processes such as perspective taking are likely to increase sympathy for, and possibly reduce anger toward, potential targets of aggression, then the evidence indicating a link between these affective states and aggression raises the possibility of a central role for empathy in the inhibition of aggressive responding. However, given the absence of direct evidence, it remains a very open question as to whether a reliable link between situational empathic processes and outcomes can be empirically established.

Perspective Taking and Aggression

Thus far, evidence for links between affective outcomes, nonaffective outcomes, and aggressive behavior has been mostly suggestive. Feelings of anger and attributional judgments both seem capable of affecting aggression, and the attributional effect may be mediated through these anger feelings; however, neither outcome has been conclusively linked, within aggressive contexts, to empathy-related processes such as perspective taking. It is not clear, therefore, that such processes actually contribute to the inhibition of aggression through these intrapersonal outcomes. Three studies, however, have examined the direct link between perspective taking (induced via instructional sets) and subsequent aggression, with mixed results.

In one study (Polk, 1976), subjects served as "teachers" and had the opportunity to administer painful noise bursts to help "learners" master a task. Prior to this, subjects received instructional sets designed to induce affective role taking toward the learner, to inhibit such role taking, or received no set at all. Subjects receiving the role-taking instructions subsequently displayed less aggression toward the learner than did subjects receiving the other two instructional sets. Thus, consistent with expectations, role-taking activity did inhibit aggressiveness, and in this case, under conditions of no provocation. Eliasz (1980) also had subjects serve as "teachers" and gave them the opportunity to use electric shocks to help the "learner" master a task. In an unusual procedure, Eliasz administered a role-taking manipulation to half the subjects not at the beginning but halfway through the learning task. At that point subjects were asked to engage in affective role taking toward the "learner," and spent 10 minutes doing so, before resuming the learning task. This role-taking manipulation had no effect on the shock levels administered by the teachers. Given the unusual nature of the manipulation, however, and the fact that half the subjects had also been previously provoked (by receiving a negative evaluation from the learner), it is difficult to evaluate these results.

A recent study examined possible moderating influences on the instructions-aggression link. Richardson et al. (1992, Study 2) administered perspective-taking or control instructions to college males before they competed against another subject on a "reaction time task." As part of that task, subjects had to choose, on each of 13 trials, a shock level to be administered to their opponent should the opponent lose that trial. Early in the sequence of trials, before subjects had received shocks from their opponents, perspective-taking instructions had the anticipated effect of decreasing aggression toward the opponent. Once the subjects had received shocks from the opponent, however, perspective taking lost this inhibiting effect. This pattern can be viewed as consistent with Zillmann's belief that cognitive processes which inhibit aggression are most effective at low to moderate levels of arousal. It also further underscores the difficulty that empathy-related processes may have in reducing aggressive behavior in vivo.

Situational Factors: Observer-Target Similarity

Evidence regarding the effect of observer-target similarity on aggression-related variables is mixed. For example, two studies have had participants make causal attributions for the negative behaviors of another person. In one case (Shaver, 1970) the other person was said to be a student, and the negative behavior was carelessness which led to an accident. In the other case (Veitch & Piccione, 1978), the subjects read about a fellow college student who had served as "teacher" in a separate experiment and administered shocks to someone as part of that experience. In both cases, observers who believed they were similar to the targets made attributions which assigned the targets less responsibility for their actions. In neither case did the target's negative behaviors have any implications for the observers themselves. In a third study (Nesdale, Rule, & Hill, 1978), subjects worked on a task while being "supervised" by someone they believed to be either attitudinally similar or dissimilar to them. For half the subjects, the supervisor (actually a confederate) made sarcastic and irritating remarks whereas for the other half, no such remarks were made. Afterward, subjects attributed causality for the supervisor's behaviors. When no sarcastic comments were made, perceived similarity led to more dispositional attributions for the supervisor's behavior; for those who had been insulted, however, similarity had no such effect. Thus, when the target's negative behavior had personal implications for the observer, perceived similarity lost its effect.

Similar results have emerged from two studies which manipulated observer-target similarity and assessed its impact on actual aggressive behavior. Rein (1974) found no effect of perceived personality similarity on the level of electric shock that subjects would administer to targets during a learning task. Hendrick and Taylor (1971) manipulated the apparent similarity between observer and target on a "beliefs questionnaire," and then allowed observers to choose the level of electric shock to be received by that opponent-target during a reaction-time experiment. Similarity to the target had no effect on the level of shocks chosen by the observer. What did have an effect was the shock level, apparently chosen by the target, which the observer himself received. Those receiving more intense shocks in turn chose more intense shocks for their opponent. While there was a slight tendency for those receiving the weaker shocks to display leniency toward a similar opponent, this effect was not significant. Thus, as with the attribution findings, similarity was found to have essentially no impact on aggressive behavior.

Individual Differences in Empathy and Aggression

As noted previously, many more studies have explored the associations between aggression and dispositional empathy than have examined any other type of empathy/aggression link. The remainder of this chapter will discuss this research, and for simplicity's sake will separately present the evidence regarding individual differences in role taking capacity/tendency ("cognitive empathy") and that regarding individual differences in affective responding ("emotional empathy").

Role-Taking Measures

At least a dozen studies have explicitly examined the link between antisocial behavior and the dispositional ability or tendency to entertain the psychological perspective of others. These investigations have assessed both perspective taking and aggression in a variety of ways; the most common approach, however, has been to compare the role-taking capacity of groups that are known to differ in their degree of antisocial behavior. What this has most frequently meant in operational terms is a comparison of delinquent and nondelinquent youths.

Chandler (1973), for example, studied 11 to 13 year old delinquent and nondelinquent boys. The delinquents were chosen from a police registry, based on their "lengthy police and court records," with each delinquent having committed at least one crime which would have constituted a felony if committed by an adult. The measure of perspective taking was based on a "privileged information" procedure (Flavell et al., 1968) in which respondents are shown a sequence of cartoons and asked to tell a story about the sequence first from their own perspective and then from the perspective of another person who has not seen the full sequence. Greater perspective taking is evidenced by the ability to suppress the privileged information they possess when telling the story from the other's viewpoint. As expected, the nondelinquents were much better at this task than the delinquents. Similar differences between delinquents and nondelinquents have been found by Rotenberg (1974), using a different role-taking task, and in two investigations (Hogan, 1969; Deardorff, Finch, Kendall, Lira, & Indrisano, 1975) using Hogan's EM scale as a measure of role taking. Kaplan and Arbuthnot (1985), however, found no difference between delinquents and nondelinquents while using the same role-taking measure as Chandler (1973), and Kendall, Deardorff, and Finch (1977) found no differences when using the EM scale.

A pair of studies have employed the same fundamental strategy but have distinguished more specifically among categories of delinquency. Jurkovic and Prentice (1977) and Lee and Prentice (1988) used a typology of delinquent youth which identifies three distinct subgroups within the delinquent population: *unsocialized-psychopathic, neurotic-disturbed,* and *socialized-subcultural* delinquents (Quay & Parsons, 1971). Psychopathic delinquents are characterized by poor impulse control and a lack of guilt for their antisocial behavior; neurotic delinquents are more socialized, and experience high levels of guilt, anxiety, and depression; the subcultural delinquents are also well socialized, but are more responsive to their delinquent peer group than to legitimate authority. Of the three groups, it might be expected that the poorly socialized psychopathic group would be most deficient in the ability to entertain others' points of view. In fact, neurotic and psychopathic male delinquents were found in both studies to be equally poor at role taking, assessed by means of Flavell et al.'s (1968) "nickel-dime" task (described in Chapter 3), and both groups were significantly worse than a control group of nondelinquent males. Role-taking performance of the subcultural delinquents fell between these two extremes. It should be noted, however, that Lee and Prentice (1988) failed to find significant differences across delinquent groups for another measure of role taking— the PT scale from the IRI.

In an interesting study, Ellis (1982) employed the same typology, and found that nondelinquent adolescents scored predictably higher on the EM scale than both neurotic and psychopathic delinquents, replicating the pattern already described. In addition, however, Ellis also categorized delinquents according to the level of aggression displayed in their delinquent "career," distinguishing between nonaggressive (those who had never been arrested for any crime involving violence against persons or property), aggressive-against-persons (those arrested for crimes including assault, rape, and murder), and aggressive-against-property delinquents (those arrested for such crimes as arson and malicious trespass). This categorization therefore allows a more direct examination of the key question, namely, is role taking directly related to aggressive behavior per se? The level of aggression previously displayed by the delinquents was in fact associated with scores on the EM scale. The nondelinquents and nonaggressive delinquents scored similarly on this scale, and both scored significantly higher than the aggressive-against-person and the aggressive-against-property groups, which did not differ.

Two studies have employed a strategy similar to those already described, but have examined an aggressive group other than delinquents. Letourneau (1981) and Wiehe (1987) both compared samples of physically abusive and non-abusive mothers with regard to cognitive role taking (EM scale). In each case the abusive mothers were drawn from the registry of child protective services agencies, and the non-abusive mothers were chosen so as to be equivalent to the abusive mothers in race, education, and income. Both investigations found the EM scale scores of abusive mothers to be significantly lower. In addition, Letourneau (1981) had all the mothers respond to a role-play inventory initially developed by Rothbart and Maccoby (1966). In this inventory respondents describe what their immediate reactions would be to a series of hypothetical situations in which their child sought comfort or became angry; these reactions are then coded for the presence of several themes, including aggression. Consistent with the group differences in empathy already reported, higher scores on the EM scale were also substantially associated with less aggressive responses on the role-play inventory.

The evidence reviewed thus far clearly supports the view that individual variation in role taking is associated with variation in aggressive and antisocial behaviors. All of this research, however, has examined the somewhat extreme groups of juvenile delinquents and child abusers. What about mainstream populations and more normal levels of aggression? Here the picture is considerably more mixed. Rothenberg (1970), for example, studied aggressiveness (assessed by teacher ratings) and affective role taking among 3rd and 5th grade children. Greater affective role-taking ability was significantly and negatively associated with teacher ratings of aggression, but only for boys; for girls there was no significant relation at all. Kurdek (1978) administered several role-taking measures to grade school children and had their teachers rate them on several antisocial behaviors. Once the effect of age and IQ were controlled statistically, only one association between role taking and aggression was found. Surprisingly, greater role-taking skill on a privileged information task (Chandler, 1973) was positively associated with fighting/quarreling with others, meaning that better role takers were rated by the teachers as more likely to fight and argue with peers.

More recently, Richardson et al. (1992) have used the IRI's PT scale to examine perspective taking and aggression among college students in a pair of investigations. In a questionnaire study they found that high perspective-takers scored significantly lower on a number of self-report measures of hostility and aggression (Buss & Durkee, 1957) and significantly higher on several measures of constructive conflict resolution (Rahim, 1983). In a separate laboratory study, women scoring high on the PT scale administered lower levels of unprovoked verbal aggression to another subject (confederate) early in the procedure, while PT scores had no such effect among men. Later in the procedure, however, once the subjects had been provoked by the confederate, the picture changed. Under these circumstances perspective taking reduced retaliatory aggression among men who had been mildly provoked, and reduced such retaliation among women who had been severely provoked. It seems apparent, therefore, that the association between dispositional perspective taking and aggressive responding is a complex one, subject to the influence of other factors.

All told, current evidence strongly suggests that extreme forms of aggressive behavior, the sort associated with juvenile delinquency and child abuse, are reliably associated with deficits in role taking. Only three of eleven studies (Kaplan & Arbuthnot, 1985; Kendall et al., 1977; Lee & Prentice, 1988) ever failed to find this pattern, and Lee and Prentice found it for one of two role-taking measures. In contrast, the scant evidence from studies not employing such groups is less consistent. The effect of dispositional role taking varied according to gender and experimental conditions, and in one case displayed a significant association opposite to that predicted (Kurdek, 1978). It seems clear, then, that much more work is needed to evaluate the strength and limits of the relation between dispositional role taking and nonpathological variations in aggression.

Affective Measures

In considering the evidence regarding aggressive behavior and dispositional affective responsivity, we are aided by the fact that Miller and Eisenberg (1988) have recently reviewed much of this research. (Their definition of empathy as affective responding excluded the dispositional role-taking studies from their review.) As in their earlier review of empathy and helping behavior (Eisenberg & Miller, 1987), Miller and Eisenberg organized their presentation in terms of the method by which empathy was assessed. In particular, they separately examined three kinds of investigations in which the empathy measure treats affective responsivity essentially as an individual difference variable: studies using picture-story techniques, self-report questionnaires, and facial-gestural indices.

Many, though not all, of the investigations using these measures employed "normal" samples (no delinquents or abusive parents) as subjects. One set of studies, however, did compare the affective responsiveness of abusive and nonabusive parents in the same way that the research reviewed earlier compared the role-taking capacity of such groups. Consistent with those role-taking studies, abusive parents were found to generally possess lower levels of affective responsivity as well. Thus, at least for these fairly extreme aggressors, deficits exist in both the cognitive and affective empathy domains.

Turning to research which employed less extreme samples, let us first consider the investigations using picture-story indexes. This approach can be well illustrated by the Feshbach and Feshbach (1969) investigation, one of the very first to examine the empathy-aggression link. In that study two age groups were employed: 4–5 year olds and 6–7 year olds. All the children were administered the FASTE, a picture-story technique in which respondents are shown four series of slides depicting a child in an emotional situation, and are asked after each one to report on their own feelings. Aggression was assessed by teachers' ratings of each child on a nine-item rating scale asking about overt instances of verbal and physical aggression. Results were somewhat mixed. Empathy had no reliable effect at all on the aggression of girls. For boys, however, greater empathy was significantly associated with more aggression for the 4–5 year olds and less aggression among the 6–7 year olds.

These results illustrate, in a nutshell, the larger pattern which has emerged from the dozen or so picture-story investigations reviewed by Miller and Eisenberg (1988). That review found the overall evidence for an empathy-aggression link to be quite weak; as with the original Feshbach and Feshbach (1969) study, however, the hypothesized association between affective empathy and aggression was stronger and more reliable for older respondents. In fact, when studies involving preschool samples are excluded, the predicted pattern emerges quite clearly. As noted in the previous chapter, it is possible that the link between empathy and behavior is weaker among the youngest respondents simply because the integration of affective and behavioral reactions tends to increase with age. Thus, picture-story indices of empathy may produce weaker associations with aggression because these measures are so frequently used with very young samples.

This interpretation is reinforced by the largely nonsignificant pattern of results which has emerged from the use of another technique—primarily employed with younger respondents—of facial/gestural indices of empathy. This technique typically involves exposing respondents to some stimulus (e.g., a traditional picture-story measure, or films of emotionally evocative events) while simultaneously recording their facial expressions for later coding. Individual differences in facial expressions are then correlated with aggressive behaviors occurring in a separate context. A study by Ekman, Liebert, Friesen, Harrison, Zlatchin, Malmstrom, and Baron (1972) illustrates this technique. In this study 5–6 year olds were exposed to excerpts from either a violent television program (*The Untouchables*) or exciting sporting events while being secretly videotaped. Afterwards, each child had the opportunity to "help" or "hurt" another child in an adjacent room (actually there was no other child) by making it easier or more difficult for that other child to win a game s/he was playing. Of most interest is the association between facial expressions while viewing acts of aggression and later aggressive actions. While virtually no associations were found for girls between facial expressions during violence and later aggression, a number of such associations were found for boys. In general, boys whose facial expressions indicated greater happiness during the violent stimulus (and thus, it is assumed, less affective sharing, personal distress, or empathic concern) were more likely to act aggressively later; boys whose expressions indicated more pain and sadness during the violent stimulus displayed less aggression later on. The size of this latter effect, however, was fairly small.

In fact, Miller and Eisenberg's review of the few studies using this technique indicates that the overall association between the facial/gestural measures and aggression is quite small indeed. These weak results using a technique which has been employed primarily with children 7 years of age or younger, coupled with the age-related differences already noted with the picture-story indices, clearly reveals that the evidence for a link between affective empathy and aggression among preschool and early elementary children is not impressive.

In contrast, the evidence is noticeably stronger for self-report measures of dispositional affective empathy, the technique which has been most extensively used with older respondents. At the time of the Miller and Eisenberg review, almost all studies using questionnaire measures employed the same instrument, the QMEE, and many of them measured aggression with similar laboratory-based measures. Mehrabian and Epstein's (1972) original investigation is typical. In two separate studies, male and female college students, to whom the QMEE had been administered one week earlier, participated in an ostensibly unrelated experiment on "personality and learning." They were to serve in the study as "teachers," helping another subject (actually a confederate) as they tried to master a task which required making a series of predictions about a third person. In particular, the subjects were required to punish the learner by administering electric shocks, for each incorrect answer with the shock level being left to the individual teacher. When the learner and teacher were in the same room, and the learner's gasps and facial grimaces fully in evidence, high scorers on the QMEE administered significantly weaker shocks; when the learner was in a separate room, audible but no longer visible, high and low QMEE scorers did not differ in their level of aggression.

About half of these studies reviewed by Miller and Eisenberg employed students as subjects (almost always college students), while the other half used delinquents or abusive mothers. Across both populations, however, Miller and Eisenberg found a considerable association between questionnaire measures of affective empathy and aggressive behavior, a finding in sharp contrast to the low overall levels of association found for picture-story and facial/gestural measures. As noted earlier, however, the questionnaire measures are routinely employed with older rather than younger respondents. Of the nine investigations using questionnaire measures reviewed by Miller and Eisenberg, only one (Bryant, 1982) employed respondents less than 14 years of age. This pattern is therefore consistent with the idea that it may be the age of the respondent rather than the particular empathy measure which is most responsible for the size of the empathy-aggression connection.

Some more recent evidence indicates that the affective subscales of the IRI, the empathic concern and personal distress scales, may also be associated with aggressive behavior. Richardson et al. (1992) have found high scorers on the EC scale to score significantly lower on some self-report measures of hostility and aggression (Buss & Durkee, 1957) and significantly higher on measures of constructive conflict resolution (Rahim, 1983). Other recent data (Davis, 1992) partially supports this pattern. In a sample of over 280 college students, scores on the EC scale displayed primarily negative but modest associations with antisocial indices from the Buss-Durkee (Buss & Durkee, 1957) and Cook-Medley (Cook & Medley, 1954) hostility scales, but these associations only reached significance among women. Interestingly, however, scores on the PD scale displayed the opposite pattern, a series of positive associations with hostility, especially such components of hostility as irritability, resentment, and suspicion. These associations were much stronger, moreover, for men than women. Table 8.1 displays these associations, along with the comparable relations between the hostility measures and dispositional perspective taking as well.

This table contains the results of a series of multiple regression analyses in which the IRI scales served as predictor variables and the various hostility measures served as dependent variables. Among males, both PT and PD scores were significantly associated with the Buss-Durkee and Cook-Medley total scores, the most global

TABLE 8.1 Associations between dispositional empathy (IRI) and dispositional hostility measures (Cook-Medley and Buss-Durkee). Values are beta coefficients from regression analyses in which the IRI scales were entered simultaneously as predictors.

	Perspective Taking		Empathic Concern		Personal Distress	
	Males	Females	Males	Females	Males	Females
Cook-Medley	-.18+	-.02	-.02	-.15*	.29**	.02
Buss-Durkee Total	-.24*	-.07	-.05	-.15	.32***	.10
Neurotic Hostility						
Resentment	-.10	-.07	-.05	-.10	.37***	.01
Suspicion	-.14	-.14+	-.04	-.02	.26**	.19*
Antagonistic Hostility						
Assault	-.24*	-.01	-.10	-.20*	.02	-.03
Verbal Hostility	-.26**	-.04	-.05	-.25**	.12	-.07
Indirect Hostility	-.18+	-.07	.00	.01	.19*	.10

Note: *** $p < .001$ **$p < .01$ *$p < .05$ +$p < .10$

measures of hostility. For females, only EC had a significant effect on any global measure (the Cook-Medley measure). More informative is an examination of the specific hostility measures making up the Buss-Durkee total score. For both men and women, dispositional personal distress was associated with higher scores on those constructs—resentment and suspicion—which tap *neurotic hostility* (Siegman, Dembroski, & Ringel, 1987), with the relationships for men somewhat stronger. Dispositional empathy also was associated with *antagonistic hostility,* the tendency to be physically and verbally hostile to others, but the pattern varied for men and women. Women displayed significant negative associations between measures of antagonistic hostility and dispositional empathic concern while men did not. Men displayed a negative association between antagonistic hostility and dispositional perspective taking while women did not.

These results therefore suggest an important distinction between different kinds of antisocial tendencies: antagonistic (overtly hostile to other people) and neurotic (characterized by feelings of resentment and suspicion). Dispositional PT and EC generally displayed the negative associations with antagonism measures expected on the basis of theoretical analyses of the empathy-aggression relationship. In contrast, dispositional personal distress displayed a substantial positive relationship with the neurotic hostility measures, suggesting that this construct may contribute to hostile attitudes and thought processes in a way that lies outside of the theoretical linkages discussed thus far.

How can the results of the research on dispositional affective empathy best be summarized? In contrast to the dispositional role-taking literature, which rather clearly indicates that pathological aggression is associated with role-taking deficits but leaves more uncertain the relationship between role taking and more normal variations in aggressive acts, the affective responsivity evidence more clearly suggests that such responsiveness is related to aggression within ''normal'' as well as especially aggressive populations. However, this evidence is currently much stronger for adults; in fact, evidence of such associations among young children is almost non-existent at the present time.

Summary and Conclusion

Perhaps the most striking aspect of this body of research is the overwhelming focus on dispositional empathy to the near-exclusion of empathy's other facets. Investigations of aggression which have attempted to manipulate empathy-related processes through instructional sets or perceived similarity have been quite few, and attempts to link such processes with intrapersonal outcomes such as affective reactions and attributions are equally rare. As a result, current knowledge in these areas is limited, and based to large degree on speculation and conjecture. Moreover, much of the research employing dispositional measures, especially role taking, has used extreme groups such as delinquents and physically abusive parents. As a result, questions remain about the generalizability of these findings. At the present time, therefore, it is difficult to fully evaluate the strength of the evidence for empathy-aggression connections.

Given this state of affairs, one especially useful approach in future research would be to establish the parameters within which processes such as role taking might reasonably be expected to influence aggression among non-delinquent samples. Thus, it would be quite informative to conduct experiments containing these three elements: 1) the prompting (or not) of role taking via instructional set or similarity manipulations; 2) the assessment of mediating constructs such as attributions and/or affective anger reactions; and 3) the measurement of aggressive responses toward the target. Such studies would provide the kind of comprehensive test of the empathy-aggression hypothesis which has thus far been lacking. Most important, perhaps, would be to discover the boundary conditions limiting this sequence, and in particular, the levels of provocation and/or general arousal at which perspective-taking processes do and do not operate.

The evidence available at present suggests that the inhibitory effect of role taking on aggression is considerably weakened at high levels of arousal/provocation. The fact that victim distress cues lose their ability to consistently reduce aggression when the aggressor is strongly provoked (e.g., Baron, 1974; Feshbach et al., 1967; Swart & Berkowitz, 1976) is one indication of this. Richardson et al.'s (1992) finding that the inhibiting effect of dispositional and situational perspective taking on aggression is strongest before one has been provoked by the target is another. The general failure of similarity manipulations (which might prompt role taking) to influence attributions or aggression under conditions of provocation (e.g., Hendrick & Taylor, 1971; Nesdale et al., 1978) is also consistent with this conclusion. Future efforts to more systematically map the limits of the empathy-aggression connection would therefore seem to hold much merit.

Based in part on these considerations, and in part on the work of Zillmann (1988) and Richardson et al. (1992), Figure 8.1 depicts

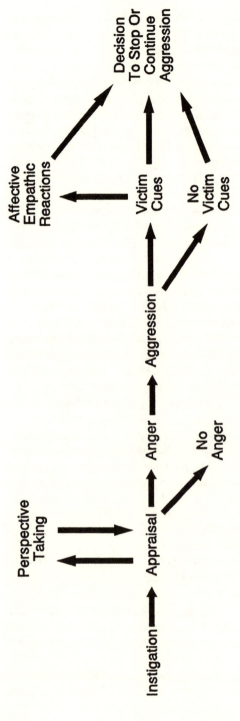

FIGURE 8.1
Possible ways in which empathic processes and reactions can enter the instigation-aggression sequence.

174

a sequence which may provide a useful way to conceive of empathy's role in affecting aggression. Early in the sequence, when the potential aggressor is being provoked, role-taking processes may play the primary role. Active role taking during the appraisal process is likely to influence how the provocation is interpreted, producing appraisals which lead to less anger, and perhaps more sympathy, and thus diminish the probability of aggression. In contrast, affective responding to victim distress cues is not especially relevant at this point, since no aggression has taken place and thus no distress is being experienced by the victim.

Once some retaliatory aggression has begun, however, affective responses to victim cues become more important in inhibiting further aggression, although such effects are also moderated by such factors as the level of prior provocation. Of course, perspective taking may also play a role at this latter point, inasmuch as this empathic process can influence the nature of the affective response to the distress cues. However, as a number of studies have indicated (e.g., Johnson & Rule, 1986; Zillmann & Cantor, 1976), mitigating information which is acquired after the provocation has relatively little effect on subsequent aggression. This suggests that there is a limited window of opportunity, early in the instigation-retaliation sequence, during which cognitive appraisals can inhibit aggression. After that time the role of cognitive processing in general, and the influence of perspective taking in particular, is likely to decline. Thus, there may be a shift from a primarily cognitive, attribution-driven reduction of aggression early in the instigation-aggression sequence to a more affective, distress-driven sequence later on. As noted above, experiments which systematically examine all elements in the sequence will be most useful in evaluating such ideas.

9

Social Relationships and Social Behavior

The previous two chapters have examined empathy's role in affecting two particular kinds of behavior: helping and aggression. The focus in this chapter will be a little different. Rather than examine a particular kind of behavior, this chapter will consider the operation of empathy-related processes and outcomes within the particular domain of social relationships. That is, we will examine empathy's impact on a variety of behaviors which all occur within the particular context of the formation and maintenance of relationships with other people. Because of this difference in focus, some of the findings discussed in the previous two chapters are also relevant here. Some helping and aggression occurs within the context of ongoing social relationships, and as a result some evidence reviewed earlier may also be mentioned in this chapter as well.

Two general approaches can be identified in the research addressing this topic. One strategy has been to examine an individual's overall evaluation of a relationship or relationships. If the focus is on marriage, for example, the connection between empathic dispositions/processes and marital satisfaction or adjustment might be examined. If the focus is on social relationships in general rather than on one relationship in particular, then the link between empathy and a subjective state such as loneliness might be considered. The second approach has been to explore the effect of empathy-related constructs on *specific behaviors* which occur within important relationships, in particular, behaviors having to do with communication, conflict, and social style. As with the research on aggression, however, almost all investigations of the empathy/social behavior question have concentrated on individual differences in empathy, with little direct attention being given to the operation of empathy-related processes, such as role taking, within social contexts.

Theoretical Links between Empathy and Social Behavior

The idea that one's social intercourse is significantly influenced by the capacity for empathy is not new. Smith (1759/1976) and Spencer (1870) both argued that important social consequences flow from our tendency to ''sympathize'' with others' experiences—that is, to share a ''fellow-feeling'' with them. Such shared feeling helps transform the interests of others, at least in part, into self-interests, and thus prompts us to act in more benevolent ways. The regular display of such benevolence towards others, in turn, generally improves the quality of our relationships with those persons.

Theorists with a decidedly more cognitive view of empathy also hold that possessing such a capacity will improve the social climate. Both Mead (1934) and Piaget (1932) have argued that the ability and willingness to step outside one's own egocentric perspective underlies much of human social capability. In fact, without a capacity to role-take, one's relations with others would be inescapably self-centered and marked by interpersonal friction, as each social participant's goals and objectives would conflict with those of others. Well-developed role-taking skills, however, allow us to effectively tailor our behaviors to the expectations of others, providing much smoother interpersonal relations.

What both approaches have in common, though perhaps more clearly with regard to the role-taking argument, is the recognition that empathy in some guise is necessary to help us deal with the fundamental obstacle in social life, namely, other people. Because other people commonly have needs, desires, and goals which differ from our own, and because the attainment of their goals is frequently incompatible with ours, a powerful tendency toward conflict is inherent in all social life. As individuals pursue their own objectives, the goals of some are on occasion thwarted by others' success. The result is a social life characterized by high levels of conflict and disagreement. Or, more accurately, the result can be such a conflict-filled existence if no mechanism, such as empathy, is available to interrupt this sequence. In recent years, several different theoretical approaches have been advanced which address, to quite varying degrees, the possible role of empathy within social relationships. Two of these are presented in the next few pages.

Davis' Mediational Model

The contemporary approach which most directly addresses the empathy/social behavior link is a model proposed by Davis and colleagues (Davis & Kraus, 1991; Davis & Oathout, 1987, 1992). This model focuses on dispositional empathy, and argues that an individual's stable tendencies in the areas of perspective taking, empathic concern, and personal distress have reliable effects on the occurrence of specific relationship behaviors. A person high in dispositional perspective taking, for example, will act in different ways towards other people, and these actions will have predictable consequences for the quality of that person's social relationships. In particular, the individual's actions will affect how others view the individual, and these perceptions by others will affect the kinds of relationships that are possible. Figure 9.1 displays this model in its simplest form.

Two points should be stressed concerning this model. First, the endpoint of the model, social outcomes, can include a wide variety of phenomena. For example, one consequence resulting from an individual's behaviors, and the subsequent perception of those behaviors by others, is a subjective feeling state in that individual. Unfavorable perceptions by others, to the degree that they are communicated, can be expected to produce in that individual feelings of anxiety, depression, and loneliness. Alternatively, social outcomes can refer to reactions, feelings, or judgments of the perceiver. Thus, an individual's behavior and the resulting perceptions by others could produce in those perceivers feelings of greater or lesser liking for the individual; such feelings, if generally held by most observers,

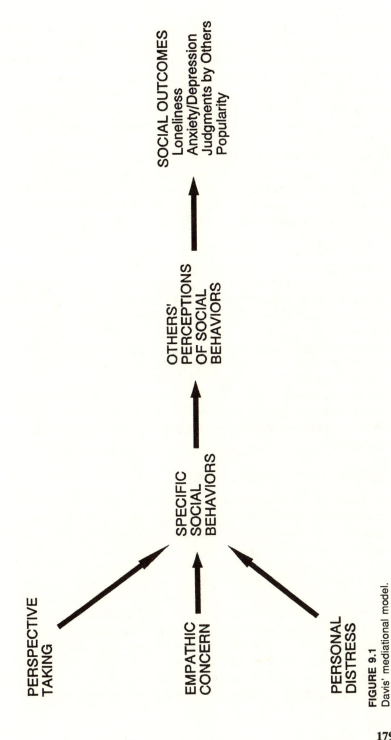

FIGURE 9.1
Davis' mediational model.

179

determine the individual's general popularity. Thus, "social outcomes" refer not only to constructs residing solely within the individual but also to those within the perceiver.

The second point to be emphasized is that this model reflects a phenomenological approach, meaning it assumes that social outcomes are directly influenced not by one's behavior, but by others' perceptions of that behavior. Certainly one's behavior has an effect on others' perceptions, but those perceptions are just as certainly influenced by other variables as well. For example, perceivers' expectations about a target, perhaps based on past experiences, can strongly affect perceptions of that target's behavior. From the perspective of the mediational model, then, the key point to remember is that perceptions of reality exert the most direct effect on social outcomes.

Finally, what of the relation between this model and the organizational model? In essence, the first two stages in the mediational model (the link between dispositional empathy and behavior) are equivalent to the link between dispositional empathy and interpersonal outcomes in the organizational model. However, the remainder of the mediational model (from behavior to others' perceptions, and from perceptions to social outcomes) lies entirely outside the scope of the organizational model. Conversely, the role of intervening empathy-related processes, and intrapersonal outcomes, is not considered in Davis' social relationships model. Because of this, one might expect the observed associations between dispositional empathy and interpersonal behaviors to be of only moderate magnitude.

Bradbury and Fincham's Model

In contrast to Davis' mediational model, which focuses explicitly on dispositional empathy's influence on social behavior and outcomes, Bradbury and Fincham have proposed a model (Figure 9.2) designed to account more generally for the integrated function of affective and cognitive processes within close relationships (Bradbury & Fincham, 1987; Fincham & Bradbury, 1988), and have begun to carry out investigations testing it (e.g., Bradbury & Fincham, 1988; Fincham & Bradbury, 1989a, 1989b). In brief, the model holds that all behavior by one partner (A) is perceived and processed by the other partner (B). In primary processing, which occurs quickly, and outside of conscious awareness, the behavior is evaluated primarily in terms of how negative, unexpected, and self-relevant it seems to be. In subsequent secondary processing a conscious attempt is made

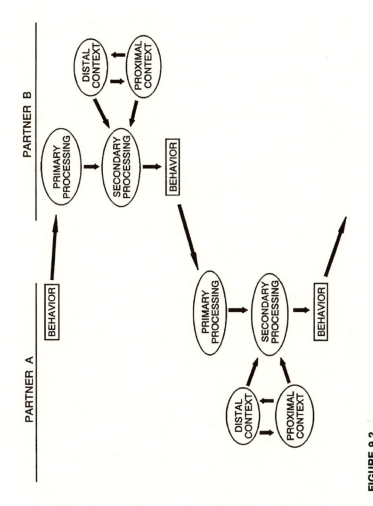

FIGURE 9.2
Bradbury and Fincham's model.

to identify a cause for A's behavior, and to characterize that cause in terms of attributional dimensions such as locus (internal-external), stability, and so forth. The result of this processing is then said to influence B's affective and behavioral responses to A, and these responses by B are then processed in a similar fashion by A.

Empathy enters this sequence through two additional constructs that Bradbury and Fincham refer to as *proximal* and *distal* contexts. Proximal context refers to thoughts and feelings experienced by B immediately prior to processing A's behavior, and distal context refers to more stable factors, including personality characteristics, which may also affect processing. Both the act of perspective taking and the temporary affective states which may result from such perspective taking (e.g., empathic concern) seem to fall under the proximal context heading. In contrast, dispositional tendencies to engage in perspective taking or to experience empathic affective responses seem to qualify as distal context variables. In either case, state or trait, greater perspective taking and/or empathic concern might be expected to influence secondary processing in a particular way by producing more "actor-like" attributional judgments (e.g., less dispositional) regarding the partner's behavior. Such evaluations would in turn be likely to foster more positive responses to the partner.

Because the Bradbury and Fincham model focuses on intrapersonal phenomena such as thoughts and feelings, it has less in common with Davis' mediational model, and is more compatible with the organizational model. In essence, the Bradbury and Fincham model encompasses dispositional empathy (distal context), role taking (proximal context), intrapersonal outcomes (attributional judgments and affective reactions), and interpersonal outcomes (overt behaviors toward partners). It therefore provides a means of analyzing relationship behavior, in general, which aligns quite well with the organizational model's specific focus on empathy-related reactions and behavior.

The Domain of Relationship Behaviors

The remainder of this chapter will follow the form of preceding ones by considering the evidence for associations between social relationship variables and a variety of empathy-related dispositions, processes, and outcomes. Because the focus is on behaviors occurring within a particular context rather than on a specific kind of behavior, a wide array of social relationship variables have been studied, and it thus seems useful to organize them in some manner. Based on prior theoretical and empirical work, four relatively clear categories seem to exist. In keeping with the distinction outlined earlier, the first three refer to classes of specific social behavior which occur within relationships, and the fourth refers to overall evaluative judgments about the relationship(s).

Conflict Avoidance/Conflict Management

Implicit in many of the theoretical treatments of empathy and social behavior (e.g., Davis & Kraus, 1991) is the notion that empathy in general and perspective taking in particular play an important role both in anticipating conflict, and thus in some cases avoiding it, and in more successfully managing conflict when it does occur. Thus, one important category of social behavior is success at avoiding or minimizing interpersonal frictions.

Good Communication

Another clear implication of theoretical treatments of empathy is that greater role taking produces better communication between social participants (e.g., Mead, 1934; Davis & Kraus, 1991). It has also been suggested that social partners characterized by high levels of warmth and compassion are especially valued as confidants (Davis & Kraus, 1991), and therefore prompt more communication from others.

Considerate Social Style

The third category is a little different. Individuals who habitually make an effort to step outside their own perspectives and entertain those of others might as a consequence exhibit behaviors reflecting a considerate, other-oriented style. By virtue of their greater understanding of others' motives, for example, such persons might be more tolerant of others, and more accommodating to their views. In general, they may act in more cooperative and less egocentric ways. Similarly, a person who regularly experiences feelings of sympathy and compassion for others might display more supportive behaviors, and act in more generous ways. It should be noted that the well-established link between empathic concern and helping behavior (Chapter 7) is consistent with this expectation.

Global Evaluation

The first three categories have all dealt with what may be considered the "micro" level of analysis, that is, the effect of empathy-related constructs on specific social behaviors. The remaining category is a more "macro" variable, the individual's global evaluation of a relationship or relationships. By far the most frequently examined evaluation is one's overall level of satisfaction with a particular relationship. Also included here would be such measures as relationship longevity/survival (whether or not a relationship is still intact after some period of time). Subjective feelings of loneliness, in contrast, provide an evaluation of one's social network as a whole, as opposed to evaluating one particular relationship.

Affective Outcomes and Social Relationships

As was the case in the previous chapter's examination of links between affective outcomes and aggression, traditional theoretical treatments of affective reactions within close relationships have not been much concerned with empathically aroused emotion. Instead, the focus has typically been on the emotional reactions, usually negative, which are directly evoked in one partner by the other's words or actions. In other words, the focus has been on affective responses in one partner (A) which result because of the direct impact on A's well-being of B's behavior.

Berscheid (1983), building on Mandler's (1975) more general framework of human emotions, has offered a theoretical account of emotions within close relationships which is reasonably representative of contemporary approaches. According to this analysis, the experience of emotion requires first that some event occurs which triggers activation of the autonomic nervous system (ANS), and, more particularly, activation of the ANS's sympathetic nervous system. The resulting, perceptible effects of such activation (dry mouth, sweaty palms, pounding heart) are a powerful signal to the individual to pay attention to the environment in order to interpret the meaning of whatever cues have prompted this physical reaction. As a result of this attentional shift, a cognitive interpretive process ensues in which available information is analyzed to determine the appropriate emotional response.

According to this model, one of the most important classes of events which can trigger ANS activity and thus produce emotions are *interruptions,* the disruption of some ongoing activity, plan, or behavioral sequence. Events which unexpectedly derail one's activities or plans are likely to be arousing, and when the interpretive analysis indicates that the interruption is threatening in some significant way, the subjective emotional reaction is likely to be negative. It may also be possible, as both Mandler and Berscheid acknowledge, for ANS arousal to occur even without an interruption; however, in most cases it is expected that arousal, and therefore emotion, will result from the interruption/interpretation sequence. Thus, the key determinants of an emotional reaction will typically be the intensity of the ANS arousal produced by the interruption and the outcome of the cognitive interpretation of that interruption. The Bradbury and Fincham model, it might be noted, offers a similar analysis of how one partner's behavior triggers a cognitive-affective sequence in the other which eventually leads to a behavioral response.

Empirically speaking, current evidence suggests that negative affect within relationships is significantly associated with the overall level of satisfaction or adjustment displayed by the couple. As Bradbury and Fincham (1987) and Rusbult, Verette, Whitney, Slovik, and Lipkus (1991) have noted, observational studies consistently indicate that distressed couples display more overt negativity, and more reciprocation of negativity, than nondistressed couples. Moreover, diary-type studies reveal that it is the occurrence of negatively valenced events, not positive ones, which most strongly affect one's day-to-day satisfaction with the relationship (e.g., Wills, Weiss, & Patterson, 1974). In fact, some research has indicated that couples' emotional arousal during a laboratory interaction, as indexed by their physiological activity (heart rate, skin conductance), is a substantial predictor not only of current relationship satisfaction (Levenson & Gottman, 1983), but of changes in satisfaction three years later (Levenson & Gottman, 1985). In a variety of ways, then, affective responses (especially negative ones) appear to have a substantial association with relationship quality.

Given this pattern, the question now becomes, are these findings regarding the affect-satisfaction link relevant to the organizational model we have been employing? As with the analysis of aggression in the previous chapter, there is virtually no direct evidence of relationship satisfaction being linked to *empathically* aroused affective states. Thus, no clear empirical links have yet been established between empathy-related processes (such as perspective taking), the resulting affective reactions, and overall satisfaction within the context of specific social relationships. All evidence consistent with such links is indirect, drawn from research not focusing on social relationships.

One source of such indirect evidence is the work on affect and helping reviewed in Chapters 6 and 7. As noted in those chapters, considerable research supports the conclusion that affective responses to another's distress, whether parallel or reactive, make helping of that other person more likely. If this research, typically conducted using strangers in the laboratory, is generalizable to long-term social relationships, and if prosocial behaviors occurring within a relationship are assumed to have a generally beneficial effect, then the operation of well-documented empathic processes are likely to play a role in enhancing the quality of close social relations. In this indirect sense, then, evidence for affective empathy's role in social relationships can be said to exist.

It should be recognized, however, that this analysis differs from traditional considerations of affect within relationships (e.g. Berscheid, 1983; Fincham & Bradbury, 1987), which are primarily concerned with explaining how the actions of one partner come to have affective consequences, usually negative, for the other. Because the other's actions are typically interpreted in terms of their direct implications for the self, concepts such as shared affect, or reactive feelings of empathic concern, are not typically part of these analyses. Empathy-related processes and outcomes might, however, have a meaningful role to play within this more traditional analysis of affect in relationships, one that becomes apparent by considering the cognitive evaluative processes which also occur in response to behaviors of relationship partners. While such processes have thus far been mentioned only in passing, it is now time to consider them more explicitly.

Non-Affective Outcomes and Social Relationships

As we have seen in the previous two chapters, a consideration of empathy's role in influencing affective and behavioral responses frequently requires some attention to the mediating role played by cognitive outcomes, most notably causal attributions. The same is true in the case of social relationships. The important role of cognitive causal analyses is clearly seen in the Bradbury and Fincham (1987) model, which assumes that behaviors by one partner trigger two kinds of cognitive processing in the other. The immediate, nonconscious *primary* processing evaluates the behavior in terms of how negative, unexpected, and self-relevant it appears to be. The most important factor is probably the degree to which the behavior deviates from some standard of appropriate behavior held by the perceiver (Fincham, Bradbury, & Grych, 1990). This stage of the process is roughly comparable to the stage in Berscheid's theory at which ANS arousal is generated by an interruption.

It is the next stage, *secondary* processing, at which more elaborate attributional judgments are made: estimates of the degree to which the partner's behavior is caused by his/her disposition, the degree to which such causes are stable over time, and the degree to which the causes have global implications for other relationship behaviors. In addition, a further analysis takes place as well, one which focuses specifically on the question of responsibility. Estimates are made at this point regarding the partner's ability and willingness to have engaged in alternative behaviors. To the degree that s/he is seen to have deliberately and freely chosen a particular behavior, s/he is held responsible for that act. The more that a partner is held responsible for negative actions, the greater the likelihood of negative affective reactions such as anger.

Based on this model, causal attributions occurring within close relationships should display an association with overall marital adjustment/satisfaction, and in fact such an association seems to exist (for a review of this literature, see Bradbury & Fincham, 1990). The strongest evidence thus far has been found for the globality dimension. Persons in distressed relationships see positive behaviors by their partners as relatively isolated events, but see partners' negative behaviors as part of larger, more global patterns. Less consistent but nevertheless notable support has also been found for the dimensions of locus (internal vs. external) and stability. Again, people in distressed relationships see bad behaviors by the partner as due to stable factors which are largely internal to the partner; partners' good behaviors, in contrast, are typically seen as resulting from unstable causes largely external to the partner (Bradbury & Fincham, 1990).

The relevance of empathic dispositions and processes to this model is represented by the constructs Bradbury and Fincham refer to as *proximal* and *distal* contexts, the thoughts, feelings, attitudes, dispositions, etc., which influence secondary processing. Greater perspective taking, either dispositional or situational, in particular seems a likely influence on secondary attributional processing, and ultimately therefore on affective and behavioral responses as well. A number of studies reviewed earlier (e.g., Gould & Sigall, 1977; Regan & Totten, 1975) have demonstrated that the process of role taking, induced via instructional sets (proximal context), does have a reliable impact on observers' attributions for targets' behavior. It must be emphasized, of course, that such investigations have typically assessed attributions for strangers rather than for significant figures in the individual's social world. To the degree that such findings can be generalized to ongoing social relationships, however, empathy-related processes such as role taking can be seen as significantly implicated in the Bradbury and Fincham model.

It should be further noted that virtually all of the studies in this tradition have focused exclusively on the locus dimension, the degree to which the target's behavior is seen as due to dispositional causes, and have largely ignored the dimensions of stability and

globality. Because globality is the dimension most strongly implicated in the relationship satisfaction literature, it is presently unclear
how substantial an impact empathy-related processes might have on
this most well-established attributional dimension. The same limitation applies to the indirect evidence from studies conducted within
the attribution-aggression research tradition (Chapter 8). Those
investigations identified controllability as a causal dimension substantially related to feelings of anger toward, and aggression
against, a misbehaving target; one study (Betancourt, 1990a) in fact
found role-taking instructions to influence these controllability attributions. Bradbury and Fincham's (1990) review of the attribution-
satisfaction literature, however, found very few studies examining
the link between relationship satisfaction and controllability attributions, and those which did yielded inconsistent results. Thus, while
the evidence suggests a reliable association between role taking and
locus attributions outside the context of social relationships, and
some association between locus attributions and satisfaction within
such relationships, the overall picture regarding empathy, satisfaction, and other attributional dimensions remains somewhat cloudy.

Role Taking and Social Relationships

Previous work on role taking and attributions, although suggesting a
reliable link between the two, has not examined this connection
within the specific context of ongoing social relationships. Most investigations (e.g., Gould & Sigall, 1977; Regan & Totten, 1975)
have had observers view unfamiliar targets for brief periods of time,
and have used instructions to induce a role-taking perceptual set. A
few studies (e.g., Taylor & Koivumaki, 1976) examined attributions
for spouses or well-known others, finding that attributions for such
targets tend to be more flattering and "actor-like" than attributions
made for less familiar others. One explanation for this pattern, although not the only one, is that observers are more likely to engage
in role taking when making attributional judgments for close associates. No investigations, however, have studied experimentally-
induced role taking, and its effect on attributions, within the context
of ongoing social relationships.

However, one study has come close. Howe (1987) manipulated role taking via instructional set and then exposed observers to
a videotaped couple engaged in a realistic conflict apparently taking
place within a marital counseling session. In particular, observers
were instructed to put themselves in the position of either the
husband, the wife, or the counselor. Afterward, observers were

asked to respond in an open-ended fashion to questions inquiring about the causes of the argument they had seen. When observers took the husband's perspective, they were significantly more likely to attribute primary causality for the conflict to the wife, and when taking the wife's perspective were more likely to attribute cause to the husband. When asked to take the counselor's perspective, in contrast, observers offered intermediate levels of attributions to both husbands and wives, and in fact made a substantial attribution to joint causes, indicating that the couple as a unit were responsible for the argument. Thus, the act of perspective taking did influence the attributions made for an apparently genuine altercation between two persons involved in a long-term relationship. However, because the attributor was not a participant in the relationship, and in fact did not know either member of the couple, this finding must also be taken as indirect support for the proposition that adopting the perspective of one's partner during "real life" behavioral episodes will influence attributions for that partner's behavior.

Dispositional Empathy and Social Relationships

The vast majority of investigations into empathy's role in social relationships have employed dispositional measures of empathy. To most effectively present this research, we will separately examine the evidence concerning the four classes of social behavior outlined earlier: global evaluation, conflict, good communication, and considerate social style.

Global Evaluation/Satisfaction

Investigations of the association between dispositional empathy and relationship satisfaction have generally focused on perspective taking. At least four studies have examined this issue in recent years. Franzoi, Davis, and Young (1985) had both members of 131 romantic couples complete questionnaires which included measures of dispositional perspective taking (the IRI's PT scale), satisfaction with the relationship, and two measures of processes which occur within the relationship—level of self-disclosure to the partner, and typical mode of conflict resolution. Males' satisfaction with the relationship was significantly and positively associated with their own PT scores and with the PT scores of their partner; females' satisfaction was similarly associated with their own PT scores, but not with the scores of their partner. More importantly, these associations remained significant even when controlling for the mediating effects of self-disclosure and conflict resolution. In a somewhat similar investigation, however, Fincham and Bradbury (1989a) found conflicting results. As part of a larger study, perspective taking (PT scale) and marital satisfaction were assessed for both members of 43 married couples. Husbands' satisfaction was significantly and positively related to their own PT scores, but their wives' satisfaction was unrelated to PT scores of either spouse.

Long and Andrews (1990) examined this issue in a more comprehensive fashion. Spouses in 159 married couples completed a questionnaire which included a measure of marital adjustment and three perspective taking scales: 1) the PT scale, 2) a scale assessing one's tendency to specifically adopt the perspective of one's marital partner (rather than people in general), and 3) a measure of the respondents' perceptions of their partners' perspective-taking tendency. Analyses were conducted in which one spouse's (A's) satisfaction was predicted by the other spouse's (B's) general PT, partner-specific PT, and by A's perceptions of B's PT. For both husbands and wives, marital adjustment was significantly associated with all three perspective-taking indices. In keeping with the logic of the Davis model, moreover, perceptions of one's partner's perspective taking displayed the strongest association with one's marital adjustment. Perceiving one's partner to be high in perspective taking tendency was associated with better adjustment. The partner's self-reported tendency to role take within the relationship was similarly, albeit less strongly, associated. Unexpectedly, however, once the effects of these two variables were statistically accounted for, partner's general perspective taking was negatively associated with one's marital adjustment.

Finally, Rusbult et al. (1991), within a larger investigation examining accommodation in close relationships, had a sample of 171 individuals (not couples) complete measures of relationship satisfaction, general perspective taking (PT scale), a measure of partner-specific perspective taking similar to the measure used by Long and Andrews, and a measure of dispositional empathic concern (the IRI's EC scale). Multiple regression analyses revealed that partner-specific perspective taking was significantly and positively related to one's own satisfaction, while general perspective taking and empathic concern were not. Thus, the greater one's tendency to entertain the specific perspective of one's romantic partner, the greater one's own satisfaction.

Taken as a whole, the results of these four studies reveal an interesting pattern. A dispositional tendency to take the specific perspective of one's relationship partner was consistently positively associated with one's own satisfaction (Rusbult et al. 1991) and that of one's partner (Long & Andrews, 1990). Measures of global perspective taking, on the other hand, tended to display similar but weaker patterns (Franzoi et al., 1985; Rusbult et al., 1991). This suggests the real value of assessing dispositional empathy in a way which is most appropriate to the social context in question. When the context is a particular relationship, then a measure of empathic tendencies specific to that relationship is likely to be most useful.

A pair of studies have also examined the links between dispositional empathy and feelings of loneliness, a more global indicator of satisfaction with one's social relationships. Davis (1983b) administered a battery of questionnaires, including the IRI and the UCLA Loneliness Scale (Russell, Peplau, & Cutrona, 1980), to a sample of over 400 college undergraduates. Higher PT and EC scores were significantly though modestly associated with lower levels of loneliness, while higher PD scores were associated with greater loneliness. More recently, Bruch, Kaflowitz, and Pearl (1988) also reported a significant negative association between PT scores and loneliness, using Schmidt and Sermat's (1983) Differential Loneliness Scale. Consistent with the logic of Davis' mediational model, however, this effect appears to be the result of other intervening theoretical constructs; once the effects of social anxiety, social skills, and self-disclosure were accounted for, the relation between perspective taking and loneliness dropped to nonsignificance.

Considerate Social Style

This section and the two that follow will consider associations between dispositional empathy and specific classes of social behavior. The first to be examined is the *considerate social style* which those dispositionally high in perspective taking and empathic concern might be expected to display. As noted earlier, such a social style could encompass heightened tolerance for others, greater cooperation, active support for others, and a general lack of egocentrism in thought and deed.

One relevant body of evidence consists of those studies examining dispositional empathy's effect on helping behavior. As noted in Chapter 7, evidence suggests a reliable association between role taking and helping (Underwood & Moore, 1982), and a similar reliable association, for adults, between affective responsivity and helping (Eisenberg & Miller, 1987). To the degree that dispositional empathy enhances helping behavior within ongoing relationships in the same way that it does outside of such relationships, support for an empathy-based considerate social style can be claimed. Another source of support can be found in the studies which have examined empathy's influence on tolerance for stigmatized groups (Chapter 5). Dispositional perspective taking and empathic concern were both associated with holding more tolerant, less punitive attitudes toward members of outgroups (Underwood & Briggs, 1980; Sheehan et al., 1989).

Another set of relevant findings comes from three studies which have examined, among college populations, the associations between IRI scores and a variety of self-reported traits and behaviors reflecting a considerate social style. In two of these studies (Davis & Oathout, 1987; 1992) respondents completed the IRI and a second questionnaire which assessed the frequency with which they engage in a number of specific behaviors within their romantic relationships. Included were behaviors tapping such "considerate style" constructs as warmth (e.g., affectionate, supportive, generous), even temper (e.g., patient, understanding), insensitivity (e.g., rude, critical, selfish), and positive outlook (e.g., friendly, positive, dependable). In the third study (Davis, 1983b), subjects completed two measures of traits relevant to the considerate social style, the Femininity and Negative Masculinity scales from the Extended Personal Attributes Questionnaire (Spence, Helmreich, & Holohan, 1979). The Femininity scale assesses a set of other-oriented characteristics including "aware of feelings of others," and "understanding of others," and the Negative Masculinity scale taps such negative interpersonal qualities as "arrogant," "boastful," and "dictatorial." Thus, these two scales tap dimensions which are directly reflective, in opposite ways, of the social style under investigation.

Table 9.1 displays some of the results of these three investigations. One striking feature of the table is that dispositional perspective taking and empathic concern are rather consistently associated with self-reported traits and behaviors indicative of a considerate social style; dispositional personal distress, on the other hand, is much less strongly related. There are also some differences apparent between perspective taking and empathic concern. PT but not EC scores are significantly associated with more even temper and with less insensitive behavior; EC scores, in contrast, are substantially associated with more warm and supportive behavior in romantic relationships, with PT scores less strongly related. Thus, within the general context of both perspective taking and empathic concern predicting a considerate social style, empathic concern is more strongly associated with demonstrative, other-oriented generosity and warmth, while perspective taking is more associated with a less demonstrative avoidance of rude and egotistical acts.

TABLE 9.1 Associations between dispositional empathy (IRI) and measures of a considerate social style.

	Perspective Taking		Empathic Concern		Personal Distress	
	Males	*Females*	*Males*	*Females*	*Males*	*Females*
Traits[1]						
Femininity	.37***	.33***	.58***	.55***	ns	-.12*
Negative Masculinity	-.30***	-.28***	-.30***	-.35***	-.11*	ns
Behaviors[2]						
Warmth	ns	ns	.32**	.46**	ns	ns
	—	.27**	—	.45**	—	-.24**
Positive Outlook	ns	.19*	.20*	.23**	-.28**	-.24**
	—	.31**	—	.36**	—	-.18*
Insensitivity	-.20*	-.23**	ns	-.18*	ns	ns
	—	-.36**	—	ns	—	ns
Even Temper	.19*	.26**	ns	ns	ns	ns
	—	.32**	—	ns	—	ns

[1]These values are zero-order correlation coefficients taken from Davis (1983b).

[2]These values are regression coefficients from analyses in which the three empathy measures were entered simultaneously as predictors. For each behavior, the first row provides results from Davis and Oathout (1987) and the second row from Davis and Oathout (1992).

*Note:*** $p < .001$ ** $p < .01$ * $p < .05$ ns = nonsignificant

One final way in which a non-egocentric style has been conceptualized is in attributional terms. Some research (Ross & Sicoly, 1979; Thompson & Kelley, 1981) has demonstrated an egocentric bias in the responsibility judgments which are offered for events occurring within close relationships. In short, each person in the relationship tends to claim more responsibility for relationship events than the partner is willing to grant. This tendency to overestimate one's own importance may in part be due to a failure to recognize and appreciate the partner's perspective on events. Fincham and Bradbury (1989b, Study 2) tested this notion by having both members of 25 married couples make separate estimates of the degree to which self and partner contribute to four positive (e.g., being affectionate) and four negative (e.g., criticizing) relationship behaviors.

Fincham and Bradbury found the typical egocentric bias for the negative behaviors, with husbands and wives in general claiming more responsibility for negative behaviors than their spouses assigned to them. For positive behaviors, however, the opposite bias was found. People generally claimed less responsibility for positive events than spouses were willing to grant. Thus, the overall pattern suggests a "niceness" bias, as spouses generally took more blame for negative events and offered more credit to their partners for positive ones. More relevant for our purposes, a significant association was found between the combined PT score of the couple and the amount of responsibility for positive events assigned to one's spouse ($r = .47$). Thus, greater perspective taking was associated with a tendency to give one's partner credit for positive relationship events. No relationship at all was found, however, between couple PT scores and the assignment of responsibility for negative events. Further, the overall bias scores (obtained by subtracting spouses's attributions from one's own) were unrelated to couple PT scores for either positive or negative behaviors.

Finally, in a separate investigation, Fincham and Bradbury (1989a) examined the impact of dispositional perspective taking on a different kind of attributional judgment. Both spouses in 43 marriages were asked to make causal analyses of two specific kinds of disagreements which they had actually experienced. They were to rate the cause of each disagreement in terms of its locus (was it due to the partner), globality (was it likely to affect other aspects of the marriage), and stability (was it likely to persist in the future). An index was then calculated by summing these three ratings, with higher scores therefore indicating more maladaptive (internal, global, stable) attributions. For neither husbands nor wives was there a significant association between dispositional perspective taking and this attributional index.

Taken as a whole, evidence regarding the link between dispositional empathy and a considerate social style is reasonably strong. Dispositional perspective taking and empathic concern are consistently associated with self-reported traits and behavior reflecting a tactful, tolerant, and even-tempered approach to social relationships. Dispositional personal distress, in contrast, appears to be much less related to such a style. Although only two studies have thus far addressed the issue of dispositional empathy's impact on a non-egocentric attributional style, the evidence in this area is not encouraging. One hint of an effect of dispositional PT on responsibility judgments has been found (Fincham & Bradbury, 1989b), but most of the evidence fails to support such an effect. It may be that situational (proximal) perspective taking will be more strongly related to attributional judgments, but this link has not yet been examined in social relationships.

Good Communication

Another domain of social behavior theoretically related to dispositional empathy is the *degree and quality of communication* between members of a social relationship. In one early study, Feffer and Suchotliff (1966) examined this issue by means of an ingenious laboratory measure of effective communication, success at the game "Password." In this study college students were placed into two-person groups on the basis of their scores on Feffer and Gourevitch's (1960) role-taking task, a measure of cognitive role-taking capacity. Groups then played "Password," a game in which one player, the "receiver," tries to guess an unknown stimulus word based on the one-word clues provided by the other player, the "sender." As expected, groups made up of higher scorers on the role-taking task generally performed more successfully at Password, ostensibly because of their superior ability to understand their partners' perspective and to use that information when sending and interpreting clues.

More recent attempts to examine this issue have taken a different approach, focusing not on the effectiveness of communication but instead on the extent to which members of a relationship disclose to one another. One set of studies (Davis & Franzoi, 1986; Franzoi & Davis, 1985; Davis, Franzoi, & Wellinger, 1985) has examined the connections, among high school students, between dispositional empathy and self-reported disclosure to peers. The pattern emerging across these investigations is relatively clear. Neither perspective taking nor personal distress were found to have any reliable effect on reported self-disclosure to peers; empathic concern, on the other hand, displayed a positive association with disclosure to females (Davis et al., 1985). In other words, males' empathic concern was positively related to disclosure to opposite-sex peers, and females' empathic concern was related to disclosure to same-sex peers.

A second cluster of studies (Davis & Oathout, 1987; 1992; Franzoi et al., 1985) has examined this issue within the context of romantic relationships. Consistent with the high school investigations, Franzoi et al. (1985) found that college students' dispositional perspective taking was essentially unrelated to their reported disclosure to romantic partners (no other dimension of empathy was assessed in that study). In the two Davis and Oathout investigations, however, dispositional perspective taking, empathic concern, and personal distress were all included. Communication was assessed in these studies through a four item index tapping the degree to which the respondent reported "opening up" and "readily listening" to one's partner. This measure therefore includes being a willing recipient of disclosure as well as a willing discloser. Across these two studies, it was found that all three measures of empathy were generally associated with women's self-reports of being a good communicator. Greater perspective taking and empathic concern, and lower personal distress, were associated with being a better communicator, with empathic concern displaying the strongest association. For males, neither perspective taking nor personal distress were significantly associated with the communication index, but empathic concern was significantly and positively related.

Taken as whole, then, these studies suggest that the most reliable association between dispositional empathy and good communication involves empathic concern. EC scores were consistently associated with good communication in romantic relationships, and were associated to some degree with disclosure to peers in high school. Perspective taking and personal distress displayed more sporadic patterns of association. Neither was related to self-disclosure to high school peers, but they displayed an association, for women, with good communication in romantic relationships. One factor contributing to empathic concern's importance in this area may be the attractiveness of warm, sympathetic persons as recipients for self-disclosure. Hill (1991), for example, has demonstrated that subjects who anticipate discussing an emotional problem with another person display a clear preference for doing so with someone described as warm and understanding. Thus, dispositionally compassionate people may be especially likely to receive frequent, intimate communication from others.

Conflict and Conflict Management

The tendency to have fewer conflicts with others, and to resolve conflicts more quickly or harmoniously, is another feature of social life thought to result from high levels of dispositional empathy, especially perspective taking. One body of research consistent with this view, the investigations linking dispositional empathy and hostility (Richardson et al., 1992; Davis, 1992), has already been mentioned in our previous discussion of aggression. In particular, measures of antagonistic hostility (e.g., assaultiveness, verbal aggression) were significantly and negatively related to dispositional perspective taking, although this association held primarily among males (see Table 8.1). Empathic concern displayed a similar pattern, for females, with personal distress largely unrelated to these measures for both sexes. If it can be assumed that persons characterized by high levels of antagonistic hostility are somewhat more likely to experience interpersonal conflicts, then a case can be made that both dispositional perspective taking and empathic concern are associated with less social conflict.

This reasoning is supported, at least for perspective taking, by data reported in Davis and Kraus (1991). In two different samples, one consisting of adolescent and pre-adolescent boys attending a summer camp, and the other consisting of high school students, respondents were asked to separately report on the number of angry arguments and physical fights they had engaged in with peers during the previous two years. Because the two measures were significantly correlated in each sample, they were summed into a single composite. As expected, dispositional perspective taking was negatively associated with such conflict. Greater perspective taking was significantly associated with less conflict for campers ($r = -.25$), high school males ($-.19$), and high school females ($-.17$). No other empathy measure was significantly related to conflict in either sample.

Once conflict does arise, how is it resolved? Two studies provide some indication of how high perspective takers handle social conflicts. In the Franzoi et al. (1985) investigation mentioned earlier, both members of romantic couples completed the PT scale, a measure of relationship satisfaction, and an item asking about the way in which the partners resolved conflicts. In particular, this item asked respondents to indicate whether one partner typically "gives in,'' or whether agreement is reached through "mutual give and take.'' It was found that higher perspective-taking scores of males were associated with the couple reporting more "mutual give and take''; females' PT scores were also positively related, but not significantly so. Thus, a more democratic style of conflict resolution was found among those couples whose male partner was higher in a dispositional tendency to entertain others' perspectives.

Rusbult et al. (1991) have approached the conflict question from a slightly different angle, through their focus on *accommodation* in close relationships. Rusbult et al. assume that when one partner in a close relationship behaves badly, whether through omission (e.g., forgetting an anniversary) or commission (e.g., yelling at one's spouse), the primitive, unprocessed impulse of the other partner is typically to retaliate. Thus, destructive acts by one partner generally produce an impulse toward reciprocity in the other. In many instances, however, such retaliation never takes place. Instead, the wronged party inhibits the immediate destructive impulse and instead acts in a constructive fashion, perhaps ignoring the transgression or treating it as only a minor annoyance. Rusbult et al. (1991) term this constructive reaction accommodation. Because accommodation is defined as a willingness by one partner to respond in a constructive way to the negative actions of the other partner, it seems reasonable for our present purposes to consider it a means of conflict management.

Rusbult et al. presented subjects with a series of hypothetical destructive acts that could be committed by one's partner (e.g., ignoring you, criticizing you), and asked them to report their most likely response to such acts. The tendency to make accommodating responses was most powerfully influenced by the subjects' commitment to the relationship, with those more committed to the relationship more likely to accommodate. Above and beyond the effect of commitment, however, a greater self-reported tendency to role take within the relationship was also associated with greater accommodation. Dispositional empathic concern had no such effect. If accommodation is assumed to make overt conflict less frequent, then high perspective takers, it can be argued, probably have fewer conflicts.

Finally, a quite different examination of the perspective taking/ conflict resolution question has been offered by Neale and Bazerman (1983), who investigated the bargaining process as it occurs in labor-management negotiations. In this study pairs of undergraduate students took part in an elaborate simulated contract negotiation between "union" and "management." After being given extensive background information on the simulated negotiation, the participants were urged to be as effective as possible in negotiating for their side. Prior to the session, all participants completed the PT scale.

In terms of overall outcome, a negotiator's success at achieving a contract favorable to his or her side was significantly influenced by the PT scores of both self and opponent. The overall value of the contract (a measure of bargaining success) was greater for those with higher PT scores, and lower for those whose opponents had higher PT scores. Thus, dispositional perspective taking appears to facilitate the negotiation of a favorable contract. Interestingly, however, when participants were asked after the procedure how much they "agreed with" the contract they had negotiated, greater agreement was voiced by those who had faced high PT opponents. Despite the fact that high PT opponents were more successful in negotiating good contracts for their side, facing such an opponent led one to feel more in agreement with the overall deal. It is tempting to interpret this pattern as further evidence that high perspective takers possess an interpersonal style, marked by tact and consideration, which produces greater satisfaction in their interaction partners even when the nature of that interaction is clearly adversarial.

Thus, the evidence regarding conflict avoidance and conflict management generally supports the prediction that perspective taking will be associated with less interpersonal friction. Those high in perspective taking score lower on measures of antagonistic hostility, report engaging in fewer fights and arguments, and show some tendency to settle potential conflicts through constructive actions such as mutual give and take. Evidence regarding empathic concern and personal distress is less plentiful, and also less impressive. Although EC and PD scores are to some degree associated with dispositional hostility, they bear no relation to self-reports of fights and arguments.

Evaluation of the Models

The two contemporary models dealing with empathy's role in social relationships are Davis' mediational model and the Bradbury and Fincham model. The final issue to be addressed, therefore, is the degree to which current evidence supports or fails to support these models. Overall, the Bradbury and Fincham model, with its focus on intrapersonal processes and outcomes, has received encouraging support. Attributional processes do appear to be reliably associated with marital satisfaction, as the model proposes, and seem in fact to have a causal impact on such satisfaction (see Bradbury & Fincham, 1990). Some research (Bradbury & Fincham, 1988) has also revealed satisfaction to be influenced not only by proximal variables such as attributions, but by distal variables (e.g., personality traits) as well.

With regard to the specific role played by empathy-related processes and dispositions, however, the jury is still out. While manipulations of role-taking set, a proximal influence, have been found to influence causal attributions in previous research (e.g., Betancourt, 1990a; Gould & Sigall, 1977; Regan & Totten, 1975), this effect has not been demonstrated within ongoing social relationships. Moreover, the previous research has examined very few dimensions of causal attributions, focusing almost exclusively on locus and controllability. The two studies which have examined dispositional perspective taking as a distal influence on attributions within marital relationships (Fincham & Bradbury, 1989a, 1989b) have reported almost no support for this notion. Thus, while the Bradbury and Fincham model is quite compatible with the organizational model of empathy we have been employing, much work remains to be done in evaluating empathy's place within the Bradbury and Fincham approach.

The evidence is more plentiful, and stronger, regarding Davis' mediational model. This model's focus is less on intrapersonal processes and is more on interpersonal behavior. As noted throughout this chapter, there is good evidence for the first stage of the model; dispositional empathy displays significant associations with a number of specific behaviors implied by the model. One study, Davis and Oathout (1987), has tested and supported the model's contention that behaviors by one social partner will then be predictive of the other partner's perceptions of that behavior. That investigation, along with Long and Andrews (1990), has also supported the model's final stage, the link between partner perceptions and social outcome variables. More generally, the idea that dispositional empathy influences outcome variables such as satisfaction and loneliness through the mediating role of specific relationship behaviors has also been supported (Bruch et al., 1988; Davis & Oathout, 1987; Davis et al., 1985; Davis & Kraus, 1991; Franzoi et al., 1985). Taken as a whole, then, the evidence is generally consistent with the idea that empathic tendencies exert an influence on social relationships and outcomes through their impact on the frequency of specific relationship behaviors and the perceptions those behaviors create in social partners.

Where We Have Been and Where We Should Go

We have in this volume approached the question of empathy from a variety of directions: cognitive and affective, dispositional and situational, genetic and environmental. We have reviewed the results of dozens of empirical investigations and numerous theoretical approaches, trying to assess their strengths and weaknesses. We have organized these sometimes contradictory approaches within a general model which views empathy as a set of related constructs all concerned with the reactions experienced by an observer to the experiences of a target. Within any particular empathy "episode," the model identifies antecedents (situational and individual), processes (more and less cognitive in nature), intrapersonal outcomes (affective and non-affective), and a variety of possible interpersonal outcomes. In the previous nine chapters, some of our questions about empathy were at least partially answered, while others were not. This final chapter, then, will attempt to summarize what we know about the constructs making up the organizational model, and to suggest productive areas for future work.

Where We Have Been

The best evidence suggests that our ancestors evolved as pack-hunting, group-living primates in the African savanna approximately two million years ago. The harsh environmental conditions facing them, including predators, famine, natural disaster, and competitors both inside and outside the pack, were powerful forces in shaping the evolution of capacities and abilities which today make up the constructs which we roughly label empathy. Specifically, the high level of genetic relatedness among members of the same pack means that offering help to in-group members probably conferred an evolutionary advantage because of its contribution to inclusive fitness. As a result, altruism directed toward familiar, similar others was in all likelihood "selected for" by environmental conditions.

As Rushton (1991) has noted, however, genes do not produce social behaviors directly. Instead, "genes code for enzymes which, under the influence of the environment, lay down tracts in the brains and neurohormonal systems of individuals, thus affecting people's minds and the choices they make about behavioral alternatives" (p. 142). Thus, the most likely mechanism for producing altruism among early hominids was probably the evolution of brain structures which make altruism possible, in particular, structures which facilitate the process by which one individual comes to experience an emotional response to the observed experiences of another. In terms of the organizational model, then, altruism was probably fostered by the evolution of mechanisms which make possible a particular intrapersonal outcome. As we have seen (Chapter 7), affective responding to a needy other, whether parallel or reactive, can indeed make help more likely. Thus, the evolutionary advantages of offering help to kin and in-group members in all likelihood contributed to the development of the human capacity for affective reactivity.

At the same time, the need to achieve status and popularity within the pack also placed a premium on early primates' abilities to anticipate and respond to the behavior of other members of the group. This environmental pressure may have therefore contributed to the evolution of a separate empathy-related construct, namely, a non-affective role-taking capacity. In contrast to affective responsivity, however, the development of role-taking capacity may have occurred in large part because of the survival advantages it afforded to individuals who were competing with peers for valuable resources. Thus, present day role-taking capacity may be the result of an earlier evolution of "Machiavellian" intelligence in primates. Today, these two capacities make up what most consider to be the domain of empathy: the ability and/or tendency to understand the thoughts and feelings of others, and our affective responsivity to the experiences of those others.

While evolutionary forces have led to a situation in which the vast majority of humans possess these two important capacities, there are also large individual differences in the degree to which they are utilized. Part of this variation seems due to genetic factors. Twin studies of self-reported affective empathy have produced heritability estimates as high as 70 percent, although such estimates are certainly inflated to some degree (Plomin et al., 1990). Much less is currently known regarding the heritability of role-taking tendencies, although the little available evidence (Davis et al., in press) suggests that it may be lower than that of affective responsiveness.

Individual differences in empathy are not solely the result of genetic influences. Environmental factors, especially those related to parental characteristics and behavior, also play an important role. For example, children raised in close and secure families generally display heightened affective responsivity to others, perhaps because their own emotional needs have been satisfied and they are consequently less preoccupied with self-oriented concerns. Greater affective responsivity is also found in those children whose parents, especially the mother, make use of inductive discipline techniques stressing the consequences to other people of the child's actions. Again, this may result from creating in the child an other-oriented rather than self-oriented view of the world. Finally, although little research has yet addressed this issue, it appears that children's role taking, as opposed to affective responding, may be enhanced by parenting strategies which encourage stepping outside one's usual perspective.

Our discussion thus far has focused on empathic capacities and dispositions. It is now time to direct our attention to the variety of empathy-related processes contained within the organizational model. The most primitive of these require little meaningful cognitive activity. Motor mimicry, for example, provides a fairly direct mechanism by which others' affect can be shared by the observer, without the necessity of higher-order cognitive activity. Other processes rely on increasingly sophisticated cognitive capacities. Conditioning processes, for example, require that the observer be able to associate target cues with one's own prior experiences, and role taking requires that observers deliberately suppress their own perspectives in order to imagine the internal states of the target.

The evidence indicates that both processes which have received significant study, mimicry and role taking, generally increase the likelihood that an observer will experience a parallel affective response to the observed distress of another. The more cognitively advanced process of role taking has an additional effect as well, as it helps transform parallel responses into reactive ones. In particular, role taking by the observer reliably increases the likelihood of a sympathetic, other-oriented concern for the target, and somewhat less reliably increases the likelihood of personal feelings of unease and distress.

The role-taking process affects non-affective outcomes as well. Most strikingly, role taking leads observers to produce attributional explanations for the target's behavior which parallel the target's own—explanations which emphasize situational forces, downplay dispositional ones, and see the target's behavior as somewhat less controllable. However, while role taking may lead observers to see the world as targets do, it is not at all clear that role taking makes observers' judgments about targets any more accurate. Investigations of the link between empathy and accuracy have typically found only weak associations. It might be noted, however, that virtually all contemporary investigations of empathy and accuracy have employed dispositional measures of empathy, and thus have not examined the effects on accuracy of the process of role taking.

Finally, empathic dispositions, processes, and intrapersonal outcomes have all been shown to display a reliable pattern of associations with several interpersonal outcomes. Specifically, greater role taking and stronger affective responsivity are associated with more *helpful* behavior toward others; greater dispositional empathy is for the most part associated with less *aggressive* behavior toward others; and a variety of *social behaviors* occurring within close relationships are significantly influenced by dispositional role taking, empathic concern, and personal distress. Thus, consistent with the view that empathic capacities evolved to foster altruism and enhance social success, empathic dispositions, processes and outcomes are generally associated with exactly such behavioral outcomes.

Where We Should Go

Although prior work has led to some reasonable conclusions regarding the origins and nature of empathy, much remains to be done. In fact, too much remains to be completely addressed in this chapter. However, several issues seem especially worthy of attention, and some of them will be noted in the following pages. This is by no means an exhaustive list, of course, but is a collection of issues which seem both important and underexamined. Let us begin with our poor understanding of empathy-related processes, which may be the single biggest shortcoming of empathy research to date.

Empathy-Related Processes

One key feature of the organizational model is its clear separation of empathy-related outcomes and processes. One somewhat unanticipated consequence of using the model was the degree to which it highlighted deficiencies in our understanding of these processes. These deficiencies take several forms. Some of the processes from which empathic outcomes are said to result have been virtually ignored in empirical work, while others are understood partially at best. Further, the relations among these processes, and the circumstances under which they are triggered by situational and/or personal antecedents, have received only scant attention. Let us examine these shortcomings in turn.

Some Processes have not been Studied

Both Hoffman (1984) and Eisenberg (Eisenberg, Shea et al., 1991) have characterized empathy-related processes in terms of the degree and sophistication of cognitive activity required for their operation. Some empirical attention has been given to one of the least cognitive processes (motor mimicry) and to the most cognitively advanced one (role taking); however, virtually no research efforts have examined the processes in between, specifically, those based on the moderately advanced cognitive processes necessary for associative learning. Hoffman (1984), for example, describes *classical conditioning* and *direct association* as processes in which the observer experiences some emotion because target cues (facial expression, voice, posture) evoke memories of the observer's own direct experience with that emotion. Eisenberg, Shea et al. (1991) describe a related process, *labelling,* in which the observer notices a target cue and interprets it simply on the basis of basic knowledge of the cue's meaning. For example, seeing someone's downturned mouth (target cue), and knowing that such an expression denotes unhappiness (basic knowledge), allows the observer to infer the affective state of the target. In all three cases, however, the cognitive processes involved are thought to be fairly automatic, involving no conscious memory search.

Somewhat more advanced modes of processing are *language-mediated association* (Hoffman, 1984) and the use of *elaborated cognitive networks* (Eisenberg, Shea et al., 1991). In these processes the target cues do not directly and automatically produce affective reactions or inferences in the observer. Instead, with somewhat more effort by the observer, target cues activate information stored in the observer's semantic networks. These two processes are not completely equivalent. Hoffman is more concerned with how language-based cues trigger affective reactions in the observer, and Eisenberg, Shea et al. are more concerned with how the information in these semantic networks is used in forming inferences about the target. However, in each case the process is seen as more effortful and less automatic than the associative processes described earlier.

The key point for this discussion, however, is that virtually none of these hypothesized processes, classical/direct association, labeling, language-mediated association, or elaborated cognitive networks, has actually been measured or manipulated in the context of empathy research. While it makes perfect sense that these associative processes would operate in the predicted fashion, the hypothesized connection between associative processes and empathic outcomes has almost never been demonstrated.

The work of Aronfreed (1970) provides the sole exception to this pattern. In one condition, Aronfreed had child observers and adult targets simultaneously experience the same unpleasant stimulus—a loud noise delivered over earphones. During each noise presentation the adult target displayed clear distress cues. In another condition, the adult displayed the same cues, but never at a time when the child was also experiencing the stimulus. Thus, for some observers the conditions necessary for an associative empathic process were present, with the observer being repeatedly exposed to target distress cues while experiencing unpleasant affect. For other observers, the target's distress cues never co-occurred with the observer's own discomfort, and thus no direct associations between the two were formed. Later, all observers were exposed to a new target who began to display the same distress cues as the previous one. Consistent with the view that associations with prior experiences can lead to empathic outcomes, observers who had experienced distress while exposed to target distress cues later provided significantly more help to the new target; those whose own distress had never been paired with others' cues offered less help.

This experiment therefore suggests that target distress can produce empathic outcomes at least in part because of its ability to evoke affective reactions previously paired with such distress. However, subsequent research has for the most part ignored this process, focusing instead on the somewhat more easily manipulated process of role taking. More particularly, no attempts have been made to examine the operation of associative processes as they naturally occur, rather than through direct manipulation. Thus, there is at present an almost complete absence of empirical documentation of empathy-related associative processes.

Some Processes have been Studied Insufficiently

While the associative processes have generally escaped scrutiny, others have received considerable attention. For example, a number of studies have examined motor mimicry, especially with regard to facial expressions, and its relation to the subjective experience of emotion. Instructional sets designed to induce role taking have been employed even more frequently, with at least 30 investigations exploring their influence on affect, attributions, and helping behavior. Thus, in contrast to the associative processes, something is currently known about the consequences of manipulated role taking. However, the way in which instructional sets have been used has led to a quite limited understanding of the perspective-taking process itself.

In a nutshell, the problem is that researchers employing the "imagine-the-self" and "imagine-the-other" instructions initially developed by Stotland (1969) have generally assumed that observers who are given these directions do as they are told. In fact, this is probably a reasonable assumption, because observers' responses to the manipulation check items frequently employed in this work (e.g., "To what extent did you try to imagine yourself in _____'s place as you watched the videotape?") typically indicate that they followed orders. What is poorly understood, however, is exactly what observers do when attempting to comply with such instructions. For example, assume that an observer has been given "imagine the other" instructions—how exactly does she go about imagining the feelings of another person? By watching the target more intently than usual? By trying harder to interpret overt target cues? By repeatedly asking herself how the target feels? By deliberately imagining how *she* would feel in such circumstances? This final strategy, of course, is what is proposed by the other major role-taking set, the "imagine-self" instructions.

Thus, while instructional sets, especially the "imagine-the-other" set used in much of the recent work on empathy and altruism, have been found to produce quite reliable effects on affective and behavioral outcomes, remarkably little is known about the precise cognitive activities which ensue when these instructions are followed. Specifically, it is not known whether role-taking instructions also trigger the operation of other empathy-related processes, such as language-mediated association, or the use of elaborated cognitive networks. It would not be surprising to find that observers who receive explicit instructions to imagine the feelings of some target consequently increase their use of target cues to access prestored knowledge structures, and then employ that information in making inferences regarding the target. In fact, questions such as these highlight the somewhat blurry lines which separate the more cognitively advanced empathic processes from one another. Attempts to more carefully assess exactly what people do when told to engage in perspective taking might help to clarify these issues.

Relations Among Antecedents and Processes are Poorly Understood

As suggested in the previous paragraph, a relatively superficial understanding currently exists regarding the relationship between various empathy-related processes. A similar problem also applies to the links between such processes and their antecedents—both personal and situational. For example, the organizational model assumes that in any empathy episode one or more processes are activated by one or more antecedents: the disposition of the observer, the strength of target cues, the degree of observer-target similarity, and so on. Traditionally, however, the link between antecedents and processes has not been assessed. Instead, the typical approach has been to focus on how dispositional empathy or observer-target similarity or role-taking instructions influence some intrapersonal or interpersonal outcome, with no real attention given to: 1) whether or not processes actually result from antecedents, 2) if they do, which processes result, or 3) whether the operation of such processes mediates the association between antecedents and outcomes. In large part, of course, this failure has resulted from the scant attention which has in general been given to the processes.

Not only has little attention been given to the links between antecedents and processes, the links among the various processes have also received virtually no meaningful study. One aspect of this problem, the possibility that instructions designed to induce role taking might actually prompt other kinds of processes, such as the use of elaborated cognitive structures, was alluded to previously. This might occur if, as seems likely, there is a general tendency for multiple processes to be activated during empathy episodes. For example, if observer-target similarity prompts a heightened "we-feeling" or "oneness" between observer and target, this might increase the likelihood of more primitive processes such as motor mimicry and more advanced processes such as role taking and elaborated semantic networks. Another possibility is that once certain processes have been triggered, others tend to follow. For example, observers actively attempting to imagine the perspective of a target may become more likely to unconsciously engage in mimicry, or they may be especially primed to respond to target cues with their own affective associations. In any event, the possibility that various empathy-related processes both co-occur and also interact with one another seems very strong, and efforts to better understand when and how this happens would be useful.

New Measurement Methods

A second promising direction for future work lies in the development of new measurement techniques for studying empathy-related questions. In particular, important advances in measurement are now beginning to take place in the two areas of empathy-related processes and affective outcomes. Let us consider each.

Measurement of Empathy-Related Processes
The failure to adequately investigate associative processes, noted in the previous section, may have resulted at least in part from the practical difficulties associated with such research. For example, apart from manipulating the learning history of the observer, as Aronfreed (1970) did, how does an investigator study the operation of ongoing cognitive processes in the laboratory? The difficulties seem obvious. However, this problem has been made increasingly tractable in recent years by the development of techniques for assessing the cognitive processing of social information. The field of social cognition has developed and successfully employed a number of techniques designed to assess memory and judgment processes having to do with social stimuli (Srull, 1984). As such, these techniques seem perfectly designed for examining one domain of interest to empathy researchers, namely, the means by which observers encode, process, store, and retrieve information about targets. Thus, empathy researchers now have the opportunity to employ methods which will considerably improve our understanding of empathy-related processes. In particular, the methodology is available to allow the evaluation of two broad kinds of questions.

Question One: Are Cognitive Processes and Outcomes Regarding Other People Affected when We Empathize with Them?
It seems quite plausible that observers encode and process target information differently if one or more empathy-related processes are

in operation during the observer's exposure to that target, and that this encoding and processing then influences the way the target information is cognitively represented by the observer. Such encoding/storage differences might be especially likely to occur when the more cognitively-advanced processes are involved. Deliberate attempts to understand the target's feelings, for example, might lead observers to construct cognitive representations of targets which are reliably different, perhaps larger, more complex, or more multifaceted, than representations formed in the absence of such role-taking efforts.

A variety of methods are available for assessing cognitive organization of social information. For example, *free recall* methods can be used to learn something about the size and structure of cognitive representations. Some investigators (e.g., Kuiper & Rogers, 1979; Rogers, Kuiper, & Kirker, 1977) have presented subjects with a series of adjectives and asked them to evaluate each word along one of several dimensions. Some commonly used dimensions are *structural* ("Is the word long?"), *phonemic* ("Does the word rhyme with _____?"), and *self-relevant* ("Does the word describe you?"). Following this rating task, subjects are then unexpectedly asked to recall as many of the words as possible. In general, subjects are more successful at recalling words which they earlier rated for self-relevance than they are at recalling words rated along other dimensions. The most common explanation for this finding is that people have relatively large, elaborated cognitive representations of themselves, representations which are activated when subjects are required to make judgments regarding the self-relevance of stimulus words. Later recall of those words is enhanced because it is easier to recall stimuli which have been associated with larger cognitive structures. Thus, success at this free recall task is taken to indicate something about the size and complexity of the self-structure in memory.

Recently, this technique was used in a preliminary attempt to determine if those high in dispositional empathy possess representations of other people which are more "self-like," that is, larger and more detailed, than the representations possessed by those low in dispositional empathy (Davis, Salomon, Hoefer, & DuFresne, 1990). In particular, it was hypothesized that people high in dispositional perspective taking would, over time, develop more complex cognitive representations of familiar others because of their chronic tendency to view the world from others' vantage points; those low in perspective taking were expected to have less elaborate cognitive representations of others.

Undergraduate participants were exposed to 40 adjectives and asked to evaluate each word according to one of four dimensions: 1) structural ("Is the word long or short?"), 2) semantic ("Is the word meaningful to you?"), 3) self-relevant ("Does the word describe you?"), and 4) friend-relevant ("Does the word describe your best friend?"). Following this task, subjects were asked to recall as many words as possible. Consistent with previous research, subjects recalled the words rated for self-relevance significantly more often than any other type. More importantly, however, those low and high in dispositional perspective taking displayed somewhat different recall patterns. In general, those high in PT were better at recalling words in each rating category; this difference was only significant, however, for words rated according to their *friend-relevance*. Thus, individuals characterized by a tendency to imagine others' perspectives displayed a pattern of recall which suggests more extensive cognitive representations of other people.

Another technique frequently used in social cognition research, assessing the *reaction time* required by subjects to respond to some experimental request, can also be applied to empathy research. In general, reaction time is useful because it provides evidence of the operation of some mental process unobservable by any other means. The longer the latency to respond, the stronger the evidence that some mental process is occurring. Batson et al. (1988, Study 5) used this logic to assess the presence of specific empathy-related cognitions in observers following exposure to a needy target. To do so, they assessed reaction time within the context of a *Stroop color-naming task*. In a Stroop task (Stroop, 1938) the subjects name, as quickly as possible, the color of ink in which some visual stimulus (like a word) is printed. The logic of the task is that subjects will be slower to name a word's color (longer reaction times) if they have recently been thinking about something related to that word. Theoretically, this will occur because the simple task of color-naming is disrupted by the individual's processing of the word's semantic *content*. The more recently one has been thinking about a related topic, the more likely that a stimulus word's content will be processed. Someone who has been thinking a lot about Christmas, for instance, will be slower to name the color in which the word "Santa" is printed; thinking about Christmas will have no effect on the time required to name the color of an unrelated word like "baseball."

Batson et al. (1988) presented observers with "imagine-the-other" or "observe" instructions, exposed them to the Katie Banks scenario (Chapter 7), assessed their level of empathic concern, administered a Stroop task, and then gave them the opportunity to offer help to Katie. The Stroop task included words relevant to the victim's plight (e.g., needy, tragic), words relevant to self-punishment (e.g., guilt, shame), words relevant to self-reward (e.g., proud, honor), and neutral words. The reaction time necessary to name the color of the various words serves as an indicator of the degree to which subjects were thinking about these issues. The longer the reaction time, the more thought those words had received. Consistent with Batson's views on altruism, observers experiencing more empathic concern for Katie also were slower in naming the victim-related words, indicating that they had been recently thinking about issues related to the victim's need. Analyses also indicated that, for those receiving empathy instructions, the significant association between empathic concern and helping was largely mediated by the presence of these goal-relevant cognitions; when the latency of responding to victim-related words was controlled statistically, the relation between empathic concern and helping was nonsignificant. This technique therefore allowed an examination of at least some of the thought processes accompanying the experience of particular affective outcomes.

Question Two: Is the Relationship between Self-Representation and Other-Representation Affected when We Empathize?

A different way to employ social cognition assessment techniques is to focus not simply on cognitions about others or the way that information about other people is mentally represented, but on the relationship between self-information and other-information. For example, Aron et al. (1991) have argued that "much of our cognition about the other in a close relationship is cognition in which the other is treated as self or confused with self" (p. 242). That is, others who are close to us may be represented in ways which "merge" the cognitive structures corresponding to self and other. The key question, then, does not so much concern the representation of other people per se as it does the connection between self- and other-representations. Aron et al., of course, are primarily concerned with the inclusion of others within self as it occurs in close ongoing relationships. The possibility also exists, however, that empathy-related processes might also affect the nature of this self-other cognitive connection.

No research to date has explicitly addressed this notion, but some investigations have used techniques which allow an examination of self-other overlap, techniques which could easily be used in empathy contexts. Deutsch and Mackesy (1985), for example, had pairs of friends and nonfriends simply list their 10 most self-descriptive traits. Friends were found to have significantly greater overlap in the traits listed, and thus an ostensibly greater overlap in their self- and other-schemas, than nonfriends. Aron et al. (1991, Study 3) report a reaction time study in which married subjects were initially asked to rate the degree to which a series of traits were characteristic of self and of spouse. Later they were asked to make timed ''yes-no'' judgments as to whether these traits were descriptive of self. Aron et al.'s prediction was that subjects would be slower in making these judgments of self-relevance if the trait was one on which the subject and spouse differed (i.e., one spouse had the trait and the other did not). Their reasoning is that if there is a substantial degree of overlap in the cognitive representation of self and other (as Aron et al. assumed there would be for husbands and wives), then making judgments about the self-relevance of traits can be slightly confusing, and will require a memory search and a decision as to whether the trait applies to self, other, or both. The task is somewhat simpler if both self and other possess the trait (there is no need to determine which individual possesses the trait in order to answer the question), and a bit more difficult if only one possesses it (such a determination is necessary). Thus, judgments in the latter case should take more time. In fact, this is precisely the pattern which Aron et al. report. Both the Aron et al. (1991) and Deutsch and Mackesy (1985) studies, therefore, provide examples of methodologies which could be used to assess the overlap of self- and other-representations occurring within observers.

Measurement of Affective Outcomes

While the use of new techniques to study empathy-related cognitive processes is just beginning, the development of new methods for assessing affective responses to others is well underway. In recent years Nancy Eisenberg and a number of colleagues have systematically begun the task of moving beyond self-reports as the sole method of measuring emotional responses to a target, and in particular have focused on facial expression and physiological responding, methods which do not require any reporting by the observer at all.

The reason for developing such new methods is simple. While self-reported emotions are quick and easy to collect, they do have some problems. Particularly, as Eisenberg and Fabes (1990) note, they may be difficult to use with children because of their difficulty in reporting feelings accurately, and they may be subject to strong self-presentation and social desirability biases (see Chapter 3). To the degree that observers' facial expressions and physiological reactions do not require or allow the deliberate presentation of self, these measures may provide superior indices of affective responsivity. One problem with such measures, however, is that they may be too undifferentiated. In other words, it may not be possible to clearly distinguish between specific affective states without using the observer's own self-report.

In a series of recent studies, Eisenberg has provided evidence that such measures can be used to provide markers of at least two different emotional reactions: empathic concern and personal distress. For example, studies with children have found that the facial expression of sadness/concern tends to result from inductions designed to produce feelings of empathic concern (Eisenberg, Fabes et al., 1988; Eisenberg, Schaller et al., 1988), and that facial distress is somewhat more likely to result from inductions designed to induce personal distress (Eisenberg, Fabes et al., 1988; Eisenberg & Fabes, 1990). A similar though weaker pattern has been found for adults (e.g. Eisenberg, Fabes, Schaller, Miller et al., 1991; Eisenberg, Schaller et al., 1988).

Two measures of physiological responding, heart rate and skin conductance, have been used with some success in this line of research. Heart rate can be used as a marker of either affective state, as increased heart rate is thought to be a rough indicator of personal distress reactions, while decreased heart rate is said to be an indicator of empathic concern. The theoretical explanation for this is that heart rate deceleration accompanies the intake of information—the outward attention to the other person necessary for feelings of empathic concern. In contrast, heart rate acceleration accompanies the processing of self-relevant information—the anxious, apprehensive coping response that occurs when one is feeling high levels of personal distress (Eisenberg & Fabes, 1990). In fact, the results of a number of studies have generally supported this view (e.g., Eisenberg, Fabes et al., 1988; Eisenberg, Fabes et al., 1989; Eisenberg, Fabes, Schaller, Miller et al., 1991; Eisenberg, Schaller et al., 1988).

While heart rate is thought to serve as an indicator of empathic concern or personal distress largely because it indicates whether attention is focused inward (distress) or outward (concern), skin conductance is generally considered to be a more direct measure of the actual intensity of autonomic arousal. Because personal distress is thought to be a more arousing state than empathic concern (Eisenberg & Fabes, 1990), greater skin conductance may therefore be a better indicator of distress reactions than it is of empathic concern. The initial evidence tends to support this view.

Eisenberg, Fabes, Schaller, Miller et al. (1991) and Eisenberg and Fabes (1990) both report data which indicates that stimuli designed to induce distress prompted greater skin conductance in observers than did stimuli designed to induce sympathy.

Thus, the evidence available so far suggests that it is possible to assess important affective states without employing self-reports. However, much remains to be done in this area. For example, almost all of the research has so far been conducted by a single set of investigators. While the early results are encouraging, attempts by others to replicate these findings need to be made. More importantly, the connections between these physiological measures and other empathy-related constructs remain to be explored. For example, to what degree do the empathy-related processes in the organizational model influence these facial and physiological responses? To what degree are non-affective responses such as attributions related to heart rate and skin conductance? What are the links between physiological responding and interpersonal behaviors such as helping and aggression? All of these questions deserve empirical attention from empathy researchers in the years ahead.

Usefulness of the Organizational Model

A final issue to be addressed is the usefulness of the organizational model. Just what value does this model have in helping us frame the questions which will guide future empathy research? From one perspective, of course, the model has already demonstrated its usefulness by providing a framework for conceptualizing and analyzing a large number of investigations differing in their theoretical orientation and methodological approach. In fact, the vast preponderance of research we have examined was readily interpretable within this framework. Beyond this rather large advantage, however, what is the long-term utility of the organizational model likely to be? Are there further advantages resulting from its use? In what ways does it fall short of providing a truly comprehensive means of conceptualizing the field? Those are the questions to be addressed in this section.

Benefits of the Model
One benefit of the organizational model is that by carefully distinguishing among antecedents, processes, and outcomes it has been possible to discern "holes" in the body of research evidence, issues which have been relatively under-examined in previous investigations. In fact, we have already discussed one example of this, the almost complete lack of systematic study given to empathy-related

processes. The careful separation of antecedents, processes, and outcomes helped make this clear—without such an organizational device, however, this failure was not so readily apparent.

A second, related, benefit of the organizational model is that it focuses attention on the issue of proximal vs. distal influences on behavior. In particular, it raises issues about the extent to which the effects on interpersonal behavior of some constructs (e.g., antecedents such as dispositional empathy or observer-target similarity) are mediated by empathy-related processes and intrapersonal outcomes. While theoretical treatments of empathy have never completely ignored this question, many empirical investigations, especially those using dispositional empathy measures, have given it little attention. Thus, a typical research strategy has been to select some antecedent variable and assess its association with some interpersonal outcome such as helping, aggression, or social behavior. The association is taken at face value and the question of exactly how this association is produced is often overlooked. One laudable exception to this general pattern is the recent research focusing on the question of "true" altruistic helping (Chapter 7). Many of these investigations manipulated empathic antecedents or processes, and then measured both intrapersonal outcomes (usually affective) and the interpersonal outcome of helping, thus making it possible to examine the mediating role of intrapersonal outcomes.

Some of the evidence reviewed in previous chapters has generally supported the mediational logic of the organizational model. Somewhat stronger associations were found between constructs adjacent in the model (e.g., affective responses and helping) than between those more distant from one another (e.g., similarity and helping). Even so, interpersonal behavior in all the domains we examined—helping, aggression, and social behavior—has been found to display significant and sometimes considerable associations with the most distant element in the model, dispositional empathy. Logically, of course, this is not a fatal problem for the model. Substantial correlations between dispositions and behavior could still be largely mediated by the operation of empathy-related processes and the experiencing of intrapersonal outcomes. Nevertheless, the size of these associations suggests that individual differences in empathy may also affect interpersonal behavior more directly, without much mediation by other constructs in the organizational model.

To imagine how this might work, consider the case of helping behavior. One possibility is that high levels of dispositional empathy are associated with possessing *personal standards and values* which prompt behavior which is helpful, non-aggressive, and socially beneficial (e.g., Hoffman, 1987). That is, independent of the specific operation of any empathy-related process, those high in dispositional empathy may possess and act on humane, tolerant values. They may consequently engage in more helpful, less contentious behaviors for reasons which have little or nothing to do with empathy per se. Another possibility is that those high in dispositional empathy initially do act in more helpful ways because of the processes and outcomes specified by the model, and that as a result they eventually develop *characteristic patterns of behavior* which are generally prosocial. Repeated instances of these acts can eventually lead to the development of behavioral "scripts" which are then more or less automatically evoked by the appropriate social stimulus. Eventually, those high in dispositional empathy may reach the point where exposure to certain stimuli (needy targets, for instance) causes these behavioral scripts to "go off" automatically without any necessary activation of specific processes. Thus, the relationship between dispositional empathy and helping may originally be mediated by processes and outcomes in the model, but might eventually become independent of them.

A third benefit of the organizational model is that it focuses attention on some specific ways in which cognitive and affective facets of empathy interact, emphasizing the truly multidimensional nature of empathy. Of course, the notion that cognition and affect interact in the experience of empathy is not a new one. Hoffman's (1984) theory explicitly outlines how the development of increasingly sophisticated cognitive capacities transforms the affective responses we have to others' distress. Other developmental psychologists (e.g., Feshbach 1978; Iannotti, 1975) have also considered the links between cognitive abilities and affective responding. More recently, Eisenberg, Shea et al. (1991) have carefully considered ways in which cognitive processes and affective responding might influence one another within specific empathy episodes.

The organizational model focuses attention on empathy's multidimensional nature in one very specific way by highlighting the links between and among empathy-related processes, affective outcomes, and non-affective outcomes. By explicitly separating these three constructs and examining the evidence for connections between them, it becomes apparent that there are reliable associations between cognitive processes (e.g., role taking) and cognitive outcomes (e.g., attributions), and that these outcomes contribute meaningfully to the experience of particular affective outcomes (e.g., anger, empathic concern). Moreover, some research (e.g., Weiner, 1980a, 1980b; Schmidt & Weiner, 1988) suggests that the link between attributional judgments and behavioral outcomes is almost completely mediated by affective responses. Thus, research in the areas of both helping and aggression *support* the conclusion that while affective outcomes are the most important proximal influence on behavior, cognitive processes and outcomes also contribute directly and substantially to these affective reactions. The interplay between the cognitive and affective constructs in the model is therefore readily apparent.

Limitations of the Model

Although the organizational model seems to offer some clear benefits, it is by no means perfect. In particular, it seems to have at least two limitations. First, the model as it now stands is completely recursive, with the causal arrows only going in one direction, from antecedents to processes to intrapersonal outcomes to interpersonal outcomes. In general, such an approach makes sense in that it seems likely that this causal sequence will operate most of the time. Furthermore, it is reasonable, at least initially, to keep the model as simple as possible and see how well it can account for research findings. However, it seems highly likely that constructs which occur "later" in the model may also feed back into earlier constructs. Figure 10.1 displays a revised, non-recursive version of the model which illustrates some possible feedback loops.

One likely feedback loop would connect *intrapersonal outcomes with empathy-related processes*. This loop would recognize the possibility that experiencing affective reactions to targets, or reaching cognitive judgments about them, might influence subsequent processes. Eisenberg, Shea et al. (1991), for example, have proposed that experiencing parallel affective reactions (what they term empathy) will frequently prompt cognitive activity in the observer as s/he attempts to understand the origins of this vicarious emotional state. Such cognitive activity could include associative processes (such as direct association), but most frequently would consist of higher-order processes such as role taking. Depending upon a number of situational (e.g., intensity of cues) and dispositional (e.g., possessing other-oriented values) factors, this processing can lead to the subsequent experience of either empathic concern or personal distress. Therefore, according to this view, empathic concern and personal distress in many cases depend on secondary cognitive processes resulting from an earlier parallel affective response.

A second potential feedback loop would connect *interpersonal outcomes and intrapersonal outcomes*. This loop would recognize the possibility that behavior directed toward a target might have

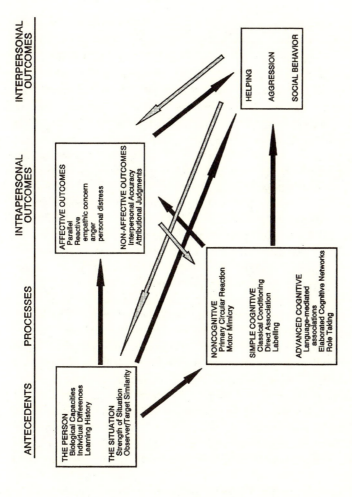

ANTECEDENTS   PROCESSES   INTRAPERSONAL OUTCOMES   INTERPERSONAL OUTCOMES

THE PERSON
Biological Capacities
Individual Differences
Learning History

THE SITUATION
Strength of Situation
Observer/Target Similarity

NONCOGNITIVE
Primary Circular Reaction
Motor Mimicry

SIMPLE COGNITIVE
Classical Conditioning
Direct Association
Labelling

ADVANCED COGNITIVE
Language-mediated
associations
Elaborated Cognitive Networks
Role Taking

AFFECTIVE OUTCOMES
Parallel
Reactive
empathic concern
anger
personal distress

NON-AFFECTIVE OUTCOMES
Interpersonal Accuracy
Attributional Judgments

HELPING

AGGRESSION

SOCIAL BEHAVIOR

FIGURE 10.1
Possible alterations in the organizational model.

effects on observers' subsequent emotions and judgments. For example, helping a distressed other may serve to reduce one's level of personal distress as the target's need is reduced; alternatively, acts of aggression (resulting from a lack of empathic reaction) might reinforce negative judgments about the target ("I hurt him, he must deserve it."). In fact, as we consider this issue, it seems that an alternative way to conceive of such feedback effects is through a loop connecting *interpersonal outcomes and situational antecedents*. That is, the result of behavior directed toward a target (helping, aggression) may have its most powerful impact on the need state of that target and the target's resulting distress cues. These cues, which constitute a powerful situational antecedent, can then significantly influence subsequent processing and outcomes. Thus, all of these proposed feedback loops point to the same conclusion: that any empathy episode is likely to consist of one or more sequences of "antecedent/process/outcome" chains, with the results of earlier sequences likely to influence subsequent ones.

A second limitation of the organizational model as it currently stands is its exclusive focus on the *individual observer*. The model identifies antecedent factors which have an impact on the observer, processes which take place within the observer, and outcomes which are experienced or performed by the observer. What is lacking is a consideration of emergent processes or outcomes resulting from the interaction of observer and target. Of course, the vast majority of empathy investigations share this individual-oriented approach. In effect, that is why the organizational model has taken the form that it has. However, some recent research illustrates another way of conceptualizing empathy which is more difficult for the model to incorporate.

Levenson and Ruef (1992), for example, found observers to be more accurate in judging targets' affective states when there was a high degree of physiological "linkage" between observer and target—that is, when observer and target displayed similar patterns of arousal on measures of heart rate and skin conductance. Thus, observer accuracy was not influenced by an individual variable (e.g., the physiological state of the observer alone), but by a dyadic variable, linkage, which depends on the responses of both observer and target. Similarly, Ickes et al. (1990) found interpersonal accuracy in mixed-sex dyads to be related to several dyadic variables such as the total number of verbalizations occurring between the two participants, number of gazes directed at each other, and total amount of smiling. Thus, characteristics of the interaction process itself were associated with the outcome of accuracy. In neither case, the

Levenson and Ruef study or the Ickes et al. investigation, can the organizational model easily incorporate these emergent, dyad-level constructs. As research findings based on this more sophisticated view of the observer-target relationship accumulate, this model, or any which seeks to account for empathy-related processes and outcomes, must be able to accommodate them.

Conclusion

We have covered a lot of ground in our attempt to understand the processes and outcomes which constitute the empathy domain. The going has occasionally been difficult, more difficult than necessary, actually, because of long-standing disagreements regarding empathy's "true" nature. As our discussion now draws to a close, it seems an appropriate time to re-emphasize the inclusive spirit which has informed the organizational model and this book. The view of empathy taken here, that it consists of a set of related constructs all having to do with the reactions of an observer to the experiences of a target, gives equal status to both cognition and emotion, process and outcome, disposition and situation. All of these constructs are necessary if we are to provide the fullest account of this complex phenomenon which helps span, at least temporarily, the perpetual gulf which lies between individual social actors.

Empathy occupies a strategically crucial location in modern psychology, lying at the border which separates the individual from the other, ego from alter. The capacity to set aside egocentric concerns and entertain the point of view of other people provides a kind of bridge which links otherwise isolated persons, allowing those separate entities, at least for a time, to share thoughts, feelings, and goals. This sharing makes possible some of the most admirable human activities, those which raise our motivations from the purely selfish to the selfless, and which give us the occasional opportunity to display a true nobility of purpose. The possession of such empathic capacities does not, of course, ensure such nobility—evidence of that is all too obvious. Our capacity for other-oriented thinking and acting, however, makes it possible, and this makes the study of empathy and related phenomena a most worthy one for modern psychology.

REFERENCES

Adelmann, P. K., & Zajonc, R. B. (1989). Facial efference and the experience of emotion. *Annual Review of Psychology, 40,* 249–280.

Aderman, D. (1972). Elation, depression, and helping behavior. *Journal of Personality and Social Psychology, 24,* 91–101.

Aderman, D., Brehm, S. S., & Katz, L. B. (1974). Empathic observation of an innocent victim: The just world revisited. *Journal of Personality and Social Psychology, 29,* 342–347.

Ainsworth, M. D. S., Bell, S. M. V., & Stayton, D. J. (1971). Individual differences in strange situation behavior of one-year-olds. In H. R. Schaffer (Ed.), *The origins of human social relations,* pp. 17–57. London: Academic Press.

Ainsworth, M. D. S., & Wittig, B. A. (1969). Attachment and exploratory behavior of one-year-olds in a strange situation. In B. M. Foss (Ed.), *Determinants of infant behavior,* (Vol. 4), pp. 113–136. New York: Barnes & Noble.

Archer, R. L., Foushee, H. C., Davis, M. H., and Aderman, D. (1979). Emotional empathy in a courtroom simulation: a person-situation interaction. *Journal of Applied Social Psychology, 9,* 275–291.

Aron, A., Aron, E. N., Tudor, M., & Nelson, G. (1991). Close relationships as including other in the self. *Journal of Personality and Social Psychology, 60,* 241–253.

Aronfreed, J. (1970). The socialization of altruistic and sympathetic behavior: Some theoretical and experimental analyses. In L. Macauley & L. Berkowitz (Eds.), *Altruism and helping behavior: social psychological studies of some antecedents and consequences,* pp. 103–126. New York: Academic Press.

Averill, J. R. (1982). *Anger and aggression: An essay on emotion.* New York: Springer-Verlag.

Bandura, A. (1973). *Aggression: A social learning analysis.* Englewood Cliffs, NJ: Prentice-Hall.

Barnett, M. A. (1987). Empathy and related responses in children. In N. Eisenberg & J. Strayer, (Eds.) *Empathy and its development,* pp. 146–162. Cambridge: Cambridge University Press.

Barnett, M. A., Howard, J. A., King, L. M., & Dino, G. A. (1980). Antecedents of empathy: Retrospective accounts of early socialization. *Personality and Social Psychology Bulletin, 6,* 361–365.

Barnett, M. A., King, L. M., Howard, J. A., & Dino, G. A. (1980). Empathy in young children: Relation to parents' empathy, affection, and emphasis on the feelings of others. *Developmental Psychology, 16,* 243–244.

Baron, R. A. (1971a). Aggression as a function of magnitude of victim's pain cues, level of prior anger arousal, and aggressor-victim similarity. *Journal of Personality and Social Psychology, 18,* 48–54.

Baron, R. A. (1971b). Magnitude of victim's pain cues and level of prior anger arousal as determinants of adult aggressive behavior. *Journal of Personality and Social Psychology, 17,* 236–243.

Baron, R. A. (1974). Aggression as a function of victim's pain cues, level of prior anger arousal, and exposure to an aggressive model. *Journal of Personality and Social Psychology, 29,* 117–124.

Baron, R. A. (1977). *Human aggression.* New York: Plenum Press.

Baron, R. A. (1979). Effects of victim's pain cues, victim's race, and level of prior instigation upon physical aggression. *Journal of Applied Social Psychology, 9,* 103–114.

Baron, R. A., & Ransberger, V. M. (1978). Ambient temperature and the occurrence of collective violence: The "long hot summer" revisited. *Journal of Personality and Social Psychology, 36,* 351–360.

Batson, C. D. (1987). Prosocial motivation: is it ever truly altruistic? In L. Berkowitz (Ed.), *Advances in experimental social psychology,* (Vol. 20), pp. 65–122. New York: Academic Press.

Batson, C. D. (1991). *The altruism question: Toward a social-psychological answer.* Hillsdale, NJ: Lawrence Erlbaum Associates.

Batson, C. D., Batson, J. G., Griffitt, C. A., Barrientos, S., Brandt, J. R., Sprengelmeyer, P., & Bayly, M. J. (1989). Negative-state relief and the empathy-altruism hypothesis. *Journal of Personality and Social Psychology, 56,* 922–933.

Batson, C. D., Batson, J. G., Slingsby, J. K., Harrell, K. L., Peekna, H. M., & Todd, R. M. (1991). Empathic joy and the empathy-altruism hypothesis. *Journal of Personality and Social Psychology, 61,* 413–426.

Batson, C. D., Bolen, M. H., Cross, J. A., & Neuringer-Benefiel, H. (1986). Where is the altruism in the altruistic personality? *Journal of Personality and Social Psychology, 50,* 212–220.

Batson, C. D., Duncan, B. D., Ackerman, P., Buckley, T., & Birch, K. (1981). Is empathic emotion a source of altruistic motivation? *Journal of Personality and Social Psychology, 40,* 290–302.

Batson, C. D., Dyck, J. L., Brandt, J. R., Batson, J. G., Powell, A. L.,
McMaster, M. R., & Griffitt, C. (1988). Five studies testing two new
egoistic alternatives to the empathy-altruism hypothesis. *Journal of
Personality and Social Psychology, 55,* 52–77.

Batson, C. D., Fultz, J., & Schoenrade, P. A. (1987). Distress and empathy:
Two qualitatively distinct vicarious emotions with different
motivational consequences. *Journal of Personality, 55,* 19–39.

Batson, C. D., O'Quin, K., Fultz, J., Vanderplas, M., & Isen, A. M. (1983).
Influence of self-reported distress and empathy on egoistic versus
altruistic motivation to help. *Journal of Personality and Social
Psychology, 45,* 706–718.

Bavelas, J. B., Black, A., Lemery, C. R., MacInnis, S., & Mullett, J. (1986).
Experimental methods of studying "elementary motor mimicry."
Journal of Nonverbal Behavior, 10, 102–119.

Bavelas, J. B., Black, A., Lemery, C. R., & Mullett, J. (1986). "I *show*
how you feel": Motor mimicry as a communicative act. *Journal of
Personality and Social Psychology, 50,* 322–329.

Bavelas, J. B., Black, A., Lemery, C. R., & Mullett, J. (1987). Motor mimicry
as primitive empathy. In N. Eisenberg & J. Strayer (Eds.), *Empathy and
its development,* pp. 317–338. Cambridge: Cambridge University Press.

Baylis, G. C., Rolls, E. T., & Leonard, C. M. (1985). Selectivity between
faces in the responses of a population of neurons in the cortex in the
superior temporal sulcus of the monkey. *Brain Research, 342,* 91–102.

Berkowitz, L. (1962). *Aggression: A social psychological analysis.* New
York: McGraw-Hill.

Berkowitz, L. (1969). Resistance to improper dependency relationships.
Journal of Experimental Social Psychology, 5, 283–294.

Berkowitz, L. (1978). Whatever happened to the frustration-aggression
hypothesis? *American Behavioral Scientist, 21,* 691–708.

Berkowitz, L. (1982). Aversive conditions as stimuli to aggression. In
L. Berkowitz (Ed.), *Advances in experimental social psychology* (Vol. 15),
pp. 249–288. New York: Academic Press.

Berkowitz, L. (1984). Some effects of thoughts on anti- and pro-social
influences of media events: A cognitive neo-association analysis.
Psychological Bulletin, 95, 410–427.

Berkowitz, L. (1989). Frustration-aggression hypothesis: Examination and
reformulation. *Psychological Bulletin, 106,* 59–73.

Bernstein, W. M., & Davis, M. H. (1982). Perspective-taking,
self-consciousness, and accuracy in person perception. *Basic and
Applied Social Psychology, 3,* 1–19.

Bernstein, W. M., McGuire, T. V., Raskin, P. M., Ganzach, Y., & Thiry, C. P.
(1988). Perspective taking increases both differential and stereotypic
accuracy. Unpublished manuscript.

Berscheid, E. (1983). Emotion. In H.H. Kelley, E. Berscheid, A.
Christensen, J. H. Harvey, T. L. Huston, G. Levinger, E. McClintock,
L. A. Peplau, & D. R. Peterson (Eds.) *Close Relationships,*
pp. 110–168. New York: W. H. Freeman and Co.

Betancourt, H. (1990a). An attribution-empathy model of helping behavior: Behavioral intentions and judgments of help-giving. *Personality and Social Psychology Bulletin, 16,* 573–591.

Betancourt, H. (1990b). An attributional approach to intergroup and international conflict. S. Graham & V. Folkes (Eds.), *Attribution theory: Applications to achievement, mental health, and interpersonal conflict.* Hillsdale, NJ: Lawrence Erlbaum Associates.

Betancourt, H., & Blair, I. (1992). A cognition (attribution)-emotion model of violence in conflict situations. *Personality and Social Psychology Bulletin, 18,* 343–350.

Block, J. (1961). *The Q-sort method in personality assessment and psychiatric research.* Springfield, IL: Charles C. Thomas.

Block, J. H. (1976). Assessing sex differences: Issues, problems, and pitfalls. *Merrill-Palmer Quarterly, 22,* 283–308.

Borke, H. (1971). Interpersonal perception of young children: Egocentrism or empathy? *Developmental Psychology, 5,* 263–269.

Borke, H. (1973). The development of empathy in Chinese and American children between three and six years of age: A cross-culture study. *Developmental Psychology, 9,* 102–108.

Borman, W. C. (1977). Consistency of rating accuracy and rating errors in the judgement of human performance. *Organizational Behavior and Human Performance, 20,* 238–252.

Borman, W. C. (1979). Individual differences correlates of accuracy in evaluating others' performance effectiveness. *Applied Psychological Measurement, 3,* 103–115.

Bradbury, T. N., & Fincham, F. D. (1987). Affect and cognition in close relationships: Towards an integrative model. *Cognition and Emotion, 1,* 59–87.

Bradbury, T. N., & Fincham, F. D. (1988). Individual difference variables in close relationships: A contextual model of marriage as an integrative framework. *Journal of Personality and Social Psychology, 54,* 1–9.

Bradbury, T. N., & Fincham, F. D. (1990). Attributions in marriage: Review and critique. *Psychological Bulletin, 107,* 3–33.

Brehm, S. S., & Aderman, D. (1977). On the relationship between empathy and the actor versus observer hypothesis. *Journal of Research in Personality, 11,* 340–346.

Brehm, S. S., Fletcher, B. L., & West, V. (1981). Effects of empathy instructions on first-grader's liking of other people. *Child Study Journal, 11,* 1–15.

Brehm, S. S., Powell, L. K., & Coke, J. S. (1984). The effects of empathic instructions upon donating behavior: Sex differences in young children. *Sex Roles, 10,* 405–416.

Brothers, L. (1989). A biological perspective on empathy. *American Journal of Psychiatry, 146,* 10–19.

Bruch, M. A., Kaflowitz, N. G., & Pearl, L. (1988). Mediated and nonmediated relationships of personality components to loneliness. *Journal of Social and Clinical Psychology, 6,* 346–355.

Bryant, B. K. (1982). An index of empathy for children and adolescents. *Child Development, 53,* 413–425.

Buck, R. (1980). Nonverbal behavior and the theory of emotion: the facial feedback hypothesis. *Journal of Personality and Social Psychology, 38,* 811–824.

Buss, A. H. (1966a). The effect of harm on subsequent aggression. *Journal of Experimental Research in Personality, 1,* 249–255.

Buss, A. H. (1966b). Instrumentality of aggression, feedback, and frustration as determinants of physical aggression. *Journal of Personality and Social Psychology, 3,* 153–162.

Buss, A. H., & Durkee, M. (1957). An inventory for assessing different kinds of hostility. *Journal of Consulting Psychology, 21,* 343–348.

Buss, A. H., & Plomin, R. (1975). *A temperament theory of personality development.* New York: John Wiley & Sons.

Caplan, A. L. (1980). A critical examination of current sociobiological theory: Adequacy and implications. In G. W. Barlow & J. Silverberg (Eds.), *Sociobiology: Beyond nature/nurture?,* pp. 97–121. Boulder, CO: Westview Press, Inc.

Campos, J. J., Barrett, K. C., Lamb, M. E., Goldsmith, H. H., & Stenberg, C. (1983). Socioemotional development. In P. Mussen (Ed.), *Handbook of Child Psychology,* 4th ed. (Vol. II), pp. 784–915. New York: John Wiley & Sons.

Carlo, G., Eisenberg, N., Troyer, D., Switzer, G., & Speer, A. L. (1991). The altruistic personality: In what contexts is it apparent? *Journal of Personality and Social Psychology, 61,* 450–458.

Carlson, M., & Miller, N. (1987). Explanation of the relation between negative mood and helping. *Psychological Bulletin, 102,* 91–108.

Chandler, M. J. (1973). Egocentrism and antisocial behavior: The assessment and training of social perspective-taking skills. *Developmental Psychology, 9,* 326–332.

Chandler, M. J., & Greenspan, S. (1972). Ersatz egocentrism: A reply to H. Borke. *Developmental Psychology, 7,* 104–106.

Chapin, F. S. (1942). Preliminary standardization of a social insight scale. *American Sociological Review, 7,* 214–225.

Chlopan, B. E., McCain, M. L., Carbonell, J. L., & Hagen, R. L. (1985). Empathy: Review of available measures. *Journal of Personality and Social Psychology, 48,* 635–653.

Cialdini, R. B., Baumann, D. J., & Kenrick, D. T. (1981). Insights from sadness: A three-step model of the development of altruism as hedonism. *Developmental Review, 1,* 207–223.

Cialdini, R. B., Darby, B. L., & Vincent, J. E. (1973). Transgression and altruism: A case for hedonism. *Journal of Experimental Social Psychology, 9,* 502–516.

Cialdini, R. B., & Kenrick, D. T. (1976). Altruism as hedonism: A social development perspective on the relationship of negative mood state and helping. *Journal of Personality and Social Psychology, 34,* 907–914.

Cialdini, R. B., Schaller, M., Houlihan, D., Arps, K., Fultz, J., & Beaman, A. L. (1987). Empathy-based helping: Is it selflessly or selfishly motivated? *Journal of Personality and Social Psychology, 52,* 749–758.

Clary, E. G., & Orenstein, L. (1991). The amount and effectiveness of help: The relationship of motives and abilities to helping behavior. *Personality and Social Psychology Bulletin, 17,* 58–64.

Clary, E. G, & Snyder, M. (1991). A functional analysis of altruism and prosocial behavior: The case of volunteerism. In M. S. Clark (Ed.), *Review of personality and social psychology: prosocial behavior,* (Vol. 12), pp. 119–148. Newbury Park, CA: Sage.

Coke, J. S., Batson, C. D., & McDavis, K. (1978). Empathic mediation of helping: A two-stage model. *Journal of Personality and Social Psychology, 36,* 752–766.

Comte, I. A. (1851/1875). *System of positive polity* (Vol. I). London: Longmans, Green & Co.

Cook, W. W., & Medley, D. M. (1954). Proposed hostility and pharisaic-virtue scales for the MMPI. *The Journal of Applied Psychology, 38,* 414–418.

Costa, P. T., Jr., & McCrae, R. R. (1985). *The NEO Personality Inventory manual.* Odessa, FL: Psychological Assessment Resources.

Cronbach, L. J. (1955). Processes affecting scores on understanding of others and assuming "similarity." *Psychological Bulletin, 52,* 177–193.

Cross, D. G., & Sharpley, C. F. (1982). Measurement of empathy with the Hogan empathy scale. *Psychological Reports, 50,* 62.

Darwin, C. (1859/1966). *On the origin of species.* Cambridge, MA: Harvard University Press.

Davis, M. H. (1980). A multidimensional approach to individual differences in empathy. JSAS *Catalog of Selected Documents in Psychology, 10,* 85.

Davis, M. H. (1983a). The effects of dispositional empathy on emotional reactions and helping: A multidimensional approach. *Journal of Personality, 51,* 167–184.

Davis, M. H. (1983b). Measuring individual differences in empathy: Evidence for a multidimensional approach. *Journal of Personality and Social Psychology, 44,* 113–126.

Davis, M. H. (1992). [Dispositional empathy, dispositional hostility, and the Big Five personality dimensions]. Unpublished raw data.

Davis, M. H., & Franzoi, S. L. (1986). Adolescent loneliness, self-disclosure, and private self-consciousness: a longitudinal investigation. *Journal of Personality and Social Psychology, 51,* 595–608.

Davis, M. H., & Franzoi, S. L. (1991). Stability and change in adolescent self-consciousness and empathy. *Journal of Research in Personality, 25,* 70–87.

Davis, M. H., Franzoi, S. L., & Wellinger, P. (1985). *Personality, social behavior, and loneliness.* Presented at the 93rd annual convention of the American Psychological Association, Los Angeles.

Davis, M. H., Hull, J. G., Young, R. D., & Warren, G. G. (1987). Emotional reactions to dramatic film stimuli: The influence of cognitive and emotional empathy. *Journal of Personality and Social Psychology, 52,* 126–133.

Davis, M. H., & Kraus, L. A. (1991). Dispositional empathy and social relationships. In W. H. Jones & D. Perlman (Eds.), *Advances in Personal Relationships* (Vol. 3), pp. 75–115. London: Jessica Kingsley Publishers.

Davis, M. H., Luce, C., & Kraus, S. J. (in press). The heritability of dispositional empathy. *Journal of Personality.*

Davis, M. H., & Oathout, H. A. (1987). Maintenance of satisfaction in romantic relationships: Empathy and relational competence. *Journal of Personality and Social Psychology, 53,* 397–410.

Davis, M. H., & Oathout, H. A. (1992). The effect of dispositional empathy on romantic relationship behaviors: Heterosocial anxiety as a moderating influence. *Personality and Social Psychology Bulletin, 18,* 76–83.

Davis, M. H., Salomon, K., Hoefer, P., & Dufresne, D. (1990). *The effects of perspective taking on schemata: Encoding self- and other-relevant information.* Unpublished manuscript.

Dawkins, R. (1976). *The selfish gene.* Oxford: Oxford University Press.

Deardorff, P. A., Finch, A. J., Kendall, P. C., Lira, F., & Indrisano, V. (1975). Empathy and socialization in repeat offenders, first offenders, and normals. *Journal of Counseling Psychology, 22,* 453–455.

Deutsch, F. M., & Mackesy, M. E. (1985). Friendship and the development of self-schemas: The effects of talking about others. *Personality and Social Psychology Bulletin, 11,* 399–408.

Deutsch, F. M., & Madle, R. A. (1975). Empathy: Historic and current conceptualizations, measurement, and a cognitive theoretical perspective. *Human Development, 18,* 267–287.

de Waal, F. (1982). *Chimpanzee politics.* London: Jonathan Cape.

Dlugokinski, E. L, & Firestone, I. J. (1974). Other centeredness and susceptibility to charitable appeals: Effects of perceived discipline. *Developmental Psychology, 10,* 21–28.

Dollard, J., Doob, L., Miller, N., Mowrer, O., & Sears, R. (1939). *Frustration and aggression.* New Haven: Yale University Press.

Dollinger, S. J., & Riger, A. L. (1984). On penetrating the ''mask'': The role of sagacity and acumen in a word-association/clinical-judgment task. *Journal of Personality and Social Psychology, 46,* 145–152.

Dovidio, J. F., Allen, J. L., & Schroeder, D. A. (1990). Specificity of empathy-induced helping: Evidence for altruistic motivation. *Journal of Personality and Social Psychology, 59,* 249–260.

Dunn, J., Brown, J., & Beardsall, L. (1991). Family talk about feeling states and children's later understanding of others' emotions. *Developmental Psychology, 27,* 448–455.

Dyck, R. J., & Rule, B. G. (1978). Effect on retaliation of causal attributions concerning attack. *Journal of Personality and Social Psychology, 36,* 521–529.

Dymond, R. F. (1948). A preliminary investigation of the relation of insight and empathy. *Journal of Consulting Psychology, 12,* 228–233.

Dymond, R. F. (1949). A scale for the measurement of empathic ability. *Journal of Consulting Psychology, 13,* 127–133.

Dymond, R. F. (1950). Personality and empathy. *Journal of Consulting Psychology, 14,* 343–350.

Eisenberg, N. (1986). *Altruistic emotion, cognition, and behavior.* Hillsdale, NJ: Lawrence Erlbaum Associates.

Eisenberg, N., & Fabes, R. A. (1990). Empathy: Conceptualization, measurement, and relation to prosocial behavior. *Motivation and Emotion, 14,* 131–149.

Eisenberg, N., Fabes, R. A., Bustamante, D., Mathy, R. M., Miller, P. A., & Lindholm, E. (1988). Differentiation of vicariously induced emotional reactions in children. *Developmental Psychology, 24,* 237–246.

Eisenberg, N., Fabes, R. A., Carlo, G., Speer, A. L., Switzer, G., Karbon, M. & Troyer, D. (1993). The relations of empathy-related emotions and maternal practices to children's comforting behavior. *Journal of Experimental Child Psychology,* ss, 131–150.

Eisenberg, N., Fabes, R. A., Carlo, G., Troyer, D., Speer, A. L., Karbon, M., & Switzer, G. (1992). The relations of maternal practices and characteristics to children's vicarious emotional responsiveness. *Child Development, 63,* 583–602.

Eisenberg, N., Fabes, R. A., Miller, P. A., Fultz, J., Shell, R., Mathy, R. M., & Reno, R. R. (1989). Relation of sympathy and personal distress to prosocial behavior: A multimethod study. *Journal of Personality and Social Psychology, 57,* 55–66.

Eisenberg, N., Fabes, R. A., Schaller, M., Carlo, G., & Miller, P. (1991). The relations of parental characteristics and practices to children's vicarious emotional responding. *Child Development, 62,* 1393–1408.

Eisenberg, N., Fabes, R. A., Schaller, M., Miller, P., Carlo, G., Poulin, R., Shea, C., & Shell, R. (1991). Personality and socialization correlates of vicarious emotional responding. *Journal of Personality and Social Psychology, 61,* 459–470.

Eisenberg, N., & Lennon, R. (1983). Sex differences in empathy and related capacities. *Psychological Bulletin, 94,* 100–131.

Eisenberg, N., & Miller, P. A. (1987). Empathy and prosocial behavior. *Psychological Bulletin, 101,* 91–119.

Eisenberg, N., Miller, P. A., Schaller, M., Fabes, R. A., Fultz, J., Shell, R., & Shea, C. L. (1989). The role of sympathy and altruistic personality traits in helping: A reexamination. *Journal of Personality, 57,* 41–67.

Eisenberg, N., & Mussen, P. H. (1989). *The roots of prosocial behavior in children.* Cambridge: Cambridge University Press.

Eisenberg, N., Schaller, M., Fabes, R. A., Bustamante, D., Mathy, R. M., Shell, R., & Rhodes, K. (1988). Differentiation of personal distress and sympathy in children and adults. *Developmental Psychology, 24,* 766–775.

Eisenberg, N., Shea, C. L., Carlo, G., & Knight, G. P. (1991). Empathy-related responding and cognition: a "chicken and the egg" dilemma. In W. Kurtines & J. Gewirtz (Eds.), *Handbook of moral behavior and development. Volume 2: Research,* pp. 63–88. Hillsdale, NJ: Lawrence Erlbaum Associates.

Eisenberg, N., & Strayer, J. (1987). Critical issues in the study of empathy. In N. Eisenberg & J. Strayer (Eds.), *Empathy and its development,* pp. 3–13. Cambridge: Cambridge University Press.

Eisenberg-Berg, N., & Lennon, R. (1980). Altruism and the assessment of empathy in the preschool years. *Child Development, 51,* 552–557.

Eisenberg-Berg, N., & Mussen, P. (1978). Empathy and moral development in adolescence. *Developmental Psychology, 14,* 185–186.

Ekman, P., Liebert, R. M., Friesen, W. V., Harrison, R., Zlatchin, C., Malmstrom, E. J., & Baron, R. A. (1972). Facial expressions of emotion while watching televised violence as predictors of subsequent aggression. In G. A. Comstock, E. A. Rubinstein, & J. P. Murray (Eds.), *Television and Social Behavior: Reports and Papers* (Vol. V), pp. 22–58. Washington, DC: U.S. Government Printing Office.

Eliasz, H. (1980). The effect of empathy, reactivity, and anxiety on interpersonal aggression intensity. *Polish Psychological Bulletin, 11,* 169–178.

Ellis, P.L. (1982). Empathy: A factor in antisocial behavior. *Journal of Abnormal Child Psychology, 10,* 123–134.

Englis, B. G., Vaughan, K. B., & Lanzetta, J. T. (1982). Conditioning of counter-empathetic emotional responses. *Journal of Experimental Social Psychology, 18,* 375–391.

Enright, R. D., & Lapsley, D. K. (1980). Social role-taking: A review of the constructs, measures, and measurement properties. *Review of Educational Research, 50,* 647–674.

Eysenck, H. J. (1967). *The biological basis of personality.* Springfield, IL: Charles C. Thomas.

Eysenck, H. J., & Eysenck, M. W. (1985). *Personality and individual differences: A natural science approach.* New York: Plenum Press.

Eysenck, S. B. G., & Eysenck, H. J. (1978). Impulsiveness and venturesomeness: Their position in a dimensional system of personality description. *Psychological Reports, 43,* 1247–1255.

Eysenck, S. B. G., & McGurk, B. J. (1980). Impulsiveness and venturesomeness in a detention center population. *Psychological Reports, 47,* 1299–1306.

Fabes, R. A., Eisenberg, N., & Miller, P. A. (1990). Maternal correlates of children's vicarious emotional responsiveness. *Developmental Psychology, 26,* 639–648.

Feffer, M. H., & Gourevitch, V. (1960). Cognitive aspects of role-taking in children. *Journal of Personality, 28,* 383–396.

Feffer, M. & Suchotliff, L. (1966). Decentering implications of social interactions. *Journal of Personality and Social Psychology, 4,* 415–422.

Ferguson, T. J., & Rule, B. G. (1983). An attributional perspective on anger and aggression. In R. G. Geen & E. I. Donnerstein (Eds.), *Aggression: theoretical and empirical reviews* (Vol. 1), pp. 41–74. New York: Academic Press.

Feshbach, N. D. (1978). Studies of empathic behavior in children. In B. A. Maher (Ed.), *Progress in experimental personality research* (Vol. 8), pp. 1–47. New York: Academic Press.

Feshbach, N. D., & Feshbach, S. (1969). The relationship between empathy and aggression in two age groups. *Developmental Psychology, 1,* 102–107.

Feshbach, N. D., & Roe, K. (1968). Empathy in six- and seven-year-olds. *Child Development, 39,* 133–145.

Feshbach, S. (1964). The function of aggression and the regulation of aggressive drive. *Psychological Review, 71,* 257–272.

Feshbach, S., Stiles, W. B., & Bitter, E. (1967). The reinforcing effect of witnessing aggression. *Journal of Experimental Research in Personality, 2,* 133–139.

Fincham, F. D., & Bradbury, T. N. (1987). The impact of attributions in marriage: A longitudinal analysis. *Journal of Personality and Social Psychology, 53,* 510–517.

Fincham, F. D., & Bradbury, T. N. (1988). The impact of attributions in marriage: Empirical and conceptual foundations. *British Journal of Clinical Psychology, 27,* 77–90.

Fincham, F. D., & Bradbury, T. N. (1989a). The impact of attributions in marriage: An individual difference analysis. *Journal of Social and Personal Relationships, 6,* 69–85.

Fincham, F. D., & Bradbury, T. N. (1989b). Perceived responsibility for marital events: Egocentric or partner-centric bias? *Journal of Marriage and the Family, 51,* 27–35.

Fincham, F. D., Bradbury, T. N., & Grych, J. H. (1990). Conflict in close relationships: The role of intrapersonal phenomena. In S. Graham & V. Folkes (Eds.), *Attribution theory: Applications to achievement, mental health, and interpersonal conflict,* pp. 161–184. Hillsdale, NJ: Lawrence Erlbaum Associates.

Fiske, S. T., & Taylor, S. E. (1991). *Social Cognition,* 2nd ed. New York: McGraw-Hill.

Flavell, J. H., Botkin, P. T., Fry, C. L., Wright, J., & Jarvis, P. (1968). *The development of role taking and communication skills in children.* New York: Wiley.

Ford, M. E. (1979). The construct validity of egocentrism. *Psychological Bulletin, 86,* 1169–1188.

Franzoi, S.L., & Davis, M. H. (1985). Adolescent self-disclosure and loneliness: Private self-consciousness and parental influences. *Journal of Personality and Social Psychology, 48,* 768–780.

Franzoi, S. L., Davis, M. H., & Young, R. D. (1985). The effects of private self-consciousness and perspective taking on satisfaction in close relationships. *Journal of Personality and Social Psychology, 48,* 1584–1594.

Freedman, J. L. (1970). Transgression, compliance, and guilt. In J. R. Macaulay & L. Berkowitz (Eds.), *Altruism and helping behavior,* pp. 155–161. New York: Academic Press.

Fultz, J., Batson, C. D., Fortenbach, V. A., McCarthy, P. M., & Varney, L. L. (1986). Social evaluation and the empathy-altruism hypothesis. *Journal of Personality and Social Psychology, 50,* 761–769.

Fultz, J., & Cialdini, R. B. (1986). Focus of attention, sadness, and the empathy-helping relationship: Evidence for a negative-state relief explanation. Presented at the 94th Annual Convention of the American Psychological Association, Washington, DC.

Funder, D. C. (1987). Errors and mistakes: Evaluating the accuracy of social judgment. *Psychological Bulletin, 101,* 75–90.

Funder, D. C., & Harris, M. J. (1986). On the several facets of personality assessment: The case of social acuity. *Journal of Personality, 54,* 528–550.

Gaertner, S. L., & Dovidio, J. F. (1977). The subtlety of white racism, arousal, and helping behavior. *Journal of Personality and Social Psychology, 35,* 691–707.

Gaertner, S. L., Dovidio, J. F., & Johnson, G. (1979). Race of victim, nonresponsive bystanders, and helping behavior. Paper presented at the 87th Annual Convention of the American Psychological Association, New York.

Gage, N. L., & Cronbach, L. J. (1955). Conceptual methodological problems in interpersonal perception. *Psychological Review, 62,* 411–422.

Gage, N. L., Leavitt, G. S., & Stone, G. C. (1956). The intermediary key in the analysis of interpersonal perception. *Psychological Bulletin, 53,* 258–266.

Galper, R. E. (1976). Turning observers into actors: Differential causal attributions as a function of "empathy." *Journal of Research in Personality, 10,* 328–335.

Geen, R. G. (1970). Perceived suffering of the victim as an inhibitor of attack-induced aggression. *The Journal of Social Psychology, 81,* 209–215.

Gergen, K., Gergen, M., & Meter, K. (1972). Individual orientations to prosocial behavior. *Journal of Social Issues, 8,* 105–130.

Glucksberg, S., Krauss, R. M., & Weisberg, R. (1966). Referential communication in nursery school children: Method and some preliminary findings. *Journal of Experimental Child Psychology, 3,* 333–342.

Goldsmith, H. H. (1983). Genetic influence on personality from infancy to adulthood. *Child Development, 54,* 331–355.

Gough, H. G. (1987). *California Psychological Inventory: Adminstrator's guide.* Palo Alto, CA: Consulting Psychologists Press.

Gough, H. G, & Heilbrun, A. L. (1980). *The Adjective Check List Manual.* Palo Alto, CA: Consulting Psychologists Press.

Gould, R., & Sigall, H. (1977). The effects of empathy and outcome on attribution: An examination of the divergent-perspectives hypothesis. *Journal of Experimental Social Psychology, 13,* 480–491.

Gould, S. J. (1980). Sociobiology and the theory of natural selection. In G. W. Barlow & J. Silverberg (Eds.), *Sociobiology: Beyond nature/nurture?*, pp. 257–269. Boulder, CO: Westview Press, Inc.

Greenwell, J., & Dengerink, H. A. (1973). The role of perceived versus actual attack in human physical aggression. *Journal of Personality and Social Psychology, 26*, 66–71.

Greif, E. B., & Hogan, R. (1973). The theory and measurement of empathy. *Journal of Counseling Psychology, 20*, 280–284.

Gruen, R. J., & Mendelsohn, G. (1986). Emotional responses to affective displays in others: The distinction between empathy and sympathy. *Journal of Personality and Social Psychology, 51*, 609–614.

Hall, J. A. (1978). Gender effects in decoding nonverbal cues. *Psychological Bulletin, 85*, 845–858.

Hall, J. A. (1979). Gender, gender roles, and nonverbal communication skills. In R. Rosenthal (Ed.), *Skill in Nonverbal Communication*, pp. 32–67. Cambridge, MA: Oelgeschlager, Gunn & Hain, Publishers.

Hamilton, W. D. (1964). The genetic evolution of social behavior. *Journal of Theoretical Biology, 7*, 1–51.

Hart, A. J., & Rosenthal, R. (1988). *Improving sensitivity to nonverbal communication.* Unpublished manuscript.

Hartshorne, H., & May, M. A. (1928). *Studies in the nature of character: Studies in deceit* (Vol. 1). New York: Macmillan.

Hartshorne, H., May, M. A., & Maller, J. B. (1929). *Studies in the nature of character: Studies in self-control* (Vol. II). New York: Macmillan.

Hartshorne, H., May, M. A., & Shuttleworth, F. K. (1930). *Studies in the nature of character: Studies in the organization of character* (Vol. III). New York: Macmillan.

Hastorf, A. H., & Bender, I. E. (1952). A caution respecting the measurement of empathic ability. *Journal of Abnormal and Social Psychology, 47*, 574–576.

Hendrick, C., & Taylor, S. P. (1971). Effects of belief similarity and aggression on attraction and counteraggression. *Journal of Personality and Social Psychology, 17*, 342–349.

Higgins, E. T. (1987). Self-discrepancy: A theory relating self and affect. *Psychological Review, 94*, 319–340.

Higgins, E. T., Feldman, N. S., & Ruble, D. N. (1980). Accuracy and differentiation in social prediction: A developmental perspective. *Journal of Personality, 48*, 520–540.

Hill, C. A. (1991). Seeking emotional support: The influence of affiliative need and partner warmth. *Journal of Personality and Social Psychology, 60*, 112–121.

Hinchey, F. S., & Gavelek, J. R. (1982). Empathic responding in children of battered mothers. *Child Abuse and Neglect, 6*, 395–401.

Hobbes, T. (1651). *Leviathan: Or the matter, form, and power of a commonwealth, ecclesiastical and civil.* London: A. Crooke.

Hoffman, M. L. (1975). Altruistic behavior and the parent-child relationship. *Journal of Personality and Social Psychology, 31,* 937–943.

Hoffman, M. L. (1977). Sex differences in empathy and related behaviors. *Psychological Bulletin, 84,* 712–722.

Hoffman, M. L. (1978). Psychological and biological perspectives on altruism. *International Journal of Behavioral Development, 1,* 323–339.

Hoffman, M. L. (1982a). Development of prosocial motivation: Empathy and guilt. In N. Eisenberg (Ed.), *The development of prosocial behavior,* pp. 281–313. New York: Academic Press.

Hoffman, M. L. (1982b). The measurement of empathy. In C. E. Izard (Ed.), *Measuring emotions in infants and children,* pp. 279–296. Cambridge: Cambridge University Press.

Hoffman, M. L. (1984). Interaction of affect and cognition in empathy. In C. E. Izard, J. Kagan, & R. B. Zajonc (Eds.), *Emotions, cognition, and behavior,* pp. 103–131. Cambridge: Cambridge University Press.

Hoffman, M. L. (1987). The contribution of empathy to justice and moral judgment. In N. Eisenberg & J. Strayer (Eds.), *Empathy and its development,* pp. 47–80. Cambridge: Cambridge University Press.

Hoffman, M. L., & Saltzstein, H. D. (1967). Parent discipline and the child's moral development. *Journal of Personality and Social Psychology, 5,* 45–57.

Hogan, R. (1969). Development of an empathy scale. *Journal of Consulting and Clinical Psychology, 33,* 307–316.

Hogan, R. (1983). A socioanalytic theory of personality. In M. Page (Ed.), *Nebraska Symposium on Motivation,* pp. 55–89. Lincoln: University of Nebraska Press.

Hornstein, H. A. (1991). Empathic distress and altruism: Still inseparable. *Psychological Inquiry, 2,* 133–135.

Houston, D. A. (1990). Empathy and the self: Cognitive and emotional influences on the evaluation of negative affect in others. *Journal of Personality and Social Psychology, 59,* 859–868.

Howe, G. W. (1987). Attributions of complex cause and the perception of marital conflict. *Journal of Personality and Social Psychology, 53,* 1119–1128.

Howe, N., & Ross, H. S. (1990). Socialization, perspective-taking, and the sibling relationship. *Developmental Psychology, 26,* 160–165.

Hume, D. (1739/1968). *A treatise of human nature,* 3rd. ed. H.A. Selby-Bigge (Ed.). Oxford: Clarendon Press.

Humphrey, N. K. (1976). The social function of intellect. In P. P. G. Bateson & R. A. Hinde (Eds.), *Growing points in ethology,* pp. 303–317. Cambridge: Cambridge University Press.

Iannotti, R. J. (1975). The nature and measurement of empathy in children. *The Counseling Psychologist, 5,* 21–24.

Ickes, W. (in press). Empathic accuracy. *Journal of Personality.*

Ickes, W., & Kidd, R. F. (1976). An attributional analysis of helping behavior. In J. H. Harvey, W. J. Ickes, & R. F. Kidd (Eds.) *New directions in attribution research,* (Vol. 1), pp. 311–334. Hillsdale, NJ: Lawrence Erlbaum Associates.

Ickes, W., Stinson, L., Bissonnette, V., & Garcia, S. (1990). Naturalistic social cognition: Empathic accuracy in mixed-sex dyads. *Journal of Personality and Social Psychology, 49,* 730–742.

Isen, A. M. (1970). Success, failure, attention and reaction to others: the warm glow of success. *Journal of Personality and Social·Psychology, 15,* 294–301.

Isen, A. M., Shalker, T. E., Clark, M., & Karp, L. (1978). Affect accessibility of material in memory and behavior: A cognitive loop? *Journal of Personality and Social Psychology, 36,* 1–12.

Izard, D. E. (1977). *Human emotions.* New York: Plenum.

Jackson, D. N. (1974). *Personality Research Form manual,* 2nd ed. Port Huron, MI: Research Psychologists Press.

Johnson, J. A., Cheek, J. M., & Smither, R. (1983). The structure of empathy. *Journal of Personality and Social Psychology, 45,* 1299–1312.

Johnson, T. E., & Rule, B. G. (1986). Mitigating circumstance information, censure, and aggression. *Journal of Personality and Social Psychology, 50,* 537–542.

Jones, E. E., & Nisbett R. E. (1971). *The actor and the observer: Divergent perceptions of the causes of behavior.* Morristown, NJ: General Learning Press.

Jurkovic, G. J., & Prentice, N. M. (1977). Relation of moral and cognitive development of dimensions of juvenile delinquency. *Journal of Abnormal Psychology, 80,* 414–420.

Kalliopuska, M. (1984). Relation between children's and parents' empathy. *Psychological Reports, 54,* 295–299.

Kaplan, P. J., & Arbuthnot, J. (1985). Affective empathy and cognitive role-taking in delinquent and nondelinquent youth. *Adolescence, 20,* 323–333.

Kendall, P. C., Deardorff, P. A., & Finch, A. J., Jr. (1977). Empathy and socialization in first and repeat juvenile offenders and normals. *Journal of Abnormal Child Psychology, 5,* 93–97.

Kenny, D. A., & Albright, L. (1987). Accuracy in interpersonal perception: A social relations analysis. *Psychological Bulletin, 102,* 390–402.

Kenrick, D. T., Baumann, D. J., & Cialdini, R. B. (1979). A step in the socialization of altruism as hedonism: Effects of negative mood on children's generosity under public and private conditions. *Journal of Personality and Social Psychology, 37,* 747–755.

Kerr, W. A., & Speroff, B. G. (1954). Validation and evaluation of the empathy test. *Journal of General Psychology, 50,* 369–376.

Kestenbaum, R., Farber, E. A., & Sroufe, L. A. (1989). Individual differences in empathy among preschoolers: Relation to attachment history. *New Directions for Child Development, 44,* 51–64.

Koestner, R., Franz, C., & Weinberger, J. (1990). The family origins of empathic concern: A 26–year longitudinal study. *Journal of Personality and Social Psychology, 58,* 709–717.

Kohler, W. (1929). *Gestalt psychology.* New York: Liveright.

Krebs, D. L. (1970). Altruism: an examination of the concept and a review of the literature. *Psychological Bulletin, 73,* 258–302.

Krebs, D. L. (1975). Empathy and altruism. *Journal of Personality and Social Psychology, 32,* 1134–1146.

Krebs, D. L. (1978). A cognitive-developmental approach to altruism. In L. Wispé (Ed.), *Altruism, sympathy, and helping: Psychological and sociological principles,* pp. 141–164. New York: Academic Press.

Krebs, D. L. (1983). Commentary and critique: sociobiological approaches to prosocial development. In D. L. Bridgeman (Ed.), *The nature of prosocial development: Interdisciplinary theories and strategies,* pp. 61–69. New York: Academic Press.

Krebs, D. L. (1991). Altruism and egoism: A false dichotomy? *Psychological Inquiry, 2,* 137–139.

Krebs, D. L., & Russell, C. (1981). Role-taking and altruism: when you put yourself in the shoes of another, will they take you to their owner's aid? In J. P. Rushton & R. M. Sorrentino (Eds.) *Altruism and helping behavior: Social, personality, and developmental perspectives,* pp. 137–165. Hillsdale, NJ: Lawrence Erlbaum Associates.

Kremer, J. F., & Stephens, L. (1983). Attributions and arousal as mediators of mitigation's effect on retaliation. *Journal of Personality and Social Psychology, 45,* 335–343.

Kuiper, N. A., & Rogers, T. B. (1979). Encoding of personal information: Self-other differences. *Journal of Personality and Social Psychology, 37,* 499–514.

Kurdek, L. A. (1978). Relationship between cognitive perspective taking and teachers' ratings of children's classroom behavior in grades one through four. *The Journal of Genetic Psychology, 132,* 21–27.

Kurdek, L. A., & Rodgon, M. M. (1975). Perceptual, cognitive, and affective perspective taking in kindergarten through sixth-grade children. *Developmental Psychology, 11,* 643–650.

Laird, J. D. (1974). Self-attribution of emotion: The effects of expressive behavior on the quality of emotional experience. *Journal of Personality and Social Psychology, 29,* 475–486.

Lanzetta, J. T., & Englis, B. G. (1989). Expectations of cooperation and competition and their effects on observers' vicarious emotional responses. *Journal of Personality and Social Psychology, 56,* 543–554.

Larsen, R. J., & Diener, E. (1987). Affect intensity as an individual difference characteristic: A review. *Journal of Research in Personality, 21,* 1–39.

Latané, B., & Darley, J. M. (1970). *The unresponsive bystander: Why doesn't he help?* New York: Appleton-Century-Crofts.

Leak, G. K. & Christopher, S. B. (1982). Empathy from an evolutionary perspective. *Journal of Theory and Social Behaviour, 11,* 79–82.

Lee, M., & Prentice, N. M. (1988). Interrelations of empathy, cognition, and moral reasoning with dimensions of juvenile delinquency. *Journal of Abnormal Child Psychology, 16,* 127–139.

Lerner, M. J., & Miller, D. T. (1978). Just world research and the attribution process: Looking back and ahead. *Psychological Bulletin, 85,* 1030–1051.

Lerner, M. J., & Simmons, C. (1966). Observer's reaction to the "innocent victim": Compassion or rejection? *Journal of Personality and Social Psychology, 4,* 203–210.

Letourneau, C. (1981). Empathy and stress: How they affect parental aggression. *Social Work, 26,* 383–389.

Levenson, R. W., & Gottman, J. M. (1983). Marital interaction: Physiological linkage and affective exchange. *Journal of Personality and Social Psychology, 45,* 587–597.

Levenson, R. W., & Gottman, J. M. (1985). Physiological and affective predictors of change in relationship satisfaction. *Journal of Personality and Social Psychology, 49,* 85–94.

Levenson, R. W., & Ruef, A. M. (1992). Empathy: A physiological substrate. *Journal of Personality and Social Psychology, 63,* 234–246.

Levine, L., & Hoffman, M. L. (1975). Empathy and cooperation in 4–year-olds. *Developmental Psychology, 11,* 533–534.

Lipps, T. (1903). Einfühlung, inner Nachahmung, und Organempfindaungen. *Archiv für die gesamte psychologie, 2,* 185–204.

Lipps, T. (1905). Das Wissen von fremden Ichen. *Psychologische Untersuchungen, 4,* 694–722.

Lipps, T. (1926). *Psychological studies.* Baltimore, MD: Williams and Wilkens.

Loehlin, J. C., & Nichols, R. C. (1976). *Heredity, environment, and personality: A study of 850 sets of twins.* Austin: University of Texas Press.

Loehlin, J. C., Willerman, L., & Horn, J. M. (1988). Human behavior genetics. In M.R. Rosenzweig and L.W. Porter (Eds.), *Annual review of psychology* (Vol. 39), pp. 101–133. Palo Alto, CA: Annual Reviews Inc.

Long, E. C. J., & Andrews, D. W. (1990). Perspective taking as a predictor of marital adjustment. *Journal of Personality and Social Psychology, 59,* 126–131.

Macaulay, J., & Berkowitz, L. (Eds.). (1970). *Altruism and helping behavior: Social psychological studies of some antecedents and consequences.* New York: Academic Press, 1970.

Maccoby, E. E., & Jacklin, C. N. (1974). *The psychology of sex differences.* Stanford: Stanford University Press.

Main, M., & George, C. (1985). Responses of abused and disadvantaged toddlers to distress in agemates: A study in the day care setting. *Developmental Psychology, 21,* 407–412.

Mandler, G. (1975). *Mind and emotion.* New York: Wiley.

Marangoni, C., Garcia, S., & Ickes, W. (1993). *Empathic accuracy in a clinically-relevant setting.* Unpublished manuscript.

Marks, E. L., Penner, L. A., & Stone, A. V. W. (1982). Helping as a function of empathic responses and sociopathy. *Journal of Research in Personality, 16,* 1–20.

Matthews, K. A., Batson, C. D., Horn, J., & Rosenman, R. H. (1981). "Principles in his nature which interest him in the fortune of others . . .": The heritability of empathic concern for others. *Journal of Personality, 49,* 237–247.

McDougall, W. (1908). *An introduction to social psychology.* London: Methuen.

McHugo, G. J., Lanzetta, J. T., Sullivan, D. G., Masters, R. D., & Englis, B. G. (1985). Emotional reactions to a political leader's expressive displays. *Journal of Personality and Social Psychology, 49,* 1513–1529.

Mead, G. H. (1934). *Mind, self, and society.* Chicago: University of Chicago Press.

Mehrabian, A. (1977). Individual differences in stimulus screening and arousability. *Journal of Personality, 45,* 237–250.

Mehrabian, A. (1980). *Basic dimensions for a general psychological theory: Implications for personality, social, environmental, and developmental studies.* Cambridge, MA: Oelgeschlager, Gunn & Hain.

Mehrabian, A., & Epstein, N. (1972). A measure of emotional empathy. *Journal of Personality, 40,* 525–543.

Mehrabian, A., & O'Reilly, E. (1980). Analysis of personality measures in terms of basic dimensions of temperament. *Journal of Personality and Social Psychology, 38,* 492–503.

Mehrabian, A., Young, A. L., & Sato, S. (1988). Emotional empathy and associated individual differences. *Current Psychology: Research & Reviews, 7,* 221–240.

Melburg, V., Rosenfeld, P., Riess, M., & Tedeschi, J. T. (1984). A reexamination of the empathic observers paradigm for the study of divergent attributions. *The Journal of Social Psychology, 124,* 201–208.

Meyer, J. P., & Mulherin, A. (1980). From attribution to helping: An analysis of the mediating effects of affect and expectancy. *Journal of Personality and Social Psychology, 39,* 201–210.

Milgram, S. (1965). Some conditions of obedience and disobedience to authority. *Human Relations, 18,* 57–76.

Miller, P. A., & Eisenberg, N. (1988). The relation of empathy to aggressive and externalizing/antisocial behavior. *Psychological Bulletin, 103,* 324–344.

Miller, P. A., Eisenberg, N., Fabes, R. A., Shell, R. & Gular, S. (1989). Mothers' emotional arousal as a moderator in the socialization of children's empathy. In N. Eisenberg (Ed.), *Empathy and related emotional responses,* pp. 65–83. San Francisco: Jossey-Bass.

Miller, R. S. (1987). Empathic embarrassment: situational and personal determinants of reactions to the embarrassment of another. *Journal of Personality and Social Psychology, 53,* 1061–1069.

Mussen, P., & Eisenberg-Berg, N. (1977). *Caring, sharing, and the roots of prosocial behavior in children.* San Francisco: Freeman.

Neale, M. A., & Bazerman, M. H. (1983). The role of perspective-taking ability in negotiation under different forms of arbitration. *Industrial and Labor Relations Review, 36,* 378–388.

Nesdale, A. R., Rule, B. G., & Hill, K. (1978). The effect of attraction on causal attributions and retaliation. *Personality and Social Psychology Bulletin, 4,* 231–234.

Nisbett, R. E., Caputo, G. C., Legant, P., & Marecek, J. (1973). Behavior as seen by the actor and as seen by the observer. *Journal of Personality and Social Psychology, 27,* 154–164.

Oakley, K. (1959). *Man the tool-maker.* Chicago: University of Chicago Press.

Passingham, R. E. (1982). *The human primate.* New York: W. H. Freeman.

Perrett, D. I., Rolls, E. T., & Caan, W. (1982). Visual neurons responsive to faces in the monkey temporal cortex. *Experimental Brain Research, 47,* 329–342.

Perrett, D. I., Smith, P. A. J., & Potter, D. D. (1985). Visual cells in the temporal cortex sensitive to face view and gaze direction. *Proceedings of the Royal Society of London (Biology), 223,* 293–317.

Peterson, C. & Skevington, S. (1988). The relation between young children's cognitive role-taking and mothers' preference for a conflict-inducing childrearing method. *Journal of Genetic Psychology, 149,* 163–174.

Piaget, J. (1932). *The moral judgment of the child* (trans.). London: Kegan Paul, Trench, Trubner.

Piaget, J. & Inhelder, B. (1956). *The child's conception of space.* London: Routledge & Kegan Paul.

Piliavin, J. A., Dovidio, J. F., Gaertner, S. L., & Clark, R. D. (1981). *Emergency intervention.* New York: Academic Press.

Plomin, R. (1986). Behavioral genetic methods. *Journal of Personality, 54,* 226–261.

Plomin, R., Chipeur, H. M., & Loehlin, J. C. (1990). Behavioral genetics and personality. In L. A. Pervin (Ed.), *Handbook of personality: theory and research,* pp. 225–243. New York: The Guilford Press.

Plomin, R., DeFries, J. C., & McClearn, G. E. (1990). *Behavioral genetics: A primer* (2nd ed.). New York: W. H. Freeman.

Plomin, R., & Rowe, D. (1977). A twin study of temperament in young children. *Journal of Psychology, 97,* 107–113.

Polk, W. M. (1976). Perceptual orientation, empathy, and the inhibition of aggression (Doctoral dissertation, North Carolina State University, Raleigh, 1976). *Dissertation Abstracts International, 37,* 4225B.

Quay, H. C., & Parsons, L. B. (1971). *The differential behavioral classification of the juvenile offender.* Washington, DC: U.S. Bureau of Prisons.

Rahim, M. A. (1983). A measure of styles of handling interpersonal conflict. *Academy of Management Journal, 26,* 368–376.

Regan, D. T., Straus, E., & Fazio, R. (1974). Liking and the attribution process. *Journal of Experimental Social Psychology, 10,* 385–397.

Regan, D. T., & Totten, J. (1975). Empathy and attribution: Turning observers into actors. *Journal of Personality and Social Psychology, 32,* 850–856.

Regan, D., Williams, M., & Sparling, S. (1972). Voluntary expiation of guilt: A field replication. *Journal of Personality and Social Psychology, 24,* 42.

Rein, B. A. (1974). The effects of empathy, similarity, and attraction on level of aggression (Doctoral dissertation, University of California, Riverside, 1974). *Dissertation Abstracts International, 35,* 1395B.

Reisenzein, R. (1986). A structural equation analysis of Weiner's attribution-affect model of helping behavior. *Journal of Personality and Social Psychology, 50,* 1123–1133.

Richardson, D. R., Hammock, G. S., Smith, S. M., Gardner, W., & Signo, M. (1992). *Empathy as a cognitive inhibitor of impulsive aggression.* Unpublished manuscript.

Riggio, R. E., Tucker, J., & Coffaro, D. (1989). Social skills and empathy. *Personality and Individual Differences, 10,* 93–99.

Roe, K. V. (1980). Toward a contingency hypothesis of empathy development. *Journal of Personality and Social Psychology, 39,* 991–994.

Rogers, T. B., Kuiper, N. A., & Kirker, W. S. (1977). Self-reference and the encoding of personal information. *Journal of Personality and Social Psychology, 35,* 677–688.

Rosenthal, R., Hall, J. A., DiMatteo, M. R., Rogers, P. L., & Archer, D. (1979). *Sensitivity to nonverbal communication: The PONS test.* Baltimore: Johns Hopkins University Press.

Ross, M., & Sicoly, F. (1979). Egocentric biases in availability and attribution. *Journal of Personality and Social Psychology, 37,* 322–336.

Rotenberg, M. (1974). Conceptual and methodological notes on affective and cognitive role taking (sympathy and empathy): An illustrative experiment with delinquent and nondelinquent boys. *The Journal of Genetic Psychology, 125,* 177–185.

Rothbart, M. K., & Derryberry, D. (1981). Development of individual differences in temperament. In M. Lamb & A. Brown (Eds.), *Advances in developmental psychology* (Vol. 1), pp. 37–86. Hillsdale, NJ: Lawrence Erlbaum Associates.

Rothbart, M. K., & Maccoby, E. E. (1966). Parents' differential reactions to sons and daughters. *Journal of Personality and Social Psychology, 4,* 237–243.

Rothenberg, B. B. (1970). Children's social sensitivity and the relationship to interpersonal competence, intrapersonal comfort, and intellectual level. *Developmental Psychology, 2,* 335–350.

Rule, B. G., Dyck, R., & Nesdale, A. R. (1978). Arbitrariness of frustration: Inhibition or instigation effects on aggression. *European Journal of Social Psychology, 8,* 237–244.

Rule, B. G., & Nesdale, A. R. (1976). Emotional arousal and aggressive behavior. *Psychological Bulletin, 83,* 851–863.

Rusbult, C. E., Verette, J., Whitney, G. A., Slovik, L. F., & Lipkus, I. (1991). Accommodation processes in close relationships: Theory and preliminary empirical evidence. *Journal of Personality and Social Psychology, 60,* 53–78.

Rushton, J. P. (1981). The altruistic personality. In J. P. Rushton & R. M. Sorrentino (Eds.) *Altruism and helping behavior: Social, personality, and developmental perspectives,* pp. 251–266. Hillsdale, NJ: Lawrence Erlbaum Associates.

Rushton, J. P. (1991). Is altruism innate? *Psychological Inquiry, 2,* 141–143.

Rushton, J. P., Fulker, D. W., Neale, M. C., Nias, D. K. B., & Eysenck, H. J. (1986). Altruism and aggression: The heritability of individual differences. *Journal of Personality and Social Psychology, 50,* 1192–1198.

Rushton, J. P., Russell, R. J. H., & Wells, P. A. (1984). Genetic similarity theory: Beyond kin selection. *Behavior Genetics, 14,* 179–193.

Rushton, J. P., & Sorrentino, R. M. (1981). Altruism and helping behavior: An historical perspective. In J.P. Rushton & R.M. Sorrentino (Eds.), *Altruism and helping behavior: social, personality, and developmental perspectives,* pp. 3–16. Hillsdale, NJ: Lawrence Erlbaum Associates.

Russell, D., Peplau, L. A., & Cutrona, C. (1980). The revised UCLA Loneliness Scale: Concurrent and discriminant validity evidence. *Journal of Personality and Social Psychology, 39,* 472–480.

Sagi, A., & Hoffman, M. L. (1976). Empathic distress in newborns. *Developmental Psychology, 12,* 175–176.

Sande, G. N., Goethals, G. R., & Radloff, C. E. (1988). Perceiving one's own traits and others': The multifaceted self. *Journal of Personality and Social Psychology, 32,* 13–20.

Scarr, S., & Carter-Saltzman, L. (1979). Twin method: Defense of a critical assumption. *Behavior Genetics, 9,* 527–542.

Schaller, M., & Cialdini, R. B. (1988). The economics of empathic helping: Support for a mood management motive. *Journal of Experimental Social Psychology, 24,* 163–181.

Schmidt, G., & Weiner, B. (1988). An attribution-affect-action theory of behavior: Replications of judgments of help-giving. *Personality and Social Psychology Bulletin, 14,* 610–621.

Schmidt, N., & Sermat, V. (1983). Measuring loneliness in different relationships. *Journal of Personality and Social Psychology, 44,* 1038–1047.

Schopler, J., & Matthews, M. (1965). The influence of perceived causal locus of partner's dependence on the use of interpersonal power. *Journal of Personality and Social Psychology, 2,* 609–612.

Schroeder, D. A., Dovidio, J. F., Sibicky, M. E., Matthews, L. L., & Allen, J. L. (1988). Empathic concern and helping behavior: Egoism or altruism? *Journal of Experimental Social Psychology, 24,* 333–353.

Selman, R. L., & Byrne, D. B. (1974). A structural-developmental analysis of levels of role-taking in middle childhood. *Child Development, 45,* 803–806.

Shaver, K. G. (1970). Defensive attribution: Effects of severity and relevance on the responsibility assigned for an accident. *Journal of Personality and Social Psychology, 14,* 101–113.

Sheehan, E. P., Lennon, R., & McDevitt, T. (1989). Reactions to AIDS and other illnesses: Reported interactions in the workplace. *The Journal of Psychology, 123,* 525–536.

Shelton, M. L., & Rogers, R. W. (1981). Fear-arousing and empathy-arousing appeals to help: The pathos of persuasion. *Journal of Applied Social Psychology, 11,* 366–378.

Siegman, A. W., Dembroski, T. M., & Ringel, N. (1987). Components of hostility and the severity of coronary artery disease. *Psychosomatic Medicine, 49,* 127–135.

Simner, M. L. (1971). Newborn's response to the cry of another infant. *Developmental Psychology, 5,* 136–150.

Smith, A. (1759/1976). *The theory of moral sentiments.* Oxford: Clarendon Press.

Smith, K. D. (1992). Trait sympathy and perceived control as predictors of entering sympathy-arousing situations. *Personality and Social Psychology Bulletin, 18,* 207–216.

Smith, K. D., Keating, J. P., & Stotland, E. (1989). Altruism reconsidered: The effect of denying feedback. *Journal of Personality and Social Psychology, 57,* 641–650.

Spence, J. T., Helmreich, R. L., & Holohan, C. K. (1979). Negative and positive components of psychological masculinity and femininity and their relationships to self-reports of neurotic and acting-out behaviors. *Journal of Personality and Social Psychology, 37,* 1673–1682.

Spencer, H. (1870). *The principles of psychology.* London: Williams and Norgate.

Srull, T. K. (1984). Methodological techniques for the study of person memory and social cognition. In R. S. Wyer, Jr. & T. K. Srull (Eds.) *Handbook of Social cognition* (Vol. 2), pp. 1–72. Hillsdale, NJ: Lawrence Erlbaum Associates.

Staub, E. (1978). *Positive social behavior and morality: social and personal influences* (Vol. 1). New York: Academic Press.

Staub, E. (1979). *Positive social behavior and morality: Socialization and development* (Vol. 2). New York: Academic Press.

Staub, E. (1987). Commentary on Part I. In N. Eisenberg & J. Strayer (Eds.), *Empathy and its development,* pp. 103–115. Cambridge: Cambridge University Press.

Stinson, L., & Ickes, W. (1992). Empathic accuracy in the interactions of male friends versus male strangers. *Journal of Personality and Social Psychology, 62,* 787–797.

Storms, M. D. (1973). Videotape and the attribution process: Reversing actors' and observers' points of view. *Journal of Personality and Social Psychology, 27,* 165–175.

Stotland, E. (1969). Exploratory investigations of empathy. In L. Berkowitz (Ed.), *Advances in experimental social psychology* (Vol. 4), pp. 271–314. New York: Academic Press.

Stotland, E., & Dunn, R. E. (1963). Empathy, self-esteem, and birth order. *Journal of Abnormal and Social Psychology, 66,* 532–540.

Stotland, E., Sherman, S., & Shaver, K. (1971). *Empathy and birth order: Some experimental explorations.* Lincoln, NB: University of Nebraska Press.

Strack, F., Martin, L. L., & Stepper, S. (1988). Inhibiting and facilitating conditions of the human smile: A nonobtrusive test of the facial feedback hypothesis. *Journal of Personality and Social Psychology, 54,* 768–777.

Straker, G., & Jacobson, R. S. (1981). Aggression, emotional maladjustment, and empathy in the abused child. *Developmental Psychology, 17,* 762–765.

Strayer, J. (1983). Affective and cognitive components of children's empathy. Paper presented at the meeting of the Society for Research in Child Development, Detroit.

Strayer, J. (1987). Affective and cognitive perspectives on empathy. In N. Eisenberg & J. Strayer (Eds.) *Empathy and its development,* pp. 218–244. Cambridge: Cambridge University Press.

Strayer, J., & Roberts, W. (1989). Children's empathy and role taking: Child and parental factors, and relations to prosocial behavior. *Journal of Applied Developmental Psychology, 10,* 227–239.

Streufert, S., & Streufert, S. (1969). Effects of conceptual structure, failure, and success in attribution of causality and interpersonal attitudes. *Journal of Personality and Social Psychology, 11,* 138–147.

Stroop, J. R. (1938). Factors affecting speed in serial verbal reactions. *Psychological Monographs, 50,* 38–48.

Swart, C., & Berkowitz, L. (1976). Effects of a stimulus associated with a victim's pain on later aggression. *Journal of Personality and Social Psychology, 33,* 623–631.

Taft, R. (1955). The ability to judge people. *Psychological Bulletin, 52,* 1–23.

Taylor, S. E., & Achitoff, P. (1974). To see ourselves as others see us: Empathy, role-taking and actor-observer effects. Unpublished manuscript.

Taylor, S. E., & Koivumaki, J. H. (1976). The perception of self and others: Acquaintanceship, affect, and actor-observer differences. *Journal of Personality and Social Psychology, 33,* 403–408.

Thompson, S. C., & Kelley, H. H. (1981). Judgments of responsibility for activities in close relationships. *Journal of Personality and Social Psychology, 41,* 469–477.

Titchener, E. (1909). *Elementary psychology of the thought processes.* New York: Macmillan.

Tobias, P. V. (1983). Hominid evolution in Africa. *Canadian Journal of Anthropology, 3,* 163–185.

Toi, M., & Batson, C. D. (1982). More evidence that empathy is a source of altruistic motivation. *Journal of Personality and Social Psychology, 43,* 281–292.

Trivers, R. (1971). The evolution of reciprocal altruism. *The Quarterly Review of Biology, 46,* 35–57.

Trommsdorff, G. (1991). Child-rearing and children's empathy. *Perceptual and Motor Skills, 72,* 387–390.

Turner, C. W., & Berkowitz, L. (1972). Identification with film aggressor (covert role taking) and reactions to film violence. *Journal of Personality and Social Psychology, 21,* 256–264.

Underwood, B., & Briggs, S. R. (1980). *The influence of perspective-taking and aggressiveness on attitudes toward Iran.* Unpublished manuscript.

Underwood, B., & Moore, B. (1982). Perspective-taking and altruism. *Psychological Bulletin, 91,* 143–173.

Vaughan, K. B., & Lanzetta, J. T. (1980). Vicarious instigation and conditioning of facial expressive and autonomic responses to a model's expressive display of pain. *Journal of Personality and Social Psychology, 38,* 909–923.

Vaughan, K. B., & Lanzetta, J. T. (1981). The effect of modification of expressive displays on vicarious emotional arousal. *Journal of Experimental Social Psychology, 17,* 16–30.

Veitch, R., & Piccione, A. (1978). The role of attitude similarity in the attribution process. *Social Psychology, 41,* 165–169.

Wallach, L., & Wallach, M. A. (1991). Why altruism, even though it exists, cannot be demonstrated by social psychological experiments. *Psychological Inquiry, 2,* 153–155.

Washburn, S. L. (1960). Tools and human evolution. *Scientific American, 203,* 62–75.

Waters, E., Wippman, J., & Sroufe, L. A. (1979). Attachment, positive affect, and competence in the peer group: Two studies in construct validation. *Child Development, 50,* 821–829.

Wegner, D. M., & Finstuen, K. (1977). Observers' focus of attention in the simulation of self-perception. *Journal of Personality and Social Psychology, 35,* 56–62.

Weiner, B. (1972). *Theories of motivation.* Chicago: Rand McNally.

Weiner, B. (1980a). A cognitive (attribution)-emotion-action model of motivated behavior: An analysis of judgments of help-giving. *Journal of Personality and Social Psychology, 39,* 186–200.

Weiner, B. (1980b). May I borrow your class notes? An attributional analysis of judgments of help-giving in an achievement-related context. *Journal of Educational Psychology, 72,* 676–681.

Weiner, B. (1986). *An attributional theory of motivation and emotion.* New York: Springer-Verlag.

Weiss, R. F., Boyer, J. L., Lombardo, J. P., & Stich, M. H. (1973). Altruistic drive and altruistic reinforcement. *Journal of Personality and Social Psychology, 25,* 390–400.

Weiss, R. F., Buchanan, W., Altstatt, L., & Lombardo, P.P. (1971). Altruism is rewarding. *Science, 171,* 1262–1263.

Whiten, A., & Byrne, R. W. (1988a). The Machiavellian intelligence hypotheses: Editorial. In A. Whiten & R. W. Byrne (Eds.), *Machiavellian intelligence: Social expertise and the evolution of intellect in monkeys, apes, and humans,* pp. 1–9. Oxford: Clarendon Press.

Whiten, A., & Byrne, R. W. (1988b). The manipulation of attention in primate tactical deception. In A. Whiten & R. W. Byrne (Eds.), *Machiavellian intelligence: Social expertise and the evolution of intellect in monkeys, apes, and humans,* pp. 211–223. Oxford: Clarendon Press.

Wiehe, V. R. (1987). Empathy and locus of control in child abusers. *Journal of Social Service Research, 9,* 17–30.

Wiesenfeld, A. R., Whitman, P. B., & Malatesta, C. Z. (1984). Individual differences among adult women in sensitivity to infants: Evidence in support of an empathy concept. *Journal of Personality and Social Psychology, 46,* 118–124.

Wills, T. A., Weiss, R. L., & Patterson, G. R. (1974). A behavioral analysis of the determinants of marital satisfaction. *Journal of Consulting and Clinical Psychology, 42,* 802–811.

Wilson, E. O. (1975). *Sociobiology: The new synthesis.* Cambridge, MA: Harvard University Press.

Wise, P. S. (1985). *Empathic responsiveness and self-reported empathy in young adolescents.* Presented at the 93rd Annual Convention of the American Psychological Association, Los Angeles.

Wispé, L. (Ed.) (1978). *Altruism, sympathy, and helping: Psychological and sociological principles.* New York: Academic Press.

Wispé, L. (1986). The distinction between sympathy and empathy: To call forth a concept, a word is needed. *Journal of Personality and Social Psychology, 50,* 314–321.

Wispé, L. (1991). *The psychology of sympathy.* New York: Plenum Press.

Wolosin, R., Sherman, S., & Till, A. (1973). Effects of cooperation and competition on responsibilty attribution after success and failure. *Journal of Experimental Social Psychology, 9,* 220–235.

Wynn, T. (1988). Tools and the evolution of human intelligence. In R. Byrne & A. Whiten (Eds.), *Machiavellian intelligence: Social expertise and the evolution of intellect in monkeys, apes, and humans,* pp. 271–284. Oxford: Clarendon Press.

Zahn-Waxler, C., Radke-Yarrow, M., & King, R. A. (1979). Child rearing and children's prosocial initiations toward victims of distress. *Child Development, 50,* 319–330.

Zahn-Waxler, C., Robinson, J. L., & Emde, R. N. (1992). The development of empathy in twins. *Developmental Psychology, 28,* 1038–1047.

Zillmann, D. (1988). Cognition-excitation interdependencies in aggressive behavior. *Aggressive Behavior, 14,* 51–64.

Zillmann, D. (1990). The interplay of cognition and excitation in aggravated conflict among intimates. In D. D. Cahn (Ed.), *Intimates in conflict: A communication perspective,* pp. 187–208. Hillsdale, NJ: Lawrence Erlbaum Associates.

Zillmann, D., Bryant, J., Cantor, J. R., & Day, K. D. (1975). Irrelevance of mitigating circumstances in retaliatory behavior at high levels of excitation. *Journal of Research in Personality, 9,* 282–293.

Zillmann, D., & Cantor, J. R. (1976). Effect of timing of information about mitigating circumstances on emotional responses to provocation and retaliatory behavior. *Journal of Experimental Social Psychology, 12,* 38–55.

Zuckerman, M., Klorman, R., Larrance, D. T., & Spiegel, N. H. (1981). Facial, autonomic, and subjective components of emotion: The facial feedback hypothesis versus the externalizer-internalizer distinction. *Journal of Personality and Social Psychology, 41,* 929–944.

INDEX

Nisbett, R. E., 94, 97
Non-affective outcomes, 47, 82–103
    and adults, 52–54
    and aggression, 157–58
    and helping, 141–44
    and intrapersonal outcomes, 19
    and social relationships, 186–88
Noncognitive processes, 15–16
Non-conformity, 54
Non-verbal sensitivity, 87–88, 92

Oakley, K., 30
Oathout, H. A., 178–80, 192, 193, 196, 200
Obliging, 69
Observe instructions, 211–12
Observer
    and actor-observer differences, 94
    and individual observer, 220
    and observer set, 95
    and observer/target relationship and
        attributions, 96–99
    and observer/target similarity and
        aggression, 162–63
    and observer/target similarity and helping,
        145–46
    and parallel outcomes, 116–18
    and physiological linkage to target, 220
    and similarities between observer and
        target, 116–18
Observer set, 95
Oneness, 208
Oor, 32
Opening up, 196
O'Quin, K., 119
O'Reilly, E., 67
Orenstein, L., 146
Organizational model of empathy, 12–21,
    215–21
Other-oriented outcomes, 19
Other-representation, 212–13
Ought self, 99
Outcomes, 47, 52–53
    affective. See Affective outcomes
    and helping, 141–44
    and non-affective outcomes, 82–103
    and organizational model alterations, 219
    and parallel outcomes, 105–7, 111–18,
        122–24
    and processes, 10–11, 12, 17, 18, 19
Outgroups, tolerance for, 102
Outlook, 193
Overdetermination, 113–14

Parallel outcomes, 18, 105–7, 111–18,
    122–24, 204
Parallel responding, 105–7, 111–18, 122–24

Parental discipline, 81
Parental self-report, 71–72, 74–76
Parenting style, 77–78
Parenting techniques, 74–78
Parents' dispositional empathy, 78–80, 81
Parsons, L. B., 165
Passingham, R. E., 31
Password, 195
Past, and future, 201–21
Patient, 69
Patterns of behavior, 217
Patterson, G. R., 185
Pearl, L., 191
Peekna, H. M., 106
Peer competence, 71
Penner, L. A., 117
Peplau, L. A., 191
Perception, and interpersonal perception test,
    50–51
Perceptual inlets, 4, 6, 15, 20
Perceptual role taking, 7, 47, 48–49
Perrett, D. I., 28
Person, and antecedents, 14
Personal distress, 106, 120–22, 133–35
Personal distress scale (PD), 56, 57, 60, 67,
    68–70, 92, 102, 170–72, 193, 194,
    195, 199
Personal factors, 107–8
Personality
    socioanalytic theory of, 32–33
    and temperament, 65–67
Personal standards and values, 216–17
Person identity, 38, 42
Person permanence, 38, 41–42
Perspective, and target, 123–24
Perspective taking, 17
    and aggression, 161–62
    and helping, 144–45
Perspective taking scale (PT), 55–58, 60, 67,
    68–70, 80, 92, 102, 115, 120, 149,
    150, 165, 166, 170–72, 189–91, 192,
    193, 194, 195, 198, 199
Peterson, C., 77
Phonemic, 210
Physical punishment, 74
Physiological linkage, 91, 220
Piaget, J., 6, 7, 17, 19, 48–49, 177
Piccione, A., 163
Piliavin, J. A., 109, 131, 151
Planning, 31
Plomin, R., 63, 65–66, 67, 203
Polk, W. M., 162
Positive outlook, 193
Potter, D. D., 28
Poulin, R., 60–61, 67
Powell, A. L., 60–61
Powell, L. K., 115